About Island Press

Since 1984, the nonprofit Island Press has been stimulating, shaping, and communicating the ideas that are essential for solving environmental problems worldwide. With more than 800 titles in print and some 40 new releases each year, we are the nation's leading publisher on environmental issues. We identify innovative thinkers and emerging trends in the environmental field. We work with world-renowned experts and authors to develop cross-disciplinary solutions to environmental challenges.

Island Press designs and implements coordinated book publication campaigns in order to communicate our critical messages in print, in person, and online using the latest technologies, programs, and the media. Our goal: to reach targeted audiences—scientists, policymakers, environmental advocates, the media, and concerned citizens—who can and will take action to protect the plants and animals that enrich our world, the ecosystems we need to survive, the water we drink, and the air we breathe.

Island Press gratefully acknowledges the support of its work by the Agua Fund, Inc., The Margaret A. Cargill Foundation, Betsy and Jesse Fink Foundation, The William and Flora Hewlett Foundation, The Kresge Foundation, The Forrest and Frances Lattner Foundation, The Andrew W. Mellon Foundation, The Curtis and Edith Munson Foundation, The Overbrook Foundation, The David and Lucile Packard Foundation, The Summit Foundation, Trust for Architectural Easements, The Winslow Foundation, and other generous donors.

The opinions expressed in this book are those of the author(s) and do not necessarily reflect the views of our donors.

Coastal Governance

Foundations of Contemporary Environmental Studies

James Gustave Speth, editor

Global Environmental Governance
James Gustave Speth and Peter M. Haas

Ecology and Ecosystem Conservation
Oswald J. Schmitz

Markets and the Environment
Nathaniel O. Keohane and Sheila M. Olmstead

Water Resources
Shimon Anisfeld

COASTAL GOVERNANCE

Richard Burroughs

ISLANDPRESS

Washington | Covelo | London

ISLAND PRESS is a trademark of the Center for Resource Economics.

Library of Congress Cataloging-in-Publication Data
Burroughs, Richard,
    Coastal governance / by Richard Burroughs.
        p.   cm. — (Foundations of contemporary environmental studies)
    Includes bibliographical references and index.
    ISBN-13: 978-1-59726-484-6 (cloth : alk. paper)
    ISBN-10: 1-59726-484-9 (cloth : alk. paper)
    ISBN-13: 978-1-59726-485-3 (pbk. : alk. paper)
    ISBN-10: 1-59726-485-7 (pbk. : alk. paper)
1. Coastal zone management—Environmental aspects—United States. I. Title.
    HT392.B88 2010
    333.91'70973—dc22   2010017001

⊛ Printed on recycled, acid-free paper

Manufactured in the United States of America
10   9   8   7   6   5   4   3   2   1

KEYWORDS: ecosystem-based management, sector-based management, spatial
management, dredging, sewage, wetlands, fisheries, watersheds, Coastal Zone
Management Act, coastal policy development

To Nancy
Thank you

Contents

X CONTENTS

Preface

Most coastal policy issues start with debates about changes in the natural environment. However, ultimately the discussions revolve around the values people share and the actions they take. People affect flows of materials and energy while their actions determine populations of organisms and the state of biological systems. Individuals are the ultimate ecosystem change agents—particularly if unfettered. Conversely, their behavior, if channeled, can produce social and natural systems that deliver many of the values society seeks. Therefore, an understanding of the policy process and its application in coastal settings can make substantial contributions to practical problem solving in coastal lands and seas.

An introductory text must address the fact that effective coastal management requires integration of information across many human endeavors and that individuals usually focus on just one discipline pertinent to the topic. Furthermore, the text should recognize that institutional change, which improves the match among human activities and environmental limits, underlies contemporary discussions of coastal governance. Some students bring great enthusiasm about the importance of coasts and a substantial knowledge of the natural sciences. However, they may not have studied the policy process and can be frustrated by the seeming inability of discussions about governance to reflect the natural sciences. Other students are familiar with human dimensions and governmental processes but not comfortable with the underlying natural science pertinent to governance options and their operation.

To meet the needs of both of these groups of students, as well as professionals and interested citizens, this book identifies coastal problems, explains the policy process as a means of addressing them, and demonstrates where and how natural science can assist. It introduces how the policy process works both as an ideal and in actual practice. By delving into specific cases such as wastewater, oil, wetlands, watersheds, and fisheries, chapters ground the presentation in laws and agencies that operate in coastal lands and seas. Readers will observe firsthand the forces at play as sector-based, spatial, and ecosystem-based management are applied to specific problems, evaluated, and revised. By focusing on underlying processes, the text equips students to respond to inevitable changes that will arise as governance evolves to meet the needs and values of the increasing numbers of people who live in coastal areas. I owe a great debt to colleagues and students who have explored these topics with me, as well as the many individuals at Island Press who have helped to bring this book to fruition. The project started through the encouragement of James Gustave Speth during my sabbatical visit to the School of Forestry and Environmental Studies at Yale University. Those students for whom this material resonates have been a great inspiration through their observations and questions in class discussions, the papers and articles they write, and, most important, through the careers they lead in coastal management. Erin Jackson and Changhua Weng, graduate assistants at the University of Rhode Island, assembled key information in support of the book. Island Press provided the results from anonymous reviews of the material, which were very helpful in shaping the text. Emily Davis, the editor at Island Press, suggested changes in text and presentation that have been particularly helpful. Gaboury Benoit, Tracey Dalton, Lawrence Juda, Seth Macinko, and Robert Thompson contributed their time and insights by very thoughtfully reviewing separate chapters. The remaining omissions are the responsibility of the author alone.

Slim Chance Farm
Peacedale, Rhode Island
June 2010

1

Coastal Challenges

For many of us, the coast represents warm summer days at a welcoming beach—swimming, sea birds, and sandcastles. Yet that ideal does not reflect the full reality. Instead, water pollution, beach erosion, habitat destruction, and other forces are currently threatening coastal areas all along the United States.

These problems arise from the various, often conflicting, ways we make use of the coasts. They are not simply beautiful natural areas or family recreation spots. We also use them as a place to dispose of waste, transport goods, build houses, expand industry, and much else besides.

For example, the Gulf of Mexico spill from the Deepwater Horizon oil drilling unit highlighted the conflict between energy supply and the environment. In San Francisco Bay, the Great Lakes, and elsewhere, shipping and economic activity both depend on and collide with aquatic environments. As harbors are dredged to accommodate larger ships, contaminated sediment is unearthed at an environmental cost to the site of removal as well as to the final resting place for the dredged material. Although intertidal wetlands are valued habitats, they remain under siege because developments encroach on their area and function.

These and many other problems demand responses. Our decisions about how to address them—and how to balance conflicting coastal uses—are reflected in management practices. Conflict arises when expectations and realities diverge. The conflict exposes the extent to which we as a society understand the coast and the multiple values we bring *why not rules?*

to managing it. Ultimately the choices we make as a society, expressed through government policies, will determine the future of the coasts. This book explains those choices, how we have made them in the past, and how we can improve them for the future.

A stepping-off point for this discussion is whether our current approach is adequate. When we add up all the individual policies created to improve the coasts, can they collectively lead to success? One way to answer this question is to consider the policies' aggregate impact on ecological health. Another is to examine the policies themselves and the degree to which we apply consistent and coordinated approaches to manage coastal lands and waters. We'll do both in this chapter.

State of the coasts

The most basic measure of policy success or failure is the current state of the coasts, reflected by factors such as water quality. Unfortunately coastal waters throughout the contiguous United States are deemed fair to poor (EPA, 2008a). In figure 1.1, the overall score for each region is based largely on water and habitat quality. Waters that are murky due to solids, are low in oxygen, or have high levels of decomposing organic matter score poorly in national classifications. Sewage discharge and excess nutrients from agriculture and other sources lead to algae growth and decay, which ultimately cause water quality problems. Similarly, if sediments or organisms are contaminated and the numbers of organisms present at the ocean floor are different from what might be found there naturally, then the water body ranks poorly.

Factors considered in ranking

In addition to water quality, there are several other comprehensive indicators of the status of coastal environments, including the health of fisheries and the condition of wetlands and other habitats. More than 20,000 acres of coastal habitat disappear each year (Pew Oceans Commission, 2003, vi), and many fisheries have declined. For example, in 2008 twenty percent of the fish stocks assessed by the government were deemed to be subject to overfishing (NMFS, 2008).

Drivers for environmental change

Clearly, the ways we currently use the coasts are leading to environmental damage. Specifically, what human activities are responsible? Any activity that directly or indirectly causes a change in an ecosystem (Nelson et al., 2006) can be thought of as a "driver." Drivers of coastal change include greenhouse gas emissions, invasive species, land conversion, and fertilizer for agriculture, as well as growth in human populations along the coast.

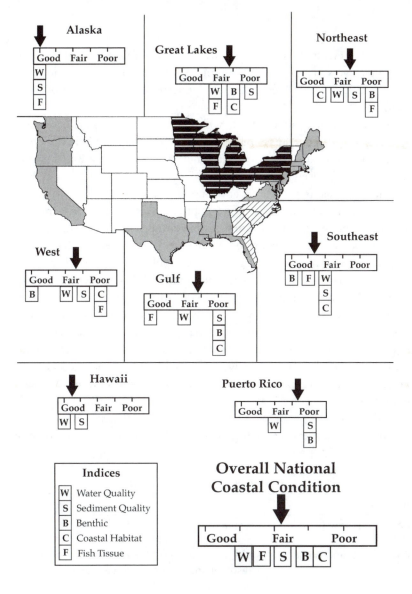

Figure 1.1. Coastal condition. By creating indices for water, sediment, benthos, habitat loss, and fish tissue contamination, the U.S. Environmental Protection Agency scored coastal condition for 2001–2002 both regionally and nationally. Nationally, coastal systems are fair, as depicted by the arrow above the bar. Regional summaries show areas ranking from good (south central Alaska, Hawaii) to poor or fair to poor (Great Lakes, Northeast, Puerto Rico, and the Gulf). More important are the scores for individual indices, shown as letters below the bar, because they lead to topics requiring additional attention. For example, when sediment quality and benthic community condition are ranked poorly, programs to limit contamination or disturbance of sediments might well be strengthened. Data from EPA, 2008a.

Table 1.1 presents the drivers that are covered in this book. The impacts of these drivers in a given situation can be influenced by economic activity, scientific discovery, technological applications, and a variety of social factors.

All future management efforts will be shaped by two key drivers: increasing human population and rising seas. Growing numbers of people choose to live next to the coast, although sea level has continued to rise. More people and encroachment by the sea increase population density and the potential for conflict. Let's consider the specifics.

Fifty-three percent of the total population of the country inhabits coastal counties, which constitute seventeen percent of the land area of the United States, when excluding Alaska (Crossett et al., 2004). The coastal counties have an average human population density of just over 300 individuals per square mile, whereas the United States as a whole averages ninety-eight persons per square mile. If we focus on density alone, we find that the six most densely populated coastal counties range from 13,000 to 68,000 persons per square mile and that nineteen of the twenty most densely populated counties in the United States are coastal (Crossett et al., 2004). Not only are coastal counties the most densely populated, densities on average are about five times the levels in inland counties.

This trend of growing population in finite coastal areas has continued for more than a half century (figure 1.2). In the fifty-five years shown in

TABLE 1.1.
Drivers of environmental change.

Activities	Impacts	Chapter
Population growth	Consumption of space and resources; conflicts	1
Fossil fuel combustion	Atmospheric composition change resulting in warming and sea level rise	1
Sewage discharge	Water quality, disease	3
Oil and gas development	Land use, environmental degradation	4
Shipping	Dredging and disposal	5
Habitat conservation	Wetlands area	6
Coastal development	Land conversion	7, 9
Farming and land development	Runoff quantity and quality	8, 9
Fishing	Ecosystems, human communities	10

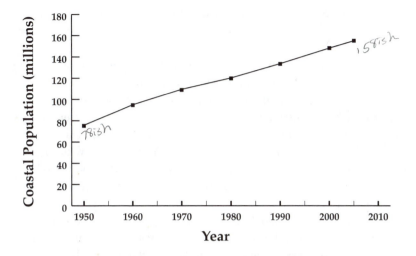

Figure 1.2. Coastal county population. The population of coastal counties has nearly doubled in just over fifty years. When human population is considered a surrogate for the number and intensity of uses, the rapid increase of stress on finite coastal lands and waters becomes apparent. Data from U.S. Census Bureau, 2007.

figure 1.2, the coastal county population has increased by 80 million individuals. Each person requires a place to live, transportation, food, waste disposal, and so on. Each of these requirements places an additional burden on the environment and ultimately drives change. And the trend of increasing coastal population shows every indication of continuing.

Research suggests that population and environmental quality are tightly linked and that as the number of people in an area increases, certain aspects of environmental quality decrease. Ehrlich and Ehrlich (1990) proposed that environmental impact changes as a function of population, affluence, and technology. Although effective technology can mitigate environmental damage, greater affluence tends to worsen it. Coastal counties have by far the highest population densities in the United States and, it turns out, higher per capita income on average than inland residents. Consequently, we should expect the greatest disruption of the environment to occur at or nearby the land/sea edge.

Increasing population triggers the need for more housing units in a finite geographic area, and in most instances the housing spreads horizontally, not vertically. To meet the growing needs, more than 1,540 single-family housing permits were issued in coastal counties each day during the early years of the twenty-first century (Pew Oceans Commission,

2003). Many additional multifamily housing permits are also issued. The increasing number of units and their sprawling nature consumes coastal land at a very high rate. One assessment found that development was consuming land at five or more times the rate of population increase in many coastal areas (Pew Oceans Commission, 2003). Those figures, if nationally representative, indicate massive changes in coastal landscapes.

Furthermore, coastal land is consumed not only by construction but also by rising seas. The two combined can rapidly transform a coastal area. Global warming triggers sea level rise. As human activities release additional greenhouse gases, such as carbon dioxide, the composition of the atmosphere changes, which traps outgoing radiation and warms the atmosphere and ocean.

To assess the consequences of this change, international scientific organizations established the Intergovernmental Panel on Climate Change (IPCC), which convenes scientists from around the world. The panel has found that over the last one hundred years the globally averaged near-surface air temperature increased 0.74 degrees Celsius. They project this metric to continue increasing at 0.2 degrees Celsius per decade for the near future (IPCC, 2007a).

Warmer air temperatures melt ice on land, which adds water to the sea. Furthermore, the seawaters themselves warm just the slightest amount and expand, which results in further sea level rise. During the twentieth century global average sea level rose at 1.7 millimeters per year, but since 1993 the rate has been 3 millimeters per year (IPCC, 2007b, 409). Projections of sea level at the end of the twenty-first century show a minimum rise of 7.1 inches (0.18 meter) and a maximum of 23.2 inches (0.59 meter), depending on what levels of greenhouse gas emissions are anticipated for the next nine decades (IPCC, 2007a, 13). These estimates do not include ice flows from continents to oceans, which will rapidly accelerate the rate of change. Furthermore, deltas and other coastal lands in certain areas are sinking due to sediment compaction and other processes that increase relative sea level rise. In sum, the IPCC projections indicate that sea level rise in the twenty-first century will at least match what has happened over the past century—a global average of 1.7 millimeters per year until 1993 and 3 millimeters per year after that. However, seas could rise at more than three times that rate and ice flows could worsen the problem further. Given the increasing rate of sea level rise in the last years of the twentieth century, the higher estimates seem more likely.

Warming and sea level rise affect coastal regions in several important ways (IPCC, 2007c). First, coastal erosion affects new areas at higher elevations along the shore. Second, wetlands are trapped and shrinking in between developed lands at their inland margins and erosion followed by inundation on the sea side. Third, the number of individuals flooded on an annual basis is expected to rise, especially in areas where the land is subsiding and tropical storms are likely. Finally, the possible increase in intense tropical storms will disrupt coastal environments and the social systems related to them. *econ effects*

A projected change of millimeters per year may sound inconsequential until you recognize that it could add up to sea level rise of almost two feet (0.61 meter) in the course of a century. A small vertical dimension in sea level elevation can become a very large horizontal encroachment of the sea if the coastal lands are relatively flat.

One recent report considering the United States as a whole found that flooding of roads, railways, and runways due to sea level rise and storm surge will be an increasing problem in future years (National Research Council, 2008). Another looked more specifically at the mid-Atlantic region (New York to North Carolina), where as much as ten percent of the total population lives on parcels or city blocks with at least some land less than thirty-nine inches (one meter) above monthly highest tides (Titus et al., 2009, 110). Episodes of this sort will no doubt be a warning of more sustained flooding to come. Currently in the mid-Atlantic, somewhere between three and ten percent of the population, or as many as 3.4 million people, live within or adjacent to land that is only thirty-nine inches (one meter) above the highest of the regularly occurring high tides (Titus et al., 2009, 26). Changes of just a few millimeters per year could affect millions of lives over time.

The ocean commissions

Environmental change persists along the coasts and in oceans. Its relationship to policy has not gone unnoticed (Cicin-Sain and Knecht, 2000). Recently two national commissions—one created by the nonprofit organization The Pew Charitable Trusts, the other formed by the federal government—have considered coastal problems and means for resolving them (box 1.1). Drawing on the opinions of diverse professionals, the commissions considered the objectives of coastal management and proposed more effective ways to reach them. Both identified serious deficiencies in current policies.

For example, the commissions found that although federal laws have reduced point source pollution significantly, they have been less effec- *CWA* tive at controlling nonpoint source pollution. Government regulations

Box 1.1. The National Commissions

America's Living Oceans: Charting a Course for Sea Change (Pew Oceans Commission, 2003) and *An Ocean Blueprint for the 21st Century* (U.S. Commission on Ocean Policy, 2004) have focused national attention on the need to improve governance of coasts and oceans. Each report assesses the national situation and provides recommendations for management. The former, commonly known as the Pew Commission Report, was overseen by eighteen commissioners, assisted by a professional staff, and supplemented by consultants who provided technical reports. The Pew Charitable Trusts financed its three-year operation ending with the publication in 2003. For the second report, the Oceans Act of 2000 established a Commission on Ocean Policy. This federally chartered effort involved sixteen commissioners, a professional staff, scientific advisors, and, like its predecessor, a series of public meetings to gather information. The final report and president's response were completed during 2004.

Together the commissions have produced hundreds of recommendations covering most areas of contemporary marine policy. The major recommendations of each group related to coastal issues overlapped in at least four areas: watershed management, water pollution discharges, creation of regional ocean councils, and fisheries management/aquaculture. Prominent action items selected by one but not both groups included coordinated management of new uses and a focus on habitat protection. To aggressively promote these actions, the commissions identified the need for enhanced science and education funding as well as coordination of coastal and ocean programs through new high-level government structures.

The completion of these reports initiated some changes in organizational structure and content for coastal management. New oversight mechanisms at the Council on Environmental Quality, a revised ocean science plan, and clarification of energy and fisheries laws arose, at least in part, from the findings of the commissions. However, the reports called for much bolder steps. Possibilities include the initiation of new coastal-ocean management entities for regions that span multiple states, ocean plans by individual states, and a federal ocean policy task force. Although it is too early to assess the overall impacts of the commissions, these accomplishments indicate the potential for substantial improvements in the future.

require that contaminants be treated before being discharged from specific sources, such as sewage or industrial plants, to rivers and estuaries. But individual pipe discharges are not the only problem. Fertilizer, manure, and other chemicals used in farming flow to the sea through groundwater and runoff after rains. Roads, parking lots, and roofs shed water faster than forests or grasslands. Consequently, suburban developments change not only the quality but the quantity of runoff. Failure to manage these and other nonpoint sources of pollution has jeopardized the gains made in controlling pipe discharges and improving coastal water quality in general. Clearly, new policies are needed. We will discuss how policy is developed, and the legal structure that orders this process, in detail in chapter 2.

[handwritten margin note: ↑coastal dev. ↑untreated NPS runoff]

This story of helpful but incomplete solutions extends to biological systems as well. In many instances piecemeal control of human activities has resulted in pollution and overharvesting. Wildlife breeding populations have declined and fisheries have become less productive. Seagrass beds and wetlands are disappearing in many coastal areas. Invasive species contribute to the decline of many ecosystems. Government has acted to alleviate these biological changes, but in each case, the commissions found the need for improvement.

Taken together, the commissions' recommendations represent the boldest changes in coastal and ocean governance to be proposed in generations. In fact, this is only the second time in the nation's history that such a shift has been attempted. A broad change in coastal governance, whether during the first phase in the early 1970s or today, forces the reexamination of current practices and the adoption of new approaches.

Management goals and processes

The Pew and the U.S. oceans commissions proposed national goals for the coast and ocean. Most broadly stated, the Pew Commission goal was "healthy, productive, and resilient marine ecosystems for present and future generations" (2002, ix). The U.S. Commission on Ocean Policy (2004, 4) similarly envisioned a future in which coastal waters "are clean, safe, prospering, and sustainably managed," and the coasts themselves "contribute significantly to the economy" while being "attractive places to live, work and play." These statements set broad goals for the coasts, but of course, the devil is in the details of how to get there.

As will be discussed in more detail in chapter 2, the policy process is a systematic way to reduce conflict and narrow the gap between present or projected circumstances and desired conditions. The process begins when a problem is identified (Lasswell, 1971; Clark, 2002; and Birkland, 2005), as we have outlined in the previous pages. Alternative solutions are then suggested, a preferred program is selected and implemented, and finally, after allowing it time to operate, the results are evaluated. Effective evaluations lead to new problem definitions and the policy process begins anew.

The policy process outlined above may operate in various contexts. In fact as we review the problems in domestic coastal management, we see three distinct frameworks for assessment and action. They are

1. *sector-based management,* which defines problems as harm resulting from single uses and seeks to restrict or modify those individual uses through regulations and permits;
2. *spatial management,* which seeks to resolve conflicts in a specific geographic area through land/sea use "zoning" plans; and
3. *coastal ecosystem governance*, which promotes sustainable natural and social systems through diverse management techniques that shape human activity in concert with the limits of natural systems.

As ecosystem governance assumes greater importance, sector-based and spatial techniques continue to contribute. Many future strategies will effectively combine the three. Recognizing these different approaches, identifying their distinctive attributes, and considering how each may contribute to coastal governance form the core of this book. Managing coastal ecosystems for the future requires the recognition of limits imposed by natural systems, effective public involvement, and the means to encourage human behavior consistent with these new realities. Furthermore, ecosystem-based management includes people—one of its key objectives is to embed sustainable human economies within overall ecosystem capabilities (Burroughs and Clark, 1995). Both of the national commissions promote ecosystem management as a crucial policy innovation.

As indicated above, sector-based, spatial, and ecosystem approaches frame coastal governance in distinctive and different ways. Interestingly, the perceived nature of the problem has shifted over time. Sector-based management defines the problem as maximizing success with a single use. In the spatial management phase, the primary focus is on recognizing the interdependence of different uses—an overlap that occurs through the coastal environmental systems. The ecosystem approach recognizes that human activity will ultimately be constrained by the capacity of natural systems. Thus, the coastal environment both connects uses and places limits on them. Ecosystem management, when effectively implemented through specific policies, holds great promise for narrowing the gap between the coast we have and the coast we want.

Organization of the book

In the following chapters I examine sector-based, spatial, and ecosystem approaches and their effectiveness at managing conflict and accommodating human activities within sustainable natural systems. But first, in chapter 2, I describe the policy process and policy analysis as a means to understand and ultimately create effective governance systems. Together these first two chapters define many of the problems of the coast and a systematic way to develop new policy solutions.

Next, the book focuses on sector-based decisions in chapters 3–5. Early on, coastal and ocean problem solving focused exclusively on individual uses or sectors. Managers viewed their task as resolving a series of independent choices that relate to different sectors. For example, dredging is controlled by issuing permits for ocean sites and individual disposal operations. Sewage discharge (chapter 3), oil development (chapter 4), dredging (chapter 5), and wetlands issues (chapter 6) have each been managed through permits related to specific actions.

However, as the number of individual sectors increased, so too did the conflicts across sectors. The second phase of coastal management recognizes that multiple sector-based programs inevitably collide in the coastal zone. Spatial planning and management look across individual sectors and create the possibility for coherent management within a politically defined geographic unit. Recognition that uses are connected through the environment changes the context for action. However, spatial management does not necessarily place environmental values above others and generally falls short of prescribing particular care for natural systems. Coastal issues cross not only sectors but regions and even the land-sea boundary. Chapters 7 and 8 demonstrate that activities on land can significantly affect coastal waters. For example, farm waste can pollute rivers that run to the sea, degrading coastal water quality and harming fisheries. Understanding the essence of these connections leads to a new approach to coastal management that promotes boundaries based on the extent of natural systems and establishes limits set by the capacity of the environment to accommodate human activities. Many refer to this new approach as ecosystem-based management.

The Pew Commission and the U.S. Commission on Ocean Policy put this concept on the national agenda for action. Proposals for ecosystem-based management abound, but effective implementation often eludes managers. Incremental changes to adopt ecosystem approaches for watersheds and bays (chapter 9) as well as fisheries (chapter 10) illuminate both the opportunities and the challenges ahead.

In chapter 11, the conclusion, we review the characteristics and suitability of sector, spatial, and ecosystem management. Each has strengths and weaknesses that warrant consideration in the design of programs. Moving ecosystem management from concept to practice requires the nesting of these perspectives to address present-day problems of the coast.

Our coasts will become what we choose to make them through the goals we establish and the governance systems we select. This book provides an introduction to governance alternatives and ways of assessing them that will equip you to participate in determining the future of our coasts.

2

Policy Process

As we seek out the shores to work, play, and live, water quality continues to decline, critical habitat is lost, and the coastal environment becomes less and less healthy. Our tendency to prize the coasts but at the same time degrade them suggests that society is not adequately planning for the future. In short, human activity is oddly mismatched with the requirements of the natural system and many human values. This situation raises two important questions. Can people collectively decide to create a different future for coastal regions? If so, how do they go about it?

Fortunately, the nation has a long history of policy development that includes issues as diverse as poverty, drug abuse, education, and health. In each instance the goal has been to change human behavior so it matches society's broadly shared goals more closely. As public concern about environmental degradation has grown over the last half century, the coast has become a significant focus of policy development. Understanding how these policies are formed is essential to changing the current trajectory of the coasts.

The idealized policy process can be viewed as a series of stages (figure 2.1): problems are defined; solutions are considered; a response is selected; a program is implemented; and finally, the program is evaluated for its effectiveness (Lasswell, 1971; Brewer and deLeon, 1983; Jones, 1984; Clark, 2002; Weimer and Vining, 1992; Birkland, 2005). Program evaluation identifies unresolved issues that shape new problem definitions, and the process repeats itself. Considering the policy process as a series of

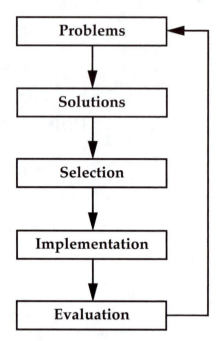

Figure 2.1. The policy process. By considering coastal policy as a sequence of stages, analysts can assess whether pertinent material is present, ascertain key factors that have influenced each stage, and consider alternative routes to solutions.

stages does not imply that each policy exhibits all of the stages or that this framework captures all the subtleties and variables of policy development and enactment. Indeed, a variety of other frameworks for understanding public policy exists. However, by considering questions pertinent to each of the stages, one gains insight into contemporary coastal problems, discovers many of the factors at work, and often finds solutions.

Because the stages framework operates at a general level, it can readily incorporate contemporary changes in who participates in creating policy and which techniques they select. For example, government officials could take a backseat as stakeholders contribute more to policy formulation. Or, during implementation, command and control regulation could diminish in importance while use of markets could increase.

In the 1970s government dominated both the design and implementation of coastal and ocean policy. Compulsory regulation of water quality is an example of this approach. The government both set limits for what contaminants may be discharged and established a permit program to ensure that the limits are met. Today, others beyond government officials often participate in conservation programs. For example, wallet cards provided by environmental groups direct seafood purchasers to species that

industry forces

are plentiful. If consumers voluntarily stop buying a threatened species of
fish, governmental regulation of that fishery becomes less important.

To change human behavior one needs to evaluate problems and opportunities, establish arrangements and institutions, and most important,
through rules and sanctions, encourage acceptable behavior related to
resource and environmental use (Juda, 1999). In the past most of these
functions occurred in government agencies. Today, the capacity to accomplish these functions outside of government is actively considered
in almost every new policy proposal that comes forward. Coastal governance is not the purview of government alone. Coastal policy instruments that operate beyond the direct purview of government are in the
realm of *governance* (Juda, 1999; Juda and Hennessey, 2001). Governance
includes arrangements and mores that structure resource use, problem
analysis, acceptable behavior, and sanctions. Voluntary organizations, private markets, and education represent some of the alternatives for management initiatives beyond government (Howlett and Ramesh, 1995).
The increased use of governance techniques promises opportunities for
program improvements in the future.

Problems

As we saw in chapter 1, the coasts are plagued by a host of problems,
large and small. Some are related to various forms of pollution: oil spills,
dead zones, invasive species, land runoff, and pipe discharges. Others are
regional or global in nature: climate change, sea level rise, and human
population growth. Still others are tied to use of resources: aquaculture,
coastal development, and overfishing. Finally, some are related to inadequate government structures: conflicting agency mandates and inability
to plan and manage regionally.

Although each of these issues deserves attention, frequently problems
remain just below the threshold of broad public notice and no action
is taken. As a result, coastal environments that no longer support natural functions and human expectations can linger in degraded conditions.
However, when large numbers of well-organized people identify a problem and solutions are apparent, change can happen.

Interest groups, whether representing a broad public interest or a special economic interest, play a large role in determining which problems
receive attention and how they are perceived. Private interest groups seek
to advance the needs of the particular industries that fund and support
them, often focusing on specific aspects of economic development. Interest groups with special economic objectives related to the coasts include

the American Association of Port Authorities, American Petroleum Institute, National Association of Realtors, National Association of Manufac-
turers, National Ocean Industry Association, and Dredging Contractors
of America, as well as many others.

privatos *but narrow issue*

Public interest groups are established to represent the broader needs
of the public with respect to the coasts and ocean. They might focus on
access to the coast, the enhancement of water quality, or the protection
of special biological resources. The Natural Resources Defense Council,
The Nature Conservancy, SeaWeb, Sierra Club, the Trust for Public Land,
and many others focus on the environment and on public use of the
coast.

Whether a particular issue gains attention and how it is addressed
depends largely on the effectiveness of the advocacy organizations involved and the political and economic feasibility of the proposed solutions. It should be no surprise that interest groups will define problems
so solutions meet their particular needs. Large, articulate groups with
effective channels of communication to government officials and other
societal leaders are most likely to be influential. Similarly, tractable solutions can gain political support for action. If, on the other hand, an issue
is poorly specified, perceived as important to a limited public, or lacking
in meaningful solution, then it will not get on the agenda for government action.

Solutions

Once a coastal problem is identified, multiple agencies, interest groups,
and levels of government propose solutions. Government can take a
number of different approaches, as is summarized in table 2.1 (Bardach,
2009). For example, to help restore a declining fishery, government may
regulate total catches so harvest does not exceed a sustainable level. Part
of the solution design process is to provide information about the total
catch a fishery can support. Fisheries scientists provide this information.

Interest groups also propose solutions based on information they have
gathered and their particular objectives. Corporations, environmental
groups, and others who have a stake in the issues engage natural scientists
as experts. For instance, environmental groups often have scientists on
staff to advise on issues such as the environmental impacts of a waste discharge or of an oil spill. The scientific information is used in identifying
a solution that the interest group is prepared to endorse.

Government involvement in solutions to public policy problems varies
in degree, as shown in table 2.1. Most commonly we think about those

TABLE 2.1.
Policy continuum.

Compulsory—High government involvement	Mixed	Voluntary—Low government involvement
①Regulation ②Public enterprises ③Direct provision of services ④Bureaucratic and political reform ⑤Agency budgeting	Information, exhortation, education, consultation Subsidies and grants Modification of property rights Tax and user charges Services Financing and contracting	Family and community Voluntary organizations Private markets

where the government regulates, requires permits, and oversees an activity in detail. High government involvement also takes the form of the government creating its own entities to deliver services, such as a sewage treatment plant. In a second category, government involvement is mixed with other nongovernmental means of changing human behavior. Certain activities may be encouraged by subsidies and grants or discouraged by taxes and charges. Alternatively, education, information, services, or contracting may nudge behavior in a new direction. Changing whether the individual or the general public owns something through a modification of property rights can have a significant impact. A third approach seeks voluntary changes through creation of private markets where economic processes channel behavior in a desired direction. Alternatively, family, community, or voluntary organizations may prescribe behavior they believe will benefit the coasts. Being familiar with all of these policy instruments as well as the circumstances under which they work well or poorly is a prerequisite for the creation of effective policies to address coastal issues.

Robust solutions are not only technically sound but take into consideration practical realities that facilitate their ultimate adoption. Among the top considerations are legality and political acceptability (Bardach, 2009). All solutions need to be seen as consistent with existing law. They also need to attract adequate political support and limited opposition. For example, restoring the oyster population is often discussed as a key part of solving the Chesapeake Bay's environmental and economic problems. First, this solution is technically sound. Oysters act as filter feeders and were once an important fishery. Restoration could mean more filtration, cleaner waters, more sea grasses, and better seafood harvests. Second, oyster population growth is consistent with both fisheries and water pollution control law. Third, it has gained political support from fishermen, water quality agencies, and, at times, farmers. By improving water quality without requiring new wastewater treatment or substantial changes in farming practices, oyster restoration has attracted constituencies beyond fishermen and environmentalists.

Selection

Many assume that when government locates a new housing development, determines discharge levels from an industrial plant, or creates a plan for fisheries that it systematically considers all possibilities and selects the one that best meets the collective needs of society. That is one ideal for how the selection process could be approached, but there are other interpretations of how decision makers act. Three types have received specific attention: (i) a rational and comprehensive approach; (ii) one that favors bounded assessment often followed by small change; and (iii) a final approach that acknowledges the serendipitous matching of solutions with problems.

To emphasize the importance of understanding process in decision making, Lasswell (1971) distinguished between knowledge *in* policy and knowledge *of* policy. For the coast, knowledge in policy consists of the physical, social, biological, or cultural information necessary to inform realistic decisions. It is the substantive knowledge about natural and social processes necessary for success. Conversely, knowledge of the decision process consists of how polices are made and subsequently implemented. Because the structure of the decision process for the coast matters as much or more than the substantive knowledge, the mechanics of how decision makers go about selecting solutions merits detailed consideration. As the following material demonstrates, knowledge of the policy process shows that there are distinctively different ways to make selections.

A *rational* and comprehensive process, the first approach, assumes that the problem has been clearly defined and a goal established (Birkland, 2005). In this context one needs only to select evaluation criteria, apply them to the policy alternatives, and recommend the solution or solutions that best meet the objectives (Weimer and Vining, 1992; Bardach, 2009). For example, construction of a new dam for hydropower illustrates how the approach works. Building the dam would provide irrigation water and electricity but at a cost to anadromous fish. In this simplified illustration, criteria such as salmon population and renewable electric power supply would be considered and the solution selected. By predicting the effects of alternative solutions and comparing across specific criteria, one identifies which policy shows the greatest promise and selects it.

Often however, selection does not present itself so cleanly, and this leads to a second approach to describe how decision makers act. In fact researchers who have carefully studied actual decision processes find actions seldom match the ideal of rationality as described above (Lindblom, 1959; March and Simon, 1958). Goals may not be clear, and they may be conflicting. This is often the case for coastal resources. In the example just mentioned, it's realistic to recognize that society, through separate laws and agencies, wants both fish and renewable power. Information may not be readily available, or it may be so diverse that establishing an effective way to use it is lacking. Complexities in goals and information cause many to consider an *incremental* or *bounded* approach. The latter is referred to as bounded rationality. March and Simon (1958) found that organizations have to simplify complex decisions to make them tractable. They observed that organizations establish boundaries of rationality by seeking only satisfactory, not optimal, results for a given criterion, and that they do this through actions that fit within a restricted range of familiar situations. In this setting, actions are goal-oriented and adaptive. In addition, solutions are adopted through a series of small changes in which each step is scrutinized for its relative effectiveness before the next step is taken (Lindblom, 1959). The concept is that if one does not have all the information necessary, but action is mandated, then small actions rather than large ones are preferred. "Muddling through" in this manner copes with information inadequacies and goal deficiencies by limiting the decision maker's liability should an initial solution prove inadequate. The concept is similar to adaptive management, as introduced by Holling (1978), which emphasizes that information is frequently inadequate, so policy interventions can usefully be viewed as experiments.

Others describing the decision-making process identify a third path that has little that could be called rational or incremental. They see that preferences have not been clearly specified, technological solutions remain unclear, and participants' involvement and effort varies (Cohen et al., 1972). They envision participants dumping problems and solutions into a *garbage can* and after matching up a problem with a solution removing both at the same time. Often the policy goals or causes of the problems are not fully specified. At moments when the organization must act, the decision maker selects among problems, solutions, participants, and choice opportunities that are in the garbage can and ready to be assembled. One could envision harmful algal blooms or oil spills forcing decision makers to hurriedly select an existing technical solution while pressure to resolve the problem is high.

Selecting significant courses of action for the coast almost always involves creating new processes for making decisions. These *constitutive* decisions determine the process by which subsequent decisions will be made (Lasswell, 1971; Clark, 2002). Constitutive decisions are the basis for fundamental changes in coastal policy and management. For example, the Energy Policy Act of 2005 obligated the U.S. Department of the Interior to lead the creation and implementation of a system to make decisions concerning the use of federal waters for wind turbine electricity generation. More broadly, the shift to ecosystem-based management for coastal environments, if fully adopted, would restructure the decision process in fundamental ways, as discussed later in this book.

Constitutive changes for coasts require a combination of majority support and technical enlightenment. The former relies on processes that involve as broad as possible a swath of individuals within the society. These majorities are at the core of democratic governance and effective processes. The latter recognizes that coastal issues often revolve around scientific and technical information. In that setting, selecting and legitimating policies depends on technical insight and administrative discretion, which are available to a far smaller number of individuals.

Let's first consider selection of coastal policies in the context of the need for majority participation. What mechanisms have been used? Ocean commissions have been charged with proposing broad policy directions for the nation and involve many stakeholders. During the 1960s it became apparent that there was a lack of coordination among ocean and coastal programs in the federal government. A commission with diverse stakeholders was mandated by law and became the basis for a national discussion on options for restructuring the federal system of governing the coasts and oceans (U.S. Commission on Marine Science, Engineering, and Resources, 1969) (Stratton Commission). They proposed the creation of a new agency to focus on ocean affairs, and, in response, the president created the National Oceanic and Atmospheric Administration (NOAA). The Stratton Commission also laid the groundwork for what became the Coastal Zone Management Act. Most recently, the Pew Oceans Commission (2003) and the U.S. Commission on Ocean Policy

(2004) have repeated a national assessment and proposed a whole new round of solutions—some of which we'll examine further in this book.

Commission reports can influence congressional activities, an additional step in involving majorities in policy selection. In the House and Senate, subcommittees focus on individual items and provide reports to the whole committee and ultimately Congress. Hearings allow discussion among interests and executive branch agencies as the issue is more fully explored. The give and take of congressional committees through hearings and drafting of legislation provides a forum for values to become evident and potential solutions to emerge.

Often the executive branch participates in creating the bill and structuring solutions that, in the case of coastal policy, are designed by the president's staff and officials in the U.S. Environmental Protection Agency, Navy, NOAA, and Interior, as well as other agencies. These executive branch findings are presented to Congress through hearings. Congress funnels all these other players into a single legislative process and produces specific results in the form of a bill for presidential consideration. Presidential approval is key not only because it is required for the bill to become law, but also because it is commonly up to the executive branch, through its administrators, to implement the solution. The steps taken following the *Exxon Valdez* oil spill clearly exemplify the selection of a new policy following congressional hearings, legislation, and presidential approval (box 2.1).

To be effective oil spill legislation requires carefully reasoned technical arguments, a second factor in selection. How do governments acquire scientific information that can be applied to identifying coastal policies most likely to succeed? Often the federal government relies on the National Academy of Sciences (NAS) to provide professional consensus on scientific issues through its National Research Council (NRC). Established by Congress around the time of the Civil War, the NAS is charged with reaching consensus on science pertinent to operation of the federal government. In recent years the NRC has reported on the loss of coastal lands to the sea, the relationship between ecosystems and fishing, the means for surveying recreational fishers, and the relationship of oil dispersants to the environment as well as stresses on Atlantic salmon, stellar sea lions, and other marine organisms to assess means for protection. In addition, technical information on the coast flows to government from other groups with a special interest in the topic. For example, The Heinz Center has prepared reports on best practices for limiting coastal hazards and on improving learning in coastal management.

Box 2.1. Oil Pollution: Changing the Rules

On March 24, 1989, the supertanker *Exxon Valdez* hit rocks in Prince William Sound, Alaska, and released more than 10 million gallons of crude oil. A major environmental crisis ensued with damage to fisheries, beaches, wildlife, and ecosystems. The nation was alerted to the need to revise the means for supervising oil transportation to reduce the possibility of spills from that and other sources. Sudden and harmful events like this that generate media coverage and subsequent public attention are referred to as focusing events. Interestingly, this one drew former adversaries in the fishing and environmental communities much closer together in their demands for policy change.

Public dismay over inadequate government supervision of the tanker industry led to congressional hearings to better understand the circumstances and identify the gaps that led to the spill. Groups with an interest in the oil spill included Cordova District Fishermen United, American Petroleum Institute, Environmental Defense Fund, American Bureau of Shipping, Wilderness Society, American Waterway Operators, and others. In very rapid succession diagnoses of the oil spill problem and possible solutions for it were reviewed through hearings of congressional committees. The congressional hearings, a forum for interest groups to propose solutions, led to creation of the Oil Pollution Act of 1990. In it Congress selected and the president endorsed specific solutions to prevent oil spills, to respond to them when they do occur, and to compensate those who suffer damages because of spills. Among various features, the law required that tankers adopt the new technology of double hulls, that shippers accept higher liability for damage, and that the industry create a trust fund in case the government is unable to collect from an entity responsible for a spill. In addition private parties may make claims for property destruction and losses that include profits, subsistence use, and earning capacity. Government agencies, referred to as federal trustees, conduct damage assessments, make claims, and use resulting settlements to restore damaged resources.

The Oil Pollution Act of 1990 also applies to oil spills from offshore facilities in state and federal waters. The law established a bureau in the Department of the Interior to be responsible for offshore spill prevention and response. Because the law applies to the April 20, 2010, oil spill caused by BP's Deepwater Horizon offshore drilling operation, the corporation is responsible for damages.

Implementation of the Oil Pollution Act of 1990 required government regulations to specify details of what was to be done by government agencies. The U.S. Coast Guard and the U.S. Environmental Protection Agency have created or enhanced capacities to confirm that vessels are designed, built, and staffed appropriately, to plan for spill avoidance and response, to receive reports of spills, to send teams of oil spill cleanup experts as needed, and to assess financial damages from spills. In Prince William Sound the new law required spill response equipment at the ready, escort tugs, vessel tracking equipment, and other features to avoid future accidents.

Although various technical experts and advocates from the private sector suggest possible solutions to coastal problems, the selection of particular policies is reserved for government officials, primarily legislators, executives, administrators, and judges.

These officials must sort through a wealth of information provided by various groups that often champion the science and policies that serve their particular interests. The interest groups inevitably have differing views about what problems require attention and what solutions should be used. Oil tanker companies may want less costly technology and operational requirements for their ships, while environmental groups may press for more stringent regulations to prevent spills.

For many issues, administrators in the executive branch of federal or state government play a pivotal role in selecting solutions. However, because technical details are frequently and appropriately omitted from the laws, senior governmental officials have significant discretionary powers concerning which technical means is most appropriate. For example, in selecting actions to meet the legislated goal of making waters swimmable, government officials have to determine safe maxima for contaminants in the water and then identify the technical means to reduce pollution to meet those levels. They have the discretion to select among different technical solutions. To protect water quality the head of the U.S. Environmental Protection Agency sets effluent limitations on discharges. Likewise, to restore fisheries, the head of NOAA selects fisheries management plans. In each case important new coastal policies are created.

Implementation

Implementation consists of actions taken to reduce or eliminate a problem. It involves government agencies, officials, budgets, administrative decisions, and the like. Coastal programs almost always involve multiple levels of government. If directives are clear and the jurisdiction and structure of the program are well established, then commitment from top officials and stakeholders will more likely result in successful implementation (Mazmanian and Sabatier, 1989). The more tractable problems have fewer technical uncertainties, small monolithic target groups, and manageable behavioral change. Success is more likely if the technology is straightforward and the socioeconomic conditions can support the behavioral change intended.

However, implementation can create debate and even lawsuits. The interest groups that weighed in about the nature of the problem and the selection of a solution also seek to influence implementation. In essence, implementation becomes interaction among special interests with often disparate goals that may or may not fit with the initial policy mandate (Bardach, 1977). The basis for a program, usually a law, is interpreted through rules, plans, and directives. When the required change in human behavior is large or costly, the parties seek the assistance of the courts to clarify the intent of the law and make sure that the regulations follow it. This discussion is fueled by unresolved issues that lurked in the background of the earlier stages of the policy process.

Conventional government programs are implemented by administrative organizations established for that purpose (Anderson, 1979; Brewer and deLeon, 1983; Jones, 1984). They are charged with putting into effect the rules that specify relationships within society. To facilitate effective programs, current federal budget allocation systems can provide enhanced funding to successful government programs as a positive incentive. Backing from well-organized interests helps because administrators consider the amount of power inherent in the program. Each of the coastal issues summarized in table 2.2 has been addressed through a law. Each law has been separately implemented with the primary objectives noted.

Many executive departments and independent agencies administer coastal and ocean activities (table 2.3). Furthermore, participants in program implementation include more than the government officials in the administrative agency charged with producing results. The "who" includes legislators, judges, private citizens, corporations, and interest groups.

TABLE 2.2.
Primary coastal issues.

Issue	Law	Objective(s)
Water quality	Clean Water Act	Restore and maintain integrity of the nation's waters
Sewage	Clean Water Act	Protect human health and the environment
Dredging	Clean Water Act/ Water Resources Development Act	Cost share environmentally acceptable disposal of dredged material
Coastal wetlands	Clean Water Act	No net loss of coastal wetlands
Oil and gas/wind	Outer Continental Shelf Lands Act	Extract energy in a way compatible with natural and social systems
Oil spills	Oil Pollution Act	Hold responsible parties liable for oil spills
Coastal development	Coastal Zone Management Act	Protect and develop the coast through planning processes and zoning
Natural hazards and environmental protection	Coastal Barrier Resources Act, Flood Disaster Protection Act	Reduce federal subsidies that encourage development on barriers
Fisheries	Fishery Conservation and Management Act	Sustain harvest and conserve habitat
Watersheds	Clean Water Act, Coastal Zone Management Act	Control land uses that affect coastal waters

Evaluation

The most basic question about a coastal policy or program is the one that began this book: does it work? Evaluation provides some answers. Systematic examination to understand a program's impact usually focuses on outcomes or how conditions have changed as a result of program activities (Hatry et al., 1981). The most effective evaluations follow a systematic approach (Jones, 1984; Brewer and deLeon, 1983). First, it's important to specify a well-defined overall goal as the basis for analysis. Obviously, it's difficult to judge whether a program met its objective if that objective

TABLE 2.3.
Federal coastal and ocean departments and agencies.

Department/Agency	Mission Example(s)
Department of Agriculture	Farm fertilization practices; growth of fish in captivity
Department of Commerce	Management of fisheries and marine sanctuaries
Department of Defense	National security and waterway development
Department of Energy	Creation of new energy systems
Department of Health and Human Services	Seafood safety
Department of Homeland Security	Hurricane response and enforcement of maritime law
Department of the Interior	Energy development, national seashores, and wildlife areas
Department of Justice	Litigation of environmental and natural resources issues
Department of Labor	Worker safety
Department of State	International ocean management and law
Department of Transportation	U.S. shipping industry
Environmental Protection Agency	Water quality management
National Aeronautics and Space Administration	Remote sensing of the ocean
National Science Foundation	Basic scientific research

is unclear or unrealistic. Measuring change reasonably attributable to the program under consideration and assigning cause form the core of the evaluation.

Evaluators can focus on efficiency, effectiveness, and equity of the program. Efficiency is judged by measures such as cost per unit, while effectiveness hinges on the total impact of the program. In the context of coastal water pollution, an efficient program provides low cost per unit of pollution removed, while an effective program removes sufficient levels of pollution for the water to be used as desired. Equity implies a fair distribution of costs and benefits across society. In the case of water pollution one might assert that those who benefit and those who pay should see equivalent burdens and benefits. Questions of environmental justice emerge when programs are not equitable and place toxics in poor neighborhoods or expect one portion of society to pay excessively for water cleanup while another portion benefits.

Evaluations assess both a program's results (outcomes) and its process (outputs) (Jones, 1984; Anderson, 1979). Outputs are defined as the actions taken by the government or some intermediary to create the desired change. Regulations, plans, establishment of governmental organizations, and permits are examples of outputs. Measured changes in the system that the program was designed to affect and that may be reasonably attributed to the program constitute the outcomes. Improved water quality due to a specific program is a successful outcome.

To see how these general principles of evaluation might be applied, let's consider a hypothetical program that seeks to limit litter on the beach. To achieve this goal, custodians of the beach may provide information to the public about how litter harms the ecosystem. The number of individuals reached by the information program is one measure of output. One hopes for a behavioral change, the program outcome, that results in less litter discarded. Assuming that beach users are the main source of litter, a decline in litter per unit of beach would constitute a favorable program outcome and the public information program or output would be deemed effective. In this example, the success in both output and outcome strongly supports continuation of public education as a means to reduce litter.

Because programs inside and outside of government affect virtually all citizens and cost large amounts of money, many entities participate in evaluation (Jones, 1984; Anderson, 1979). Congress regularly invites agencies that implement programs to report on results in oversight hearings. Congressional staff or employees of the Government Accountability Office complete evaluations that include detailed descriptions of programs. Members of Congress also hear from their constituents, particularly if a program is not working well. In some cases the appointments of program directors require approval by Congress, which provides another opportunity for evaluation and a time to discuss needed changes. Together these congressional assessments drive opinions of the program, which can influence its funding. Additionally, the interest groups that pushed for government action in the first place complete analysis of program results.

Insightful evaluation provides an avenue for improving a program—if its failures are honestly assessed. Anderson (1979) identified multiple causes for program failure. Some programs fail due to mistakes in the early stages. The problem could be plagued by a design failure in which conflicting goals are not adequately rectified and as a result working on just one of them will not create a successful result. Evaluation may also reveal an unrealistic appraisal of the situation and the potential of so-lutions. Evaluation may lead to questions about whether governmental mechanisms can achieve the results desired. One alternative is to con-sider nongovernmental policy instruments, such as voluntary programs (table 2.1). Voluntary instruments, including values instilled by family and community, charitable organizations, and private markets (Howlett and Ramesh, 1995), have grown in importance in recent years. In addition the evaluation may find a new problem attracting attention away from the original one or an erroneous interpretation of how to solve the prob-lem. Coastal governance competes for attention with related topics such as homeland security. In operation, programs can fail because resources to carry them out were limited; administration was ineffective; or the cost of the solution was simply too great. After a program has been in place for a while one may observe that the original problem has changed, and, as a result, the initial solution must be altered.

Most commonly, evaluation, by identifying weaknesses, creates the need to respond. Those responses may include a redefinition of the prob-lem followed by revisiting each of the stages (figure 2.1). In the simplest cases, the evaluation produces support without significant change (An-derson, 1979). Next and most commonly, incremental adjustment may be proposed. For example, at a five-year interval, Congress evaluates and in many instances revises federal laws related to the coast. Finally, a program shift, problem redefinition, or emergence of a new problem may trigger substantial change for a coastal program. For example, the *Exxon Valdez* oil spill triggered an evaluation of and ultimate change in the law related to oil tankers.

Each mismatch between our intentions as a society and the condi-tion of our coastal environment signals either a weakness in an existing program or the need for a new one. Evaluation specifies the nature of the remaining problems and starts another cycle of the policy process, as shown in figure 2.1. Most recently, the Pew and U.S. commissions have taken a comprehensive approach to evaluation, and their proposals for improving coastal governance will factor into our discussions in subse-quent chapters.

Summary

Growing human populations, conflicting uses, changing environmental conditions, and advancing technologies inevitably draw the government into supervising more coastal activities. This chapter presented a compre-hensive approach to understanding how coastal policies originate, what they consist of, how they are selected and carried out, and in the end, how they are evaluated. As we have seen, the policy process for coastal management may be viewed through five stages: problems, solutions, selection, implementation, and evaluation.

Given the evolving nature of policy development and enactment, how can we expect to use the stages as we examine contemporary coastal challenges? By identifying a stage or stages pertinent for a topic of interest, we can ask a number of questions. Who are the players as the problem is defined or as the solution is selected? Who carries out the program? How do the players interact at any stage? What coastal conditions are we trying to address? What are the alternatives for approaching the issues? What kinds of policy instruments can we adopt to address the problem? In each of the chapters that follow, we rely on insights from the stages framework and questions that arise from it to develop a more detailed understanding of how policy is made and implemented for specific issues. Well-informed policies hold great promise for closing the gap between the coast we have and the coast we want.

3

Wastewater

As we've discussed, coastal policy seeks to resolve conflicts among the various ways we use the land and water along our shores. Intuitively, one of the most striking conflicts is between relying on coastal waters as a source of food and a dumping ground for human waste. Yet humanity has been doing both since its earliest gatherings. As cities developed, disposing of waste in coastal waters became common, eventually contaminating seafood and causing severe illness. The following pages focus on this fundamental conflict, and the science, technology, and law to resolve it. In this chapter, we examine how the policy process, through sector-based management, has been used to address the problem.

Sewage and disease: A problem

Human health drives public policy. The installation of sewers and ultimately the development of sewage treatment in New York City illustrate this phenomenon. By 1664, the one thousand settlers of what was to become New York had established a practice of dumping chamber pots in open drainage ditches in the streets, which flowed to the rivers on either side of the island of Manhattan (Goldman, 1997; Kurlansky, 2006). By the 1830s open sewers had given way to closed systems beneath the streets, but the effect remained the same: untreated human waste was discharged to marine waters. At the time, flowing waters were presumed to purify wastes, an assumption we now know to be false.

Waste was often discharged near oyster grounds, and with many New Yorkers consuming oysters in great quantities, the contamination led to hundreds of deaths from cholera in 1832 (Kurlansky, 2006). Although this was not fully understood at the time, cholera is an infectious gastro-intestinal disease caused by bacteria. Plentiful supplies of safe drinking water, had they been available, could have averted some of the deaths. But heavy reliance on wells for drinking water limited the ability to provide uniformly safe supplies. In essence, the system to move human and animal waste off the island or treat it was not effective enough to protect groundwater. One solution was to import water.

In 1842 the Croton Aqueduct began flowing from a rural area north of the city, and in a few years nearly two hundred miles of water pipes were in operation (Goldman, 1997). Clean drinking water became available to large parts of the city. With clean water from a secure source, an important impediment to city growth had been eliminated.

However, there were consequences. Although imported water helped alleviate one aspect of the health problem, the resulting growth complicated it. More than one hundred miles of sewers collected wastewater and discharged human, animal, and other wastes without treatment. Oysters continued to be contaminated. In 1854 the death of prominent New Yorkers from cholera made people suspect that the disease might be triggered by oysters rather than by the filth and habits of the poor, as had been assumed previously. By the 1880s and 1890s, "oyster panic," as it was called, had been related to contaminated food.

The change in understanding began in 1884 when Robert Koch demonstrated that the bacterium *Vibrio cholerae* was responsible for cholera (Kurlansky, 2006). A year later, the bacterium was recovered from harbor waters in France at the same time an epidemic was occurring on land. *Salmonella bacillus*, the cause of typhoid, was also identified in water and oysters. These developments unequivocally linked two major diseases to the consumption of tainted oysters. Human disease, not to mention odor, led to demands for further change in the way human waste was handled. In terms of the policy process outlined in the last chapter, a specific problem had been identified. Now, the public needed a solution.

Sewage treatment: A solution

In this case, the solution was fairly straightforward: collect wastes from the sewers and treat them prior to discharge while at the same time discouraging consumption of shellfish from contaminated areas. In other cities the privy or outhouse had been used, and in London waste disposal had been shifted closer to the ocean. But ultimately treatment became a common technical approach to human waste.

By the early 1900s New York City had constructed three sewage treatment plants, and by 1910 a fourteen-plant system for the city had been designed and all were constructed in the following decades of the twentieth century (Bloomberg and Lloyd, 2007). Older coastal cities went through a sequence of events like those in New York. In each case, the result was a wastewater collection system similar to the one diagramed in figure 3.1. Over time enhancements at the wastewater treatment and disinfection step rendered the discharges less harmful to human health and the environment.

To see how this system works, we will follow the flow of wastewater from its origins to its eventual discharge in marine waters (Laws, 2000; Tchobanoglous and Schroeder, 1987; Mueller and Anderson, 1983). Pipes from homes, businesses, and street surfaces transport sewage and street runoff using gravity and pumps. In coastal areas surface runoff—water draining from roads, parking lots, and roofs—deserves special consideration. Originally when cities such as New York were built, it was easiest to deposit street runoff and human wastes in the same pipe, in *combined sewers*. Cracked pipes may also allow groundwater into the collection system, which adds to the volume for treatment. Because there was no treatment prior to discharge at the time the pipes were originally laid, the only constraint on the volume of water was the size of the pipe. The system worked effectively to move wastes away from people at low cost. Adding wastewater treatment changed the system. The wastewater could be purified only if it could be held for a time in tanks at a sewage treatment plant. Therefore, the size of the tanks at the plant affected how much water could be accepted. To economize, plants were constructed to handle dry weather flows only. During heavy rains the tanks at the plants were not sufficient for sewage and the large amounts of runoff from the streets. If there was a possibility of overwhelming the plant with too much wastewater, combined sewer overflows released untreated material to the estuary, causing significant contamination of marine waters and shellfish by human waste. This problem continues to the present in many U.S. cities.

Under normal conditions, as the wastewater enters the sewage treatment plant, physical, chemical, and biological processes reduce pathogens and remove materials that disrupt natural processes in the estuary. Figure 3.2 shows the techniques commonly used. First, screens remove larger

Generation ➔ Collection ➔ Treatment ➔ Use or Disposal

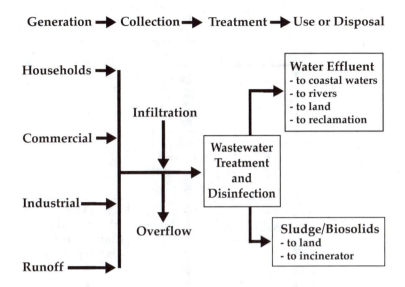

Figure 3.1. Municipal wastewater collection system. In combined sewer systems wastewater from commercial and industrial facilities as well as households and street drainage flows through pipes under urban and many suburban areas. After treatment and disinfection the effluent waters are most frequently discharged to river or coastal waters. During wet weather the capacity of the wastewater facility may be inadequate, so untreated material overflows directly to discharge waters unless special systems are constructed to control it.

materials such as garbage from the streets that has gotten into the sewers. In addition, a grit removal chamber collects sand by allowing it to quickly sink in a tank. The effluent and its load of organic particles then move to a primary sedimentation tank where, over a period of hours, the fine organic particles sink. When removed from the bottom of the tank, these particles are known as sludge. At the end of primary treatment, fifty to sixty percent of the suspended solids have been removed from the water (Mueller and Anderson, 1983). Because these particles, if released to coastal waters, would be degraded by bacteria, thereby consuming oxygen in the water, successful primary treatment reduces some of the problem of hypoxia, or low oxygen, in coastal waters. Biochemical oxygen demand (BOD), the use of oxygen in degrading wastes, is reduced by approximately thirty-five percent after primary treatment (Mueller and Anderson, 1983).

The next process, called secondary treatment, is completed in almost

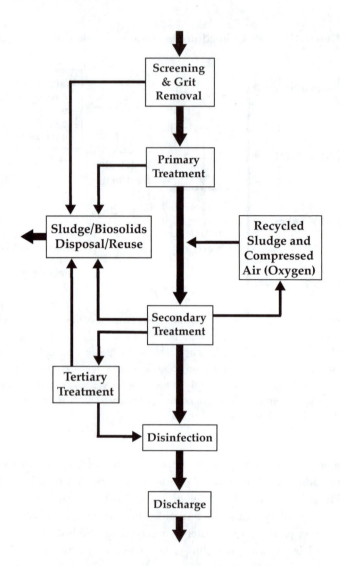

Figure 3.2. Wastewater treatment and disinfection. At treatment plants physical, chemical, and biological processes are used to separate organic materials (sludge or biosolids) from effluent waters, which are disinfected before release.

every coastal sewage treatment plant in the United States. It involves the breakdown of organic particles that remain in the effluent from primary treatment by creating conditions for bacteria to use the particles as a source of food. To accomplish this, the secondary treatment tank is inoculated with sludge containing the bacteria and provided with air to deliver oxygen for the bacteria. Under these conditions the large supply of fine organic particles from primary treatment is degraded. After the bacteria grow, secondary sedimentation or clarification separates the microbial mass from the water by allowing the mass to settle to the bottom of the tank, where it is drawn off as sludge. After primary and secondary treatment, eighty-five to ninety percent of the suspended solids have been removed along with a similar amount of the biochemical oxygen demand (Mueller and Anderson, 1983). Most of the metals, such as copper, nickel, and cadmium, reside with the organic particles. Therefore, collecting the particles as sludge can reduce the metal levels in the liquid waste stream by as much as sixty-five percent.

Two major problems remain for effluents discharged to coastal waters. One is the level of nitrogen in the water. Adding nitrogen to marine waters often produces rapid growth of algae. Tertiary treatment can reduce the amount of nitrogen in the effluent by eighty to ninety percent (Mueller and Anderson, 1983), most commonly by biologically converting it to gas through a process known as biological nitrogen removal, which relies on bacteria to assist in the conversions. Because most of the atmosphere is nitrogen, release of the gas is harmless.

The second remaining issue is control of the microorganisms found in the wastewater, some of which cause disease in humans (Tchobanoglous and Schroeder, 1987). Bacteria, fungi, algae, protozoa, worms, rotifers, crustaceans, and viruses are present in wastewater. These organisms can cause typhoid fever and cholera, as well as other diseases. The former causes high fever, diarrhea, and ulceration of the small intestine. The latter can result in heavy diarrhea, dehydration, and a high death rate. In addition, gastroenteritis and infective hepatitis, caused by viruses, result in diarrhea or jaundice and fever, respectively.

To minimize or eliminate harm, it is critical to selectively destroy disease-causing organisms (National Research Council, 1993). Popular techniques include chlorination, ozonation, and ultraviolet disinfection (EPA, 1999a–c). Chlorine, the most widely used disinfectant, oxidizes cellular material, destroying pathogenic organisms. Because the residual chlorine in the effluent is toxic to aquatic organisms, it is often removed through an additional chemical process. Alternatively, ozone gas may be used to oxidize the cell walls of the pathogenic organisms and damage their nucleic acids. This effectively destroys many bacteria and viruses without adding harmful residual chemicals to the effluent. However, it is expensive and therefore rarely used in the United States. A final alternative is to expose the wastewater to ultraviolet (UV) light using specially designed lamps. The UV light penetrates the cell wall and disrupts the genetic material of the microorganisms, which limits their ability to reproduce. UV does not produce a residual and is becoming more common in U.S. plants as chlorine is phased out.

Even successful treatment of wastewater results in a final problem: sludge. This unsavory substance is primarily water with a dilute concentration of organic particles, usually on the order of one to ten percent dry solids. As we've seen, both primary and secondary sewage treatment produces sludge, which can contain metals and synthetic organic chemicals. The management of sludge in coastal areas has gone through a number of significant changes. The nature of the material lends itself to disposal at sea, in the air (via incineration), or on the land (National Research Council, 1978a). Urban areas such as New York City at first disposed of their sludge at sea, and, as wastewater treatment improved, the amount increased (Burroughs, 1988). However, by 1988 federal law banned ocean disposal of sewage sludge because it was damaging marine resources and creating the potential for human health problems. Eliminating the sea as a final resting place for sludge put further pressure on the air and land.

A second disposal alternative is incineration, which may provide energy. However, the emissions from combustion have proven problematic, and, even with scrubbers, it was apparent many years ago that sludge incinerators would not meet air quality standards in many geographic areas (National Research Council, 1978a).

The third option includes various ways of using the material on the land. For many years, sludge has been disposed in landfills. This practice has opened the possibility for contamination of surface- or groundwater. Careful design of application approaches in these settings makes the practice viable, but many new opportunities for recycling the nutrients on land are developing.

One of the most important is the conversion of sludge into fertilizer and other usable biosolids. This has been made possible by two important transitions. First, toxic contaminants in sludge have declined due to *pretreatment*, the requirement that industries remove contaminants before discharging to the sewers. Pretreatment dramatically lowers metals and synthetic organic chemicals in the sludge. Sludge that is too high in these chemicals is not desirable because plants may assimilate toxins. Secondly, advances during the 1990s led to composting and other processing techniques that reduce pathogens after sludge is produced. As the levels of metals, synthetic organic chemicals, and pathogens decrease, sludge can increasingly be used as a biosolid. By the late 1990s, approximately 6.9 million tons of biosolids were produced annually in the United States, and about sixty percent were recycled on land. The U.S. Environmental Protection Agency (EPA) projects that the total amount of biosolids recycled will rise (EPA, 1999d). Typical reuse includes land application, composting, and landfill cover.

Making treatment a requirement: Selection and implementation

Treating wastewater remained a prerogative of states and local communities until 1972. Then the law, rules, and governmental processes for managing wastewater changed dramatically. Environmental protection had become a central, national issue for citizens and politicians, and few felt that existing water quality or pollution controls were adequate. Improving coastal water quality by managing sewage had a clear technical solution—wastewater treatment. The missing element up until 1972 was the political will to establish unequivocal rules for requiring treatment.

The goal of the Federal Water Pollution Act Amendments of 1972, now called the Clean Water Act, was to make waters "fishable and swimmable" by restoring and maintaining "the chemical, physical, and biological integrity of the nation's waters" (Federal Water Pollution Control Act Amendments of 1972; Freeman, 1990; Alder et al., 1993). The law charges individual states with identifying uses for coastal waters and, using federal assistance, with establishing water quality standards adequate to pursue those uses. In approving the legislation the government ultimately selected secondary treatment as the technical means to meet many of these goals.

By restricting the level of contaminants discharged from individual *point sources*, such as sewage treatment plants or factories, the states help maintain a level of water quality in rivers, bays, and estuaries sufficient for intended uses. In essence, the government controls the composition of the wastewater through permits as described in box 3.1. Contaminant removal levels are mostly prescribed on the basis of what specific technologies can deliver. For sewage, bacterial degradation of organic material, typically through the activated sludge process described above, constitutes the technology that must be in place for almost all plants to get a permit. To ensure that the technology is operating correctly and reducing the major contaminants, the sewage treatment plant reports monthly on flow, suspended solids, fecal coliform bacteria, and the amount of oxygen

Box 3.1 . Permits—From Concept to Practice

Major changes in water pollution control occurred through a new law passed in 1972, the Federal Water Pollution Act Amendments of 1972. The law and regulations required that each water discharge from a pipe have a permit controlling the amount and composition of the wastewater being released. Permits are reissued periodically and restrictions on the wastes discharged can be tightened. Over time more stringent government supervision results in fewer pollutants in the discharges and ultimately cleaner coastal waters.

Human uses determine goals for water quality. For example, swimming requires very different water quality than shipping. If the use was known, then a water quality criterion for a geographic area of coastal waters could be established. For toxics the criterion might be a concentration low enough that damage to biological systems does not occur. Ultimately the water quality criteria are converted into standards that specify what can be in the discharges and in the adjacent coastal waters.

Meeting the desired uses often requires a reduction in the discharges of contaminants to coastal waters. Wastewater treatment removes pollutants in the discharge. The law and regulations require treatment technologies. Secondary or biological treatment of sewage is an example of a technology that has been mandated. Other pipe discharges from industries (e.g., aluminum smelters, car factories, textile mills, etc.) meet similar technology-based regulatory requirements. This regulatory approach assumes that discharge control will result in higher ambient water quality along the coast.

A combination of scientific rationale and technological capability comes to fruition only if a clear legally enforceable process is associated with it. The National Pollutant Discharge Elimination System (NPDES) constitutes that framework. EPA establishes minimum control levels on the basis of technology. In short, the permits require that the technology and its operation reduce pollution. Furthermore, a discharger to coastal waters anywhere in the country most likely would face similar requirements. Beyond these technology-based controls the law also maintains the option for further reduction through water quality–based controls. If the initial round of technology did not result in the uses intended, then stricter controls could follow.

The NPDES permits, usually issued to dischargers for five years or less, specify effluent limits for the contaminants in the wastewater and identify monitoring and reporting requirements that apply to each pollutant.

When effluent limits are exceeded, the discharger notifies the regulators, and, if the problems persist, legal action results. Requiring permits for pipe discharges to coastal waters dramatically reduced the amount of pollution discharged.

demand removed through treatment. Values for these parameters, as well as many others, must meet specified levels for the sewage treatment plant to be in compliance with its permit.

Industries, for the most part, have elected to discharge their wastewaters to municipal sewage treatment facilities. This creates a technological and regulatory challenge. The goal of reducing or eliminating discharges of metals and synthetic organics cannot easily be met at conventional sewage treatment plants, yet the need is real. Many coastal water quality problems are related to industrial contaminants. In 1972, the law required pretreatment to substantially reduce toxins prior to discharge into the sewers.

The phrase "toxic material" refers to the impact that certain chemicals have on organisms. Acute toxicity refers to deleterious effects, including death, that occur when an organism is exposed to a substance for a relatively brief period of time (Laws, 2000). As a result of litigation the EPA was charged with developing water quality criteria for more than 120 priority toxic pollutants (Adler et al., 1993). This approach was designed to ensure that intended uses of the waters would dictate the levels of contaminants present. Because of the dangers associated with toxics in food supplies and drinking water, limiting discharge was broadly accepted as an important aspect of improving water quality.

Did sewage treatment work? Evaluation

More than thirty-five years have passed since the law was changed. Over those years, taxpayers have funded the regulatory system and its related equipment and operation, giving citizens a clear financial, as well as personal health, stake in evaluating the results. Not only did the 1972 law require consistent use of secondary treatment, but it also provided funding for the creation and upgrading of sewage treatment facilities, initially as grants and more recently as loans managed by the states. Much of the funding was directed to coastal areas. Very significant increases in capacity and level of treatment resulted from this funding. Throughout the nation, some form of wastewater treatment was available to about 140 million people prior to the revision of the act in 1972, whereas by 2000 approximately 205 million people were served (EPA, 2004). Investments in technology reduced the flow of untreated wastewater to the environment, even as the population of coastal areas increased. Examined by these measures within the sewage treatment sector, the program was a great success.

However, coastal water quality in the United States, although improved, still requires additional attention (figure 1.1). If the desired program outcome is "fishable and swimmable" waters, then existing results are not satisfactory. Data on eutrophication, sediment contamination, and fish tissue have identified a number of regional problems along the U.S. coasts (EPA, 2008a). The contaminants in treated wastewater are just one element of the many sources of contaminants flowing to coastal waters. Excess nutrients from farming or other land uses cause eutrophication. Metals and persistent organic chemicals spread through the air or released on the land ultimately contaminate sediments and fish. So although focus on a single factor, sewage treatment, has resulted in substantial gains, additional work remains to improve overall water quality (Davies and Mazurek, 1998).

Unfinished business

Combined sewer overflows (CSOs) are one major item of unfinished business for coastal wastewater systems. CSOs occur because street drains collect precipitation and combine it in one pipe with sewage from houses and industries (Burroughs, 1999). During heavy rains, the flow exceeds the sewage treatment plant capacity and is shunted to coastal waters. Pathogens from CSOs and elsewhere limit swimming at coastal beaches and, as we've seen, render shellfish unfit for human consumption. Regular water sampling and testing for *Escherichia coli* and enterococci alert communities and bathers to water quality issues as required by the Beaches Environmental Assessment and Coastal Health Act of 2000. In recent years approximately five percent of beach days nationally were affected by advisories or closings (EPA, 2008b). Keeping people out of water that contains high levels of pathogens protects human health. But clearly a better solution would be to limit the pathogens introduced in the first place.

Several technical solutions exist to solve the problem of combined sewer overflows. One possibility is separating the flows by installing a new pipe for street drainage. Another is to install limited treatment equipment at multiple locations where the combined sewers discharge to coastal waters. A third approach is to install large tanks under the city to collect the flow during heavy rains. During the periods in between the rains the wastewater would be pumped up from the deep tanks to the sewage treatment plant and upon discharge meet all the standards for secondary treatment. These and other technological approaches make it possible to nearly eliminate the problem, but the costs of constructing these new systems are high.

Sector-based management

The municipal wastewater system illustrates how technology can solve a coastal management problem for an individual *sector*, or specific use of the coasts. In this case, one sector or use of coastal waters, wastewater disposal, collides with another, food production. Environmental processes connect these two uses—that is, pathogens travel from the waste to the food supply. The introduction of treatment technology makes the two uses more compatible. Developing this sector-based management program involved a scientific understanding of the cause of disease, technological solutions, social commitment, and governmental action.

Wastewater is one example of sector-based management. Many U.S. laws address individual sectors, focusing separately on topics such as oil exploitation, fishing, coastal hazards, aquaculture, offshore ports, and species protection (U.S. Commission on Ocean Policy, 2004, appendix D). Similarly, in Europe, sector-based programs have been established for urban wastewater treatment, dangerous substances, shellfish-growing waters, and bathing waters (McLusky and Elliott, 2004). In each case, one hopes that by changing the circumstances of a single use, multiple interests within society will be served. In this chapter we have seen that sector-based management directed at wastewater has significantly reduced the discharge of pathogens to coastal waters. With refinements such as pretreatment to control toxins and treatment of wastewaters in combined sewers, this sector-based approach has covered other problems associated with wastewater discharge.

However, as coastal populations grow, uses expand in type and intensity. To complicate matters the natural and social systems connect different uses in a variety of ways. Conflicts develop. Gaps in management become apparent. In the following chapters we will consider the strengths and weaknesses of sector-based management for oil drilling, dredging, and wetlands. Your challenge will be to assess the effectiveness of sector-based management in these different settings.

Summary

The use of coastal waters for waste disposal conflicts with other uses. In New York people became ill when they ate oysters contaminated with pathogens from wastewater. A similar pattern was repeated in many other locations. Requiring sewage treatment by law limits the amount of damage to other uses of coastal waters. Focusing on an individual use and resolving issues related to it is an example of sector-based management.

In this instance technology provided a solution. Wastewater treatment uses gravity to settle organic particles in large tanks followed by a biological process that breaks down the remaining organic particles. By disinfecting the effluent prior to discharge to coastal waters, pathogens are limited, protecting public health. Cleaning wastewater creates sludge, which can be processed into biosolids and recycled. Increasingly these materials are being used to fertilize the land.

In 1972, a change in federal law required that wastewaters be treated and disinfected prior to discharge. The government mandated this sector-based program as a means of making U.S. waters fishable and swimmable. Two measures demonstrate progress: very few individuals now become ill from contaminated seafood and fewer than one in twenty beach days is affected by contaminated water. Yet, as shown in chapter 1, there remains a large gap between current and desired water quality. We still have work to do.

4

Oil

Oil and gas produced from under coastal waters contribute to domestic energy supplies. As a result, for more than a half century coastal policy and the nation's energy policy have been intertwined. The governance challenge over those decades has been to manage oil development so the coasts' natural and social systems can continue to meet the needs of all citizens. It's no secret that state governments, as well as many interest groups, object to offshore oil drilling, often because of oil spills and environmental impacts. In this chapter, we'll look at the basis for those disputes and examine whether the current sector-based management approach has proven up to the challenge of resolving them.

Oil resources: Origins and importance

Oil is solar energy provided in a liquid form. Through photosynthesis the sun powers the creation of organic materials, which, with the assistance of a series of geological events, can become oil and gas. Those accumulations are commonly found in rocks at the edge of ocean basins. Thus, crude oil is located in coastal environments where more and more people are flocking to live. The land/sea boundary has moved a lot over time, so oil deposits may be inland of or offshore from the present boundary. Nonetheless, this coincidence of oil formation and high human population densities near today's coastlines has important consequences for coastal management.

Although the details of individual oil deposits are subject to ongoing analysis, the overall process of oil formation is well understood (Deffeyes, 2005; Cook, 1976; Skinner and Turekian, 1973). The first stage is the growth of plants, compliments of solar energy and oceanic conditions that provide lots of nutrients in coastal waters. These organic materials are deposited on the ocean's bottom, where conditions are important. The ideal environment for oil formation contains low levels of oxygen, a natural condition that is observed in coastal seas and estuaries today. In this setting, the organic material is not oxidized on the bottom of the water body. The goal, if one wants oil, is to deposit organic-rich sediments, perhaps as high as ten percent organic carbon, as has happened in the Black Sea.

The next stage relies on increases in temperature to convert the organic material in the source beds to crude oil. If subsequent layers of sediments are deposited on top of the organic-rich bed, resulting in its burial to 7,500 feet (2,286 meters) or greater, the temperature rises to around 175 degrees Fahrenheit and the larger organic molecules that make up the organisms break into smaller pieces (Deffeyes, 2005). Crude oil consists of molecules with five to twenty carbon atoms. If the depth of burial is twice as great and the temperature becomes higher, the process results in molecules with five carbon atoms or fewer. These smaller molecules are natural gas at room temperature and pressure.

But creation of molecules of these highly desirable sizes is only part of the story. To be exploited, oil and natural gas must collect in deposits. It's important to recognize that roughly ninety percent of the oil formed slowly leaks to the surface of the earth and escapes as *oil seeps* because the geologic conditions to trap it at depth do not occur (Deffeyes, 2005). Oil seeps are estimated to contribute around sixty-two percent of the oil that reaches the ocean near North America today (National Research Council, 2003).

Fortunately, some of the crude oil moves within the earth but does not escape. It migrates upward mixed with salty water and, ideally, gets trapped by an impermeable layer above the porous rocks from which the oil can be extracted. These so-called *reservoir rocks* can be coral reef material or sand deposits similar to those features as they are found at the edge of oceans today. The *pore spaces* between the grains of sediment are where the oil molecules may be found. Pore spaces that are adequately connected result in more *permeable* rocks, which are desirable because oil molecules can flow from the reservoir to the oil well and be collected in tanks at the surface.

Once the oil is mobile it will reach the surface, becoming a seep, unless it encounters a *cap rock*. Cap rocks are sufficiently fine grained that the oil cannot leak upward through them. Very fine-grained mudstones or rocks formed through evaporation are nearly impermeable. With the right sequence and timing and all of these factors present, oil deposits can result, but it is a rare occurrence.

The presence of oil under marine waters has led to intense prospecting. At times the possibility of finding much more oil along the coasts has influenced energy policy. In 1974 the federal government's Project Independence declared that federal policies to lease the *outer continental shelf* (OCS) "can dramatically increase domestic oil production" (Federal Energy Administration, 1974, 8). The OCS is located seaward of state waters, which are generally limited to the first three miles (4.8 kilometers) from the shore. As the title of the 1974 report indicates, OCS leasing was offered as a means to make the United States independent of foreign oil suppliers.

An examination of the recent history of U.S. oil supply and consumption (figure 4.1)—or simply a glance at the daily headlines—reveals how well this plan turned out. Federal OCS production of crude oil and condensate had reached a plateau by the time of the Project Independence report and has only slightly increased since. Total U.S. oil production, including from the OCS, peaked in 1970 and has declined since (Hubbert, 1956; Deffeyes, 2005). If domestic production was to eliminate the need for foreign oil, or even to remain constant, dramatic increases in production from the OCS would have been needed to offset declining production onshore and under state-controlled waters. The requisite increases did not materialize, and the nation began to import ever more oil from overseas to compensate for the growing gap (figure 4.1).

The rest of U.S. demand for petroleum was made up by imports of crude oil and products (figure 4.1). Ironically, the United States has also exported as much as 0.66 billion barrels of oil per year. Although significant amounts of oil come from the OCS, the amount is nowhere near the total needed to match declines in domestic production elsewhere and growing demand (figure 4.1). In recent years OCS oil production contributed just over 2.5 percent of total U.S. energy supply or about seven percent of liquid petroleum supply (Energy Information Administration, 2009).

Oil drilling technology

Recovering oil and gas from deep water requires that the equipment necessary for drilling on land be placed on a large platform able to cope

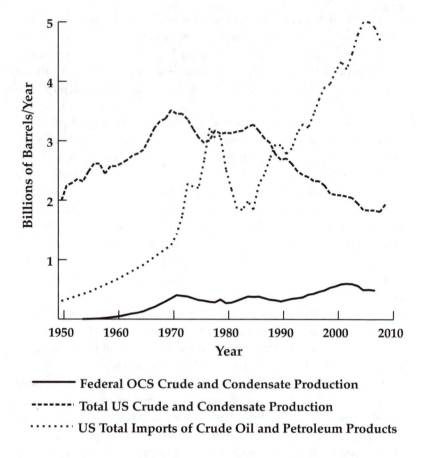

Federal OCS Crude and Condensate Production

Total US Crude and Condensate Production

US Total Imports of Crude Oil and Petroleum Products

Figure 4.1. Sources of crude oil and petroleum products for the United States. Total U.S. domestic crude oil production (dashes) has declined since the early 1970s and federal OCS oil production (solid line) has increased only slightly since that time, so imports of crude and products (dots) have risen rapidly to replace declining domestic production and increasing total demand for oil both consumed in the United States and exported from it. The peak year of OCS oil production was 2002. Data sources: Energy Information Administration, 2009.

with all the challenges of the sea. To understand the state of the art of offshore development, let's consider both drilling and the means used to respond to an oil spill should the technologies fail.

Rotary drilling, as the name implies, consists of rotating a specially de-signed *drill bit* at the end of a pipe so this *drill string* can penetrate ever deeper into the earth (Beebe, 1961; Kash et al., 1973; Raymond and

Leffler, 2006). As the drill bit "makes hole" or gets deeper into the earth, the rock chips or drill cuttings that it dislodges must be removed from the hole so the drilling apparatus does not jam. Operators use a mixture of water, clay, and a variety of additives to create *drilling mud*. The drilling mud flows down the hollow center of the drill string under high pressure, squirts out through holes in the drill bit, and carries the drill cuttings upward outside of the drill string but inside the well. For part of this journey upward the drill mud and cuttings will be contained by the rock walls of the newly created hole; above that level a *casing* of steel pipe will contain the flow. In most instances the outside of the steel casing is cemented to the rock formation. Not only do drill muds move the cuttings, but, properly formulated and delivered, they will balance the enormous pressures from the mixtures of oil, gas, and saltwater that lie deep in the earth. These *formation pressures* come about because fluids in the rocks adjacent to the hole are under the weight of what can be a mile or two of rock and liquid *overburden,* while the drill hole is potentially open to the surface.

If for some reason the pressure of the mud system becomes much less than that in the formation, then fluids from the formation will flow into the well bore. In extreme cases called *blowouts*, a mixture of oil, gas, and/ or water rushes into the well from the formation, rapidly ascends the well bore, and bursts out around the well machinery at the surface. Often at the surface a spark will set the mixture afire, and as long as fuel from the well and oxygen from the atmosphere are plentifully available, the fire will burn. Blowouts and associated fires cause loss of life and massive damage to the environment on land or at sea.

With careful monitoring of the well pressures and other factors blowouts can be prevented. However, because they do happen and the results are devastating, special safety systems have evolved to control them (National Research Council, 1981; Goins and Sheffield, 1983; Goldsmith, 2005). *Blow-out preventers* (BOPs) consist of hydraulically operated rams that close off the flow in the space between the drill string and the casing, or stop all flow in the casing by closing the well if the drill pipe has been withdrawn, or pinch/shear the drill pipe to shut it off. Given that several shut-off configurations might be required, the system consists of a BOP stack of separate preventers that, when assembled, may be dozens of feet tall. On land the BOP is located on top of the casing above the earth's surface but below the well drilling machinery. In deepwater drilling, the BOP is at the bottom of the sea.

In instances where the BOP technology fails, uncontrolled open flows may exceed 100,000 barrels per day from deepwater Gulf of Mexico reservoirs (Goldsmith, 2005). Whether at sea or on land, these situations require regaining the ability to balance formation pressure with some intervention in the well. Often the solution is to drill another well or wells to relieve formation pressure on the blowout well and ultimately inject cement into the damaged well to prevent further flow.

The complex challenges that go into well control become even more difficult when oil prospecting moves seaward. By developing technology to find and produce oil from the deeper water *continental slope* and *continental rise* portions of the *continental margin,* oil firms can search over a larger area of the earth's surface (Burroughs 1986). In the first phase of offshore drilling, land techniques migrated seaward on timber pile structures off the coasts of California and Louisiana. This early work was done right along the shore or in bays within easy reach of the shore. By the 1940s drilling had moved some distance from the shore, and steel structures to support the drill rigs became common.

Exploratory drilling expanded to ever greater depths when another innovation was adopted. By 1949 this second phase of offshore development began when the first *mobile offshore drilling unit* was introduced in the Gulf of Mexico (Graff, 1981). This barge-mounted drill rig could operate in depths of up to twenty feet (six meters) of water. When the mobile rig moved away a separate well protector platform would be erected at the casing and petroleum production activities could move ahead through surface activities located on a platform more permanently attached to the seabed.

The ability to drill in deeper waters rapidly increased with *subsea completion* of the well. The technology making a subsea completion possible consists of a system of valves placed at the seafloor to control the flow of fluids from the well to a platform or floating production facility. Free diving for maintenance is not possible due to the great depth, so equipment is lowered from the surface and tended by remotely operated submarines. Ultimately when a *subsea production system* is installed, the equipment is used to produce oil and gas from one or more wells and deliver it to the surface. Production wells are drilled in Gulf of Mexico waters that are over a mile deep, and some wells are found in waters much deeper (Paganie, 2010).

A third phase of technological development related to oil is the ability to recover it once spilled. Oil enters marine waters through a variety of pathways (table 4.1). Platform spills including blowouts, produced waters,

TABLE 4.1.
Best estimates of annual releases of petroleum in thousands of tonnes to
North American waters over the period 1990–1999. Source: National
Research Council, 2003.

Source	Release
NATURAL SEEPS	160
EXTRACTION OF PETROLEUM	
Platforms	0.16
Atmospheric deposition	0.12
Produced waters	2.7
TRANSPORTATION	
Pipeline spills	1.9
Tank vessel spills	5.3
Coastal facility spills	1.9
Atmospheric deposition	0.01
CONSUMPTION OF PETROLEUM	
Land-based (river and runoff)	54
Recreational marine vessels	5.6
Spills (non-tank vessels)	1.2
Operational discharges (vessels)	0.22
Atmospheric deposition	21
Jettisoned aircraft fuel	1.5
TOTAL	260

and pipeline ruptures contribute about five percent of the total anthropogenic load to waters around North America.

Several types of oil spill recovery equipment are used. Booms and
skimmers are the primary mechanical techniques to control or recover
oil at the surface of the sea (Office of Technology Assessment, 1990;
Clark, 2001). A boom consists of a top flotation element that rides on
the surface and a weighted skirt that extends beneath it. To the extent
that wave and current conditions allow, a boom will stop oil moving at
the surface. Booms may be used to protect shorelines or, when towed by
a vessel, collect oil on the surface. Skimmers are special vessels that collect oil by physical separation of the surface layer followed by pumping
the oil/water mixture aboard the boat or by moving an oil-absorbing
material through the oil and often squeezing the oil/water mixture into

a container on the vessel. Dispersants chemically assist in breaking up the slick into small droplets that, because of increased surface area, may be more rapidly degraded by bacterial action. Controversy concerning the toxicity of the dispersant or the dispersant/oil mixture, as well as the large amounts of the chemical that are required, has inhibited use. Another alternative is to burn the oil on the surface of the ocean. To do so it must be freshly spilled and in a layer of sufficient thickness, which can be accomplished by towing fireproof booms in the spill area and igniting the oil captured. Bioremediation has also been attempted. The goal of this technique is to create conditions, using specialized microbes and nutrients, where bacterial degradation and oxidation of oil molecules can proceed more rapidly than would naturally occur. In addition each major spill brings forward new cleanup attempts that at times have harmed marine environments. For example, chalk to sink oil, hot water to clean shorelines, and equipment on oiled marshes have resulted in significant unintended damage beyond that caused by the oil.

In contrast with advances in technology for deepwater oil drilling, oil spill recovery techniques have remained relatively unchanged over many years. Because deepwater wells are farther from the coast, sea surface conditions tend to be much rougher, which makes existing spill recovery approaches less effective. Once released in open waters, assessments show that only as much as about ten percent of the oil can be recovered by various means (National Research Council, 1985a; Office of Technology Assessment, 1990). With such low recovery rates, significant damage seems certain after most spills and prevention remains the most effective means of controlling risk.

Environmental and social impacts of offshore oil

Impacts occur both onshore and off, affecting both nature and society. Good governance demands the anticipation and avoidance of serious damage. The onshore effects of offshore oil result from ports, storage, refining, and communities to support them. Offshore impacts result from disruption and pollution of the marine environment. Both the natural areas around drilling sites and the people who live, work, and recreate there are affected in a variety of ways. For a list of significant environmental impacts, see table 4.2.

When U.S. oil development expanded from California and Louisiana to new so-called frontier areas of the coast, it became apparent that new onshore facilities and refineries would be necessary to support the extraction of oil and preparation of the crude oil for market. California and

TABLE 4.2
Significant environmental impacts associated with offshore oil activities.

Activity	Agents	Impacts
Seismic surveying	Noise	Impairment or death of organisms
Well drilling	Drill muds, cuttings, and sewage discharge; oil from operational or accidental release; air emissions	Water quality degradation; pelagic, benthic, and endangered species impacts; spatial conflicts—fishing, navigation
Drill rig and production facility fabrication	Land conversion, dredging, air and water discharges	Land use competition, workforce growth, decreased air and water quality
Separation of fluids offshore	Oil released with produced waters	Water quality and biota impacts
Enhanced recovery and/or deepwater operations	Chemical discharges	Water quality and biota impacts
Transportation/storage system construction	Dredging for pipelines and navigation; land conversion; pumping and storage facility location	Space conflicts; disturbed sediments; biota impacts
Transportation operations	Chronic and accidental discharges of oil; air emissions	Water quality and biota impacts; interference with fishing
Refining	Land use conflicts; refinery emissions and wastes	Air and water quality impacts; human health impacts; biota impacts
Decommissioning of offshore equipment	Spatial use of land or sea; contaminant release	Biota impacts

Louisiana underwent many decades of incremental change as oil technology developed and affected the coastal landscape. When new frontier areas are proposed, many residents become concerned about the potential environmental and social impacts (Council on Environmental Quality, 1974; Baldwin and Baldwin, 1975; National Research Council, 1978b; Burroughs, 1981; LaBelle, 2001).

Society and the environment are affected in different ways at each stage of oil development. In the exploration stage, geophysical surveys of the ocean floor are followed by exploratory drilling of the most promising areas. Geophysical survey ships do not require support onshore, whereas exploratory drilling operations are most efficient if bases to accommodate workers and store supplies (pipe, drill mud, chemicals, provisions, fuel, etc.) are built onshore immediately adjacent to the drilling site. These facilities consist of docks for the workboats that haul equipment and areas to store equipment near the dock. Air bases for helicopters that are used to fly crews to offshore rigs also occupy coastal lands. Because drilling rigs employ many dozens of people and all of these support facilities add jobs, coastal populations often increase at this early stage.

If commercially viable quantities of oil are found, the offshore oil field moves to the *development stage*. Construction of more permanent wells, pipelines, and perhaps ultimately refineries takes place over a few to several decades, depending on the size of the field. Although the actual construction occurs offshore, space on land is required to build the drill rigs and production facilities. Each of these land conversion activities has environmental consequences, such as marsh loss. The greater demand for land also raises real estate prices. Finally, the labor force supporting well construction grows, as can the need for schools, hospitals, police, and entertainment.

Offshore, drilling mud associated with the wells is discharged to ocean waters. Some of the additives to drilling fluids are toxic to marine organisms (Holdway, 2002). When discharged to the seabed in large amounts, drill muds and cuttings create anoxic conditions, nearly eliminating the benthos around the rigs (Clark, 2001).

During the subsequent *production stage* oil generally flows onshore for storage and distribution. To prepare for transporting the oil and gas, pipelines, handling facilities, and possibly new navigation channels are constructed. Navigation channels and pipeline corridors are often dredged through marshes, changing coastal hydrology and possibly introducing oil spills (Ko and Day, 2004). Once production begins, wells generate a mixture of oil, gas, and saltwater. These fluids are separated at the ocean's surface and the saltwater is discharged into the sea as produced formation water. Because some of the molecules that make up crude oil dissolve in saltwater, when it is returned to the sea petroleum and possibly other chemicals go with it, affecting marine organisms in a variety of ways (Holdway, 2002). The crude oil is transported to the shore by barge, pipeline, or tanker.

During production, total employment drops from the levels experienced during construction and the natural environment is affected by transportation, storage, and possibly refining. Tank farms, natural gas treatment facilities, and the pipelines that connect them to the oil wells may leak and cause damage. If an oil refinery has been built, it emits contaminants to the surrounding air, land, and water, further increasing the environmental burden.

Blowouts of oil wells, pipeline ruptures, and tanker accidents can release large amounts of oil. The first U.S. oil disaster to capture national attention occurred off the shores of Santa Barbara, California, in 1969 (Baldwin, 1970). For a period of days the well was out of control, and even after it was shut seepage continued at several points on the seafloor. Of the 1,500 birds brought to treatment centers, about ninety percent died. The broader impacts of this incident on the ecosystem are not known, but the photographs of oiled birds had a significant effect on how people viewed oil spills.

The next major incident to hit U.S. waters was a blowout at the Ixtoc exploratory well in 1979. It was drilled off the east coast of Mexico but ultimately affected the beaches of Texas (National Research Council, 1985a). The blowout started a fire that burned on the ocean surface over the well and consumed thirty to fifty percent of the oil released, while less than ten percent was recovered. At the time, high concentrations of petroleum hydrocarbons were observed at depth in the ocean at distances of up to 12.5 to 18.6 miles (twenty to thirty kilometers) from the blowout. Taken together, these observations indicate that oil did not just float on the surface but also collected on the seafloor, in the water column, and through evaporation and burning, in the atmosphere. Microbial populations near the blowout were high in organisms capable of degrading hydrocarbons, but due to nutrient limitations little degradation was noted (National Research Council, 1985a). Some three decades after Ixtoc, a similar but far more serious blowout occurred at BP Deepwater Horizon Macondo well in U.S. waters south of the Mississippi delta (box 4.1).

Oil spills have lethal and sublethal effects on broad ranges of marine organisms and environments (Laws, 2000; Clark, 2001; National Research Council, 2003). After a spill, oil not only floats on the surface but dissolves into the seawater and sinks into the water column or all the way to the bottom. As a result, its impacts are widespread. Crude oil is toxic to larval finfish at one to fifty parts per million, but individual aromatic compounds of oil are toxic at concentrations one hundred times lower (Laws, 2000). On shorelines where oil gets incorporated in fine-grained sediments, the zone of low oxygen retards bacterial degradation of the oil, which can remain in the sediments for a decade or more. When coated

Box 4.1. BP Deepwater Horizon Macondo Spill

On April 20, 2010, a blowout at the Macondo well resulted in a fire on the mobile offshore drilling unit Deepwater Horizon in the Gulf of Mexico. Eleven people were killed and control of the well was lost (Unified Command, www.deepwaterhorizonresponse.com). BP held the drilling permit for the site and had contracted Transocean, Inc., to drill the Macondo well using their dynamically positioned Deepwater Horizon drilling unit. The Department of the Interior leased the tract to BP in 2008, and the Minerals Management Service was supervising activities at the well on behalf of the federal government. The well had been drilled in about 5,000 feet (1,524 meters) of water and was located more than 40 miles (64 kilometers) from the coast of Louisiana.

High gas pressures, inadequate well control procedures, and a BOP failure contributed to the largest oil spill in the history of the nation. In the weeks after the blowout, fire, and sinking of the Deepwater Horizon, it became apparent that the well was flowing at a significant portion of its open flow potential. This continued for eighty-seven days. In early August after the flow had been stopped, a federal group reported that 4.9 million barrels of oil (206 million gallons) had been released (FRTG, 2010). The tanker *Exxon Valdez,* which prior to this incident had been responsible for the largest oil spill in U.S. waters, released only five percent of the amount attributable to the BP Macondo blowout.

Over the months of the spill various attempts were made, with limited success, to control the flow and contain and remove the oil. Finally a cap was fitted on top of the failed BOP and flow ceased. Relief wells, which potentially block the spill at the source miles below the seafloor, were viewed as the ultimate solution. While the well was flowing, devices installed above the failed BOP directed some of the oil and gas flow by pipe to a ship on the surface, where it could be burned or collected. Oil that formed slicks, mousse, and tarballs on the surface was skimmed or chemically dispersed offshore and, to the extent that the technology allowed, boomed away from sensitive inshore locations. Nonetheless, many hundreds of miles of shorelines were oiled, including particularly sensitive marshes. Booms were also used to collect freshly released oil near the well so that it could be burned while on the surface of the sea. A workforce numbering 20,000 or more was involved, and some were shown on television shoveling oil and sand mixtures for removal from Gulf Coast beaches.

The spill oiled birds, marine mammals, and turtles over large areas of the Gulf of Mexico. Plumes of oil were apparent at various depths in the water column. Marshes adjacent to the spill were oiled, and beaches in Louisiana, Mississippi, Alabama, and Florida were oiled, resulting in a steep drop-off in tourist visits to the shore. To ensure the safety of seafood, almost 87,000 square miles (more than 22.5 million hectares) of federal ocean waters were closed to fishing at one point. The combination of oil on the fishing grounds and oil on the beaches crippled important parts of the Gulf economy.

with oil, marsh plants lose the ability to effectively exchange gas with the atmosphere and cease photosynthesizing. This combined with direct tissue toxicity can result in a loss of marsh plants after a spill (Pezeshki et al., 2000). Sea birds are particularly vulnerable. After oil has coated the bird's plumage, seawater penetrates and both buoyancy and insulation disappear. As the bird attempts to remove oil, some is ingested. The combined effects result in death.

The social impacts of offshore oil disasters and development itself are equally important but less understood. Inevitably residents' stance on offshore drilling reflects how they believe it will affect their own lives. Oil development changes the environment, alters the availability and types of jobs, affects the character and amount of local growth, and influences life in coastal areas in many additional ways. Residents in many areas of the country believe the costs of oil development are too great and have sought to restrict or exclude it. Even though California has oil deposits off its shores, most citizens oppose further development.

On the other hand, Louisiana, Texas, and Alaska have been largely supportive of offshore drilling, but even those states are not free of dispute (Freudenburg and Gramling, 1994; Gramling and Freudenburg, 2006). Louisiana tends to favor oil for several reasons. Many elements of offshore technology were developed in southern Louisiana, so residents could observe incremental changes and to a certain extent participate in the development of new technologies. Also, low population density and the prevalence of marshes and potential harbors made accommodating oil easier than in other parts of the country. In addition many citizens there believe in extractive use of natural resources, have adapted to oil development, and have had positive experiences with people in the industry. Plus, many in Louisiana have gotten jobs in the industry. However, the BP Deepwater Horizon Macondo spill severely tested this goodwill, suspending fishing, damaging marshes, and threatening a way of life.

Law

Coastal law, if successful, not only governs oil sector development but also limits environmental and social damage. Development often conflicts with other uses by displacing them from scarce coastal land or degrading water quality. Consequently, the legal framework for OCS development apportions jurisdiction and establishes leasing procedures, assesses responsibility for spills and cleanup, and defines the relationship that oil developments will have with other coastal interests (table 4.3).

The need to divide federal and state ownership developed from a change in the technology itself (U.S. Commission on Ocean Policy, 2004; Juda, 1993; Mead et al., 1985; Burroughs, 1986). Because the resource extended seaward under coastal waters, the oil developers created new technology to exploit it. Initially California and Louisiana claimed the revenues from oil drilled under marine waters adjacent to their states. Not surprisingly, this became an issue for the federal government. Ultimately the Submerged Lands Act of 1953 resolved the boundary between the two domains. For most of the United States, that boundary is three nautical miles (5.6 kilometers) seaward of the *baseline*. Normally the baseline is the low or lower low-water line along the shore, or it extends across rivers and bays and across outer points of complex coastlines. The seafloor outside of state-owned submerged lands is the OCS. For historical reasons the separation along the west coast of Florida, Texas, and Puerto Rico is marked by a line nine nautical miles (16.7 kilometers) seaward of the baseline.

The Outer Continental Shelf Lands Act of 1953, revised in 1978, identifies how oil under federal OCS lands may be exploited by private corporations. The key step in the process is the leasing of three-mile by three-mile (4.8-kilometer) tracts of seafloor to a private corporation and, subject to a variety of rules, conveying rights to the oil and gas at that location. In general, corporations compete in terms of size of the *bonus bid* that the individual company is willing to pay to get access to the tract. To hold the land, the company pays a small rental fee and, as oil is produced, pays a *royalty* to the government that often amounts to 16.66 percent of the value of the oil produced (Mead et al., 1985). Other payment formulas are possible, but they should ensure that the citizens of the United States, who own the oil and gas, are adequately compensated for it. Because the amount of money collected is large—in many years second only to federal taxes—the federal government has a role as an arbiter that considers revenues from and environmental consequences of

TABLE 4.3
Laws affecting outer continental shelf oil and gas development.

Law	Federal Agency	Objective
OCS DEVELOPMENT		
Submerged Lands Act, 1953	Department of the Interior	Separate federal and state submerged lands
Outer Continental Shelf Lands Act, 1953 and 1978	Department of the Interior	Control leasing of federal offshore lands; environmental impacts
OCS Deep Water Royalty Relief Act, 1995	Department of the Interior	Encourage deepwater drilling by reducing royalties collected
Gulf of Mexico Energy Security Act, 2006	Department of the Interior	Share leasing revenues with Gulf producing states and reallocate leasing plans
OIL POLLUTION		
Federal Water Pollution Control Act Amendments, 1972 and revisions	U.S. EPA	Control operational discharges from oil and gas operations
Clean Air Act, 1990	U.S. EPA	Control air pollution from oil facilities
Oil Pollution Act, 1990	U.S. Coast Guard, Department of the Interior	Control and clean up oil spills
LINKS TO OTHER USES		
National Environmental Policy Act 1969	Department of the Interior and other federal agencies	Identify environmental consequences of federal actions
Coastal Zone Management Act 1972, 1990	Department of Commerce	Ensure that federal actions remain consistent with state plans for the coast
Rivers and Harbors Act	U.S. Army Corps of Engineers	Site offshore oil facilities away from shipping lanes
Endangered Species Act	Department of the Interior	Limit oil impacts on endangered species
Marine Mammal Protection Act	Department of Commerce	Limit oil impacts on marine mammals
Fishery Conservation and Management Act	Department of Commerce	Plan for interactions with commercial fisheries

oil development. From its inception to the mid twentieth century the revenues from OCS leasing flowed almost exclusively to the federal treasury, but the coastal states were burdened with the expenses for onshore infrastructure to support offshore oil.

The 1978 revision of the law more effectively incorporated environmental considerations (U.S. Commission on Ocean Policy, 2004). The changes mandated a schedule for the anticipated lease sales and a process for states to identify tracts or sales that, if developed, would likely cause environmental damage (figure 4.2). The revision also formalized an environmental studies program (Burroughs, 1981), further enforced the ability of states to determine if the development would be consistent with their plans, and established the means to create safer working conditions.

Key elements of the current process for leasing OCS lands were established following the 1978 revision. First, the government identifies and seeks comments on the geographic areas on the OCS for which it wishes to consider bids over a forthcoming five-year period. This process establishes a provisional list of potential areas to be leased and a schedule for considering each. Second, the department plans an individual lease sale by identifying an area, completing an environmental impact statement (EIS), and obtaining the views of the adjacent states through *federal consistency* determinations. These determinations assess whether federal plans match objectives the states have established for their coastal areas. This leads to the opening of the bonus bids and the award of the lease to the highest bidder. Third, after a company or group of companies receives a lease, exploration occurs by actually drilling in promising locations. Exploratory drilling requires a plan for activities, an environmental assessment, and permits for wells because a variety of resources are affected. Fourth, if commercially viable quantities of oil are found, a development and production plan is created. At this point, a commitment to well drilling and pipeline construction offshore and a variety of additional activities near and onshore will occur. Therefore, development activities and production plans must be consistent with state goals for the coast and require additional evaluation through the EIS processes. In short, the law demands considerable oversight by the federal government of safety and environmental protection associated with oil production.

Since 1978 there have been a number of prominent changes or additions to OCS law, including the OCS Deep Water Royalty Relief Act of 1995. By reducing the amount of the royalty due to the government, legislators tried to encourage oil firms to invest more in costly deepwater (greater than 656 feet [200 meters]) oil development. The goal was to

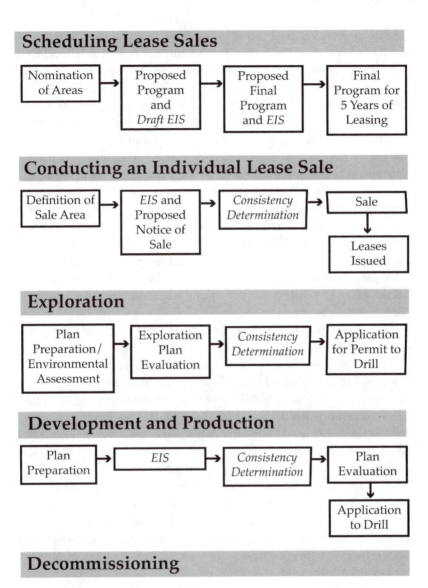

Scheduling Lease Sales

Nomination of Areas → Proposed Program and *Draft EIS* → Proposed Final Program and *EIS* → Final Program for 5 Years of Leasing

Conducting an Individual Lease Sale

Definition of Sale Area → *EIS* and Proposed Notice of Sale → *Consistency Determination* → Sale → Leases Issued

Exploration

Plan Preparation/ Environmental Assessment → Exploration Plan Evaluation → *Consistency Determination* → Application for Permit to Drill

Development and Production

Plan Preparation → *EIS* → *Consistency Determination* → Plan Evaluation → Application to Drill

Decommissioning

Figure 4.2. The leasing process. The Department of the Interior schedules and conducts lease sales and supervises exploration, development, production, and decommissioning of oil and gas fields on the OCS. EIS processes and consistency determinations, shown in italics, allow stakeholders to participate in some aspects of oil development decision making.

increase oil production. The Gulf of Mexico Energy Security Act of 2006 (PL 109-432) represented a clear recognition that coastal states bear costs and environmental damages associated with oil development and should receive some of the revenue generated. Accordingly, the act specified 37.5 percent of offshore oil revenues be apportioned to adjacent coastal states. Separate legislation awarded the states a share (twenty-seven percent) of the revenue to the federal government for oil produced from the three-mile (4.8 kilometers) wide zone that extends seaward of the state-federal line.

Most OCS law is implemented through the Department of the Interior. In 2010 after a series of management improprieties and the BP Deepwater Horizon blowout in the Gulf of Mexico, the Department of the Interior reorganized to eliminate the Minerals Management Service, the unit that had been responsible for these problems. In its place the Secretary created the Bureau of Ocean Energy Management, Regulation, and Enforcement with units to evaluate and lease resources, to ensure safety and environmental enforcement, and to collect revenues (Salazar, 2010a, b).

The second part of the legal framework governing offshore oil development addresses the response to and responsibilities for oil spills. Although multiple laws relate to spills, the Oil Pollution Act of 1990, created in response to the *Exxon Valdez* disaster, is the most important. The law empowers *natural resource trustees* in governmental entities to represent the public and ensure that the *responsible parties* for the spill restore the system damaged by it. Under the law, responsible parties are defined as those that own, operate, or charter a vessel or a facility responsible for oil discharges (U.S. Commission on Ocean Policy, 2004; National Research Council, 2003). Within some limits, the responsible parties are liable for cleanup costs and damages associated with the oil. These obligations include removal costs and compensation for damages to or loss of use of resources, destruction of private property, and loss of earning capacity, among other factors. Natural resource damage assessments quantify injuries and create a context for restorations (Grigalunas et al., 1998).

The third body of law related to offshore oil development encompasses specific provisions about its interactions with other uses of coastal lands and waters. EISs, required by the National Environmental Policy Act of 1969 (42 USC 4332), are one way to identify likely consequences of offshore oil activities. An EIS allows the Department of the Interior to compare alternatives to leasing and evaluate their relative effects on the environment.

The development of oil offshore affects navigation, environmental quality, and organisms (U.S. Commission on Ocean Policy, 2004). Each of these has attracted specific provisions in the law. The Rivers and Harbors Act gives the Corps of Engineers the responsibility to limit obstructions to navigation and therefore plays a role in the location of offshore platforms and activities. In addition the U.S. Coast Guard determines what lights and other signals the platforms should display.

Environmental quality is addressed in the Clean Air Act of 1990. A provision of this law regulates OCS air emissions and empowers the EPA to require that offshore facilities within twenty-five miles (forty kilometers) of the seaward boundary of a state adhere to the rules onshore. Because saltwater is commonly separated from oil and gas produced from wells at offshore locations, the Clean Water Act has a role in regulating the discharge.

Three prominent laws focused on the biology of coastal areas affect offshore oil (U.S. Commission on Ocean Policy, 2004). A provision of the Endangered Species Act requires federal agencies to consult the National Marine Fisheries Service and/or the U.S. Fish and Wildlife Service before undertaking any action, including oil development, that could harm a listed species. The National Marine Fisheries Service and Fish and Wildlife Service can issue a *biological opinion* to help ensure that reasonable and prudent activities are pursued before development may go forward. In the event that the oil development could affect a mammal, the Marine Mammal Protection Act applies. A letter authorizing disturbance or takes of mammals may be arranged under specific conditions. Finally, the Fishery Conservation and Management Act requires the Secretary of Commerce to advise the Secretary of the Interior about actions that can be taken to protect *essential fish habitat*.

If these laws had been able to protect the environment, while providing for harmonious uses for all coastal interests, then conflicts among users and between state and federal governments would have been minimal. However, that did not occur and the state of tension reached what some would call a rebellion.

The seaweed rebellion

By legislatively drawing a line in the water to divide state and federal control of oil and gas resources, the government resolved jurisdictional issues about what entities control and receive revenues from oil and gas development. However, natural and social systems span that line and many additional problems festered. Under the OCSLA, most benefits flow to the federal government, and most costs are the responsibility of state government. As a result many states opposed oil leasing, and their vigorous opposition to the federal government became known as the *seaweed rebellion*. Interests like oil, fishing, or tourism held diverse views about how to resolve coastal issues and gravitated to different branches and levels of government, according to which was most sympathetic. Many argue that one sector, oil, has dominated within the executive branch of the federal government and, to a large extent, within the courts. This is in spite of the fact that Congress and the Executive have enacted a number of laws to better represent the needs of other coastal users. As a result, those other coastal users, feeling disenfranchised by oil's influence at the federal level, have gravitated to state governments where their views are more likely to be supported.

The state-federal conflict grows from the distribution of costs and benefits related to oil (Fitzgerald, 2001). National benefits include federal revenue from oil sales, a domestic source of energy and jobs, and a reduction in the trade deficit because less oil is purchased from abroad. Coastal states bear most costs. Environmental damage affects fisheries, recreation, habitat, wetlands, and air quality, as well as other uses and the jobs that depend on them. These impacts are most acute during major oil spills, but normal construction and operation of oil development facilities also affect coastal lands, waters, and biota. Until recently coastal states have received negligible revenue from offshore development yet must provide infrastructure (roads, ports, hospitals, schools, etc.) to support the industry, the workers, and their families. The result has been an era of competition and conflict among the states and federal agencies that has spread from offshore oil to aquaculture, deepwater ports, and other activities in federal waters (Salcido, 2008).

The rebellion has manifested itself in a great variety of ways. We will highlight four: federal consistency, moratoria, revenue sharing, and oil spills. The Coastal Zone Management Act of 1972 (16 USC 1456) declared that if the federal government has approved a state's coastal plan, it cannot take actions that will run contrary to the state's objectives. Although the intent seems clear enough, years of controversy followed about which actions were subject to federal consistency review. States attempted to oppose certain leases or shape development activities, but the federal government was usually successful in supporting the oil industry's plans. Litigation extended all the way to the Supreme Court. Ultimately in 1990 the Coastal Zone Management Act was revised, clarifying that offshore development activities are subject to consistency reviews. In addition the law created a process for review of development and production activities (Fitzgerald, 2001). Under the consistency review guidelines, many oil development actions receive much closer scrutiny (National Oceanic and Atmospheric Administration, 2009).

Congressional moratoria on and *presidential withdrawal* of geographic areas for leasing, most commonly in deference to pressures from the states, comprise a second element of the seaweed rebellion (U.S. Commission on Ocean Policy, 2004; Fitzgerald, 2001). Congress identified regions, initially in California in 1982 and then around the nation, where federal agencies could not spend any money for lease sale preparation. Congress used its budgetary power to shape offshore oil policy, thereby addressing the needs of coastal users who had not previously been heard in the leasing process. This policy continued until 2008 when Congress failed to renew it. Starting in 1990 presidents have withdrawn geographic areas from consideration in the schedule of planned lease sales (U.S. Commission on Ocean Policy, 2004). In addition all leasing in marine sanctuaries has been prohibited. In mid-2008 the president lifted remaining withdrawals under his control. The fact that these actions were taken at all indicates the difficulty of reconciling oil development with other coastal uses. The use of direct congressional or presidential intervention to address issues that administrative or judicial procedures could not resolve signals numerous underlying conflicts on topics such as environmental impacts and revenues.

Almost all revenue from OCS development over a half century went to the federal government. In 2005 and 2006 changes in federal law clarified the arrangements so a portion of the revenues from the region just seaward of the state offshore boundary would flow to the adjacent state. Another law declared that states bordering the Gulf of Mexico would receive a percentage of all the oil revenue from the Gulf. To the extent that money was the problem, some progress has been made.

Finally, because oil spilled offshore can easily cross the state-federal line and destroy state waters, fisheries, marshes, and beaches, the question of damages and recovery remained. The Oil Pollution Act allows individuals, businesses, and governments to recover damages from the party responsible for the spill. Assuming the mechanisms are effective and equitable, problems may be diminished. If not, states may seek additional changes in how the burdens and benefits of offshore oil are distributed.

The seaweed rebellion, an event that has been many decades in the making, is far from over. Further adjustments in decisions, goals, and processes are in order. Inherent in this debate is the ability of sector-based management to harmonize the diverse interests of coastal stakeholders.

Summary

Geological processes operating millions of years ago favored oil formation on the edges of ocean basins, which makes current-day continental
margins an attractive place to prospect for oil and gas. Expansion of oil
drilling in the Gulf of Mexico and Alaska, coastal areas most likely to
produce new supplies, has continued throughout recent decades. Production of OCS oil appears to have peaked in 2002 at just over 0.6 billion
barrels of oil (figure 4.1), which is equivalent to around 2.5 percent of
U.S. energy supply.

Technological innovation allowing well drilling in ever deeper ocean
waters has been the basis of maintaining production from the OCS. Currently oil wells in the Gulf of Mexico are routinely drilled in a mile (1.6
kilometers) or more of water and reach two miles (3.2 kilometers) or
more beneath the seafloor. However, oil spill recovery technologies have
not kept pace. As a result, the risk to the environment has rapidly esca-
lated. The combination of advances in oil development technology, historical oil-sector domination of policy decisions, growing environmental
awareness, and perceived inequities in the division of risks and benefits
have created a volatile situation.

Ownership of submerged lands, and therefore control of revenues
from oil and gas, was an early and important part of the tension between
the federal and state governments. It was resolved by a 1953 law that
created a line in the water, usually at three miles (4.8 kilometers) from
shore, which divided the two claims. But resolving oil ownership still left
lingering a number of tensions, as evidenced by the seaweed rebellion.
Among the issues at stake are more equitable distribution of revenues,
offshore and onshore environmental quality, and a variety of social impacts. Decisions about drilling in the OCS pit state government against
the federal government and even one part of the federal government
against another. Behind these conflicts are individual sectors (oil, fishing,
wildlife conservation, tourism, housing, recreational boating, aquaculture,
etc.) with differing views about how the coast should be used.

By distributing more of the OCS revenues to the states, requiring
EISs for key parts of the leasing process, and clarifying the states' roles
in federal consistency determinations, the policy process for oil leasing
has begun to address key issues of the seaweed rebellion. However, the
recently tamed disputes over federal consistency, as well as moratoria/
withdrawals, indicate that conflict between state and federal government
still lingers. The BP Deepwater Horizon Macondo oil spill in the Gulf of

Mexico in 2010 brought many of the tensions to the surface. These on-going problems suggest that further policy revisions are needed and raise the question of whether managing oil development as an isolated sector is effective. In the next chapter, we'll evaluate the efficacy of a sector-based approach to managing shipping and dredging and we'll see how similar conflicts have gridlocked the policy process.

5

Dredging

People and goods have moved along coasts through most of human history. Good ports spawn cities as waterborne trade focuses economic activity in specific geographic locales. However, to carry more cargo at a reduced cost, ships have gotten bigger, in many cases outgrowing the harbors that used to accommodate them. As a result, dredging—removing sediment from the ocean floor—has become as much a part of shipping as the ever larger ships themselves. Dredging changes water quality, alters biological systems, and modifies habitat. Must the growth of ports and cities come with high costs to the environment? This chapter assesses the ability of sector-based management to address this conflict.

The growth of shipping

In 1847 San Francisco was a small village that was occasionally visited by whaling vessels. In 1849 the discovery of gold attracted more than eight hundred ships, and everything began to change (Labaree et al., 1998). The gold rush, a large harbor, and sea transportation connected coastal California with the rest of the world. Rapid growth followed. By 1860, San Francisco was the fourteenth largest city in the United States and a major port. At the time, ships fit easily into the harbor because their drafts (the distance between the waterline and the bottom of the hull) were twenty feet (six meters) or less. The vessels' relatively small size allowed them to navigate vast areas of sheltered waters, not just around San Francisco but also all along the U.S. coasts, during the first shipping boom.

By the late twentieth and early twenty-first century shipping had changed. Coal and then oil had long since replaced wind as a source of energy to power the ships. Wood hulls were traded in for steel. Most important, the vessels themselves had become much larger to transport more cargo at lower cost. By the 1980s crude oil and containerized cargoes traveled on the world's oceans in vessels that required two or three times the draft of the earlier sailing ships that called on San Francisco. In California manufactured goods from Asia were offloaded in containers at the Port of Oakland (figure 5.1).

Changes in the way cargo was handled became important for these bigger ships. Instead of loading a ship with one piece of cargo at a time, individual items were packed into containers, a process that could occur at the point of manufacture, and the containers were loaded aboard the ship using large cranes (Labaree et al., 1998). In the 1950s, the original containers were eight feet (2.4 meters) wide, eight feet tall, and twenty feet (six meters) long, and called twenty-foot equivalent units. They readily fit on wheels for over-the-road transit as trailers. Today, most containers are double that length, but the principle of the operation remains the same. Containers are efficient, but require both large ships and large areas on land for handling. In 1957 pioneers in container shipping started with a vessel that carried 226 containers and drew twenty-five feet (7.6 meters)—just a bit more than the sailing vessels. New containerships entering service today haul well over 11,000 twenty-foot equivalent units and draw fifty feet (fifteen meters) of water or more.

When vessel drafts reached forty feet (twelve meters), or double the original sailing vessel draft, almost two-thirds of San Francisco's central bay area, and large portions of the northern and southern bays, became inaccessible. Without artificially deepened channels to accommodate them, international trading ships would leave San Francisco Bay and use port facilities elsewhere. Port development rested on dredging of channels for ships to pass and frequent filling of marshes to create areas for cargo handling.

Port expansion is not only a local concern, but has national implications because of its impact on the country's economy. In 1970 the total value of international trade in the United States as a percentage of the gross domestic product was about eight percent. By 2000 it had grown to twenty percent (Juda and Burroughs, 2004). Because approximately ninety-five percent of all imports and exports move through U.S. ports, the capacity of the port system directly affects the economic well-being of the nation. And current and future port capacity depends on dredging.

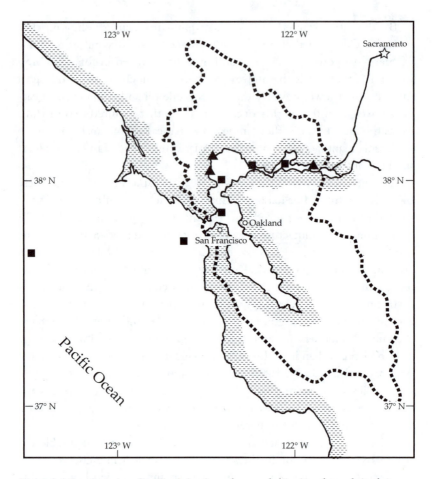

Figure 5.1. San Francisco Bay. To maintain and expand shipping channels in the bay, locations for disposal (squares) and reuse (triangles) of dredged material are designated in a planning area that includes land and water areas within the dashed line as well as adjacent coastal waters. In some circumstances dredged sediments can be used in wetland restoration at the reuse sites. Data from U.S. Army Corps of Engineers, http://www.spn.usace.army.mil/projects/ltmso&m.html.

Yet those economic considerations must be balanced with dredging's effect on coastal environmental quality.

Dredging processes

Dredging, the process of making the harbor fit the ship, started in some areas in the nineteenth century and continues today. Dredges remove material from the bottom of harbors using hydraulic or mechanical means (Randall, 2004). Hydraulic dredges operate by using digging, agitation, or water jet equipment to loosen sediment, which is then pumped as slurry of sediment and seawater through a pipeline or into a storage and transportation container known as a hopper. The pipeline carries the material to a location on land or sea for disposal. The hopper is moved from the dredging site to a disposal or reuse area to discharge sediments.

Mechanical dredges use buckets and lifting mechanisms to excavate sediment. They are able to operate near piers or jetties and may be equipped to more effectively contain contaminated sediments while removing them from the seafloor. However, mechanical dredges dig at a slower rate than hydraulic dredges.

Removal of sediment is only half of the dredging process. The other, and more difficult part, is finding a location to place the dredged material. In conventional dredge and fill operations, the site was dictated largely by economic concerns. Often, dredged material was dumped on low-lying land adjacent to the port, elevating the land and making it enormously valuable for commerce. Historical dredge and fill operations often converted salt marshes into open water or dry land with the intention of using both new environments for commerce.

Today indiscriminant land filling has given way to much more carefully selected options. In open water disposal, the material is pumped to or dumped in a body of water, where it settles to the bottom. Dredging and aquatic disposal release a cloud of fine material, which is known as a turbidity plume, in the water column. If bottom conditions at the location selected include low current and wave energies, then the material will not disperse. If, on the other hand, there are higher energy conditions on the bottom, the dredged material can spread widely in the environment. These plumes, coupled with dispersal of dredged material on the bottom during storms, can spread sediments containing toxins over a large area.

A second possibility for disposal entails walling the water or land area where the dredged material comes to rest after it is deposited. These locations, known as confined disposal facilities, allow sediments to settle in specific locations. The diked area may be located on land or near shore. In some instances they are created by dredging a deep hole, perhaps under a channel, and dumping material into it. In other cases islands have been created or enlarged. The slurry of water and sediment flows into the confined disposal facility, sediments settle out, and the water is discharged. Eventually the sediments consolidate.

Environmental impacts

The dredging that advances shipping and local economic development comes with substantial costs to the environment. It disrupts communities of organisms living on or in the seafloor as they are removed with the sediments or buried (National Research Council, 1985b). Both the salinity and circulation of coastal waters can be changed as the shape of the bottom is altered.

Turbidity plumes of suspended sediment from dredging and aquatic disposal affect both the water column and the bottom as particles settle. The plume can have an impact 1,640 feet (500 meters) or more from the dredge, and within that zone the concentration of suspended particles in the water can be four hundred times the background level (Kennish, 1991, 1997). Typically five percent or less of the volume of sediment discharged disperses away from the disposal site. Wherever they go, the particles may block out light that sea grasses depend on for photosynthesis. Plume particles settling on fish eggs may affect their viability. These and similar impacts can be felt well beyond the immediate dredging area.

Organisms directly in the path of dredging equipment are unlikely to survive. They are removed from the dredging site, often destroyed as they pass through the dredging machinery, and transported to a different location. Areas of the seafloor with reduced abundance and biodiversity of benthic organisms—those that live on or in bottom sediments—may recover over months to a decade (Newell et al., 1998). Estuarine environments with fine mobile deposits experience frequent disturbance and rapid recolonization, with reported recovery rates of six to eight months. In contrast, sands or gravels require two years or more. Coral reefs require five to ten years for recovery. Dredging and disposal have modified more than two percent of estuarine bottom areas throughout the nation, but the area affected may be as high as ten percent in certain regions (Orlando et al., 1988). In addition, dredging redistributes contaminants in the coastal environment.

Until 1972 there were only limited controls on disposal of human, manufacturing, and other liquid wastes into harbors, and consequently, coastal waters became common dumping grounds. Many of these contaminants settled with sediment particles to the seafloor, creating a record of the history of industrial development in nearby cities. Contaminated sediments show high levels of metals, hydrocarbons, synthetic organic chemicals, and/or nutrients. Dredging reintroduces these long buried pollutants to coastal waters, to biota that lives there, and to new locations where pollution levels may not be as high. Ultimately, fish and other organisms can accumulate toxins.

The level of contamination may be measured by sediment chemistry, toxicity, and impact on benthic organisms (Long and Chapman, 1985). One would expect a correlation between contamination levels and the degradation of benthic ecosystems. In fact, twenty-six percent or more of the sediment samples from U.S. estuaries had chemical concentration levels high enough to cause toxic effects (Long, 2000). When tested, samples representative of 7.5 percent of the surface area of U.S. estuaries showed acute toxic impacts on one type of common benthic organism. Furthermore, the U.S. Environmental Protection Agency (EPA) estimated that ten percent by volume of the sediment under the nation's waters is so contaminated that it poses a risk to fish, wildlife, and humans (EPA, 1998). The agency also estimated that 3 to 12 million cubic yards or one to four percent of the material dredged each year requires special handling.

In this instance, economic development rests on technology—dredging and disposal—that, if not managed effectively, has serious environmental consequences. In short, the situation presents multiple problems. As a result, the attempt to resolve them through sector-based management must now operate in several spheres. It would seem that society expects governance to simultaneously advance commerce through port development while at the same time protecting and restoring coastal environments. Furthermore, interest groups pushing either port development or environmental protection can cite ambiguous sections of federal law to favor their respective objectives. In the next portion of this chapter we examine those laws. Ultimately we will have to consider how effective sector-based management is when multiple and at times conflicting goals are advanced by society.

Law of dredging and disposal

Although naturally deep harbors were favored even very early in the development of shipping, access to the shore often depended upon creating deep water adjacent to piers. By 1824 the General Survey Act, the first of many laws related to dredging, had empowered the U.S. Army Corps of Engineers to conduct dredging operations (Juda and Burroughs, 2004). Through the 1899 Rivers and Harbors Act, the Corps was tasked with supervising dredging, filling, and the location of structures in navigable waters (table 5.1).

For much of the twentieth century dredging was synonymous with economic development through expansion of trade. Not only were

TABLE 5.1.
Dredging and disposal law

Law	Organization(s)	Focus
General Survey Act–1824	Corps	Conduct dredging operations
Rivers and Harbors Act–1899	Corps	Permit dredge, fill, and structures in navigable waters
Appropriations for public works–various years	Corps	Fund dredging, breakwaters, etc.
Fish and Wildlife Coordination Act– 1958	Fish and Wildlife Service	Coordinate with state agencies for wildlife habitat
National Environmental Policy Act–1969	Corps and others	Identify environmental consequences of dredging
Coastal Zone Management Act– 1972	National Oceanic and Atmospheric Administration (NOAA), Corps, states	Coordinate permit review with states
Marine Protection, Research, and Sanctuaries Act–1972	EPA, Corps, NOAA	Designate ocean dumping sites and permit criteria
Federal Water Pollution Control Act–1972	EPA, Corps	Regulate dredging and disposal
Fishery Conservation and Management Act–1976	NOAA-National Marine Fisheries Service (NMFS)	Regulate fisheries and impacts on habitat
Comprehensive Environmental Response, Compensation, and Liability, Act–1980	EPA	Manage highly contaminated sediments
Water Resources Development Act– 1986	Corps	Establish new funding approach for dredging
Endangered Species Act–1973	Interior/Commerce	Consult for protected and endangered species

channels deepened, but dredged material became a source of fill for land-side development. Dredged material dumped on a salt marsh or urban beach did not immediately obstruct the shipping channels, and the fill did provide more land area in crowded urban centers.

The potential for dredging and other large Corps of Engineers projects to generate wealth in specific cities drew the attention of elected officials at all levels. Because Congress determines the location of major public construction projects, its members saw the opportunity to bring large sums of federal dollars, often referred to as pork, to their districts (Ferejohn, 1974). Members frequently traded votes, supporting each other's funding bills in a process known as logrolling. For example, a representative from Arizona might vote for a dredging project in Massachusetts if he or she could expect a reciprocal vote from a Massachusetts representative for a dam in Arizona. The hierarchical structure of Congress allows committee chairs to wield extraordinary power in making these decisions about funding, and they tend to reward their home districts first. All this pork may have generated votes for representatives, but the ultimate benefit to the nation was questionable.

Public works funding rests on incentives for individual legislators and congressional subcommittees, as described above, as well as those of commercial interests associated with ports. The relationship can be seen as an iron triangle (figure 5.2). The three points of the iron triangle include the Corps of Engineers as cognizant federal agency, the congressional subcommittees with control of public works and budget, and the shipping/economic development-related interests of ports. Business groups worked with the government to identify needed channel depths and with members of Congress to ensure that planning and budgeting deliberations included the needs of the specific port. Often, those most successful at manipulating this system were focused on shipping and economic development, not environmental protection. At the second point of the triangle, the congressional subcommittees provided benefits to commercial interests while the members accepted campaign contributions from these groups. Simultaneously the subcommittee guided and budgeted the Corps with the knowledge that funding would flow to preferred congressional districts. At the third point of the triangle is the Corps. By catering to the needs of special interest groups and members of Congress, the Corps could expect to advance its budget and projects as well as the stature of the agency itself.

However, by the 1960s the general public had become concerned about dredging's environmental impacts. Many saw the intrinsic value of

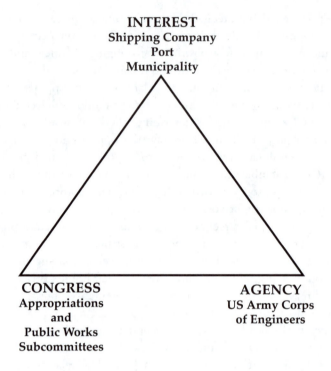

INTEREST
Shipping Company
Port
Municipality

CONGRESS
Appropriations
and
Public Works
Subcommittees

AGENCY
US Army Corps
of Engineers

Figure 5.2. The iron triangle of dredging. Private interests, ports, and municipalities assist the Corps of Engineers and influence deliberations in Congress. When successful, parties in the triangle benefit because congressional representatives gain funding for their districts by directing an enhanced Corps of Engineers dredging budget that favors communities, ports, and shipping companies that can move more cargo because of better infrastructure.

salt marshes and the diversity of benefits that they provided through food, recreation, and aesthetics. Furthermore, there was a growing perception that instead of "improving" salt marshes by burying them with dredged material, society needed to take measures to protect marshes and mud flats because of the wildlife habitat services and other values they provide. In short, stemming the overwhelming loss of marshes and other coastal systems became a priority that conflicted with the conversion of these environments to land- or seascapes that maximized commerce. This important shift in values shaped the intent of many new laws.

For example, the National Environmental Policy Act of 1969 required federal agencies to complete environmental impact statements before taking significant actions that could affect the environment. Under the new regulations, the Corps had to consult with other agencies prior to making a dredging decision (Burroughs, 2005). Instead of making determinations based solely on economics or the needs of a particular interest group, the environmental impact statement process forced the Corps to consider the health of coastal environments.

The ocean dumping provisions of the Marine Protection, Research, and Sanctuaries Act (MPRSA) of 1972 specified the manner in which environmental concerns would influence dumping of dredged material, or dredge spoil, as it was called at the time. Prior to the passage of this law, toxic materials from paint manufacture, sewage treatment, and dredged sediments were dumped in ocean waters. The president's Council on Environmental Quality (1970) noted that one-third of dredge spoil was polluted and that dredging and disposal operations resulted in a massive redistribution of pollutants, with uncertain consequences. At this point, the conflict between environmental and economic priorities became clear. To address this situation the Secretary of the Army was empowered to permit ocean dumping of dredged material only if, in the words of the law, it "will not unreasonably degrade or endanger human health, welfare, or amenities, or the marine environment, ecological systems, or economic potentialities" (MPRSA section 103 or USC 33 section 1413).

The Federal Water Pollution Control Act of 1972, now called the Clean Water Act (CWA), expanded this approach to other aspects of dredging and disposal. The law joins the activities of the EPA and the Corps for dredged material disposal inside of three miles from the shore (figure 5.3). The Secretary of the Army, to whom the Corps reports, issues general permits for dredge and fill if the actions "will cause only minimal adverse effects" (FWPCA section 404 or USC 33 section 1344e). Disposal activities that could affect water quality in state waters require approval by the state, usually through its environmental department.

Simultaneously, the EPA provides criteria that the Corps uses to assess the effects of dumping. Specifically, the Corps considers impacts on marine organisms, ecosystems, and alternate uses of ocean areas in deciding whether to issue each individual permit. The EPA may seek to block a permit issued by the Corps if it finds that it is inconsistent with the environmental protection criteria. Furthermore, the Corps and the EPA jointly oversee selection of disposal sites. By establishing a role for EPA in many aspects of ocean dumping of dredged material, the law formally recognized environmental concerns.

As shown in figure 5.3, inland waters include bays, estuaries, rivers,

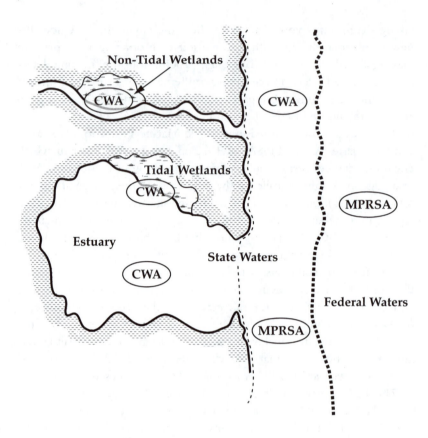

Figure 5.3. Jurisdictional boundaries for dredged material. Inside of the baseline (light dashed line that follows the shore and closes off bays) dredged material placement is managed through the Clean Water Act (CWA). Between the baseline and the seaward extent of state waters (heavy dashed line, generally three miles [4.8 kilometers] seaward of the baseline), the Clean Water Act for filling or the Marine Protection, Research, and Sanctuaries Act (MPRSA) for dumping applies. In federal waters (seaward of the heavy dashed line) the MPRSA governs dumping of dredged material. Uniform federal regulations apply to the zone where the two laws overlap.

and lakes inside of the baseline. The baseline is the mean low water line along the coast and also extends across the mouths of bays. The territorial sea stretches twelve miles (19.3 kilometers) seaward. Together the CWA and the MPRSA provide regulations for disposal or reuse in all coastal areas, as shown in figure 5.3.

Congress also passed laws that sought to protect wildlife threatened by dredging and disposal. Because waterfowl nest and feed in the same wetland areas where dredge and fill can take place, conflict was almost inevitable. The Fish and Wildlife Coordination Act of 1958 placed wildlife conservation on par with dredging by requiring that the two activities be planned jointly (Juda and Burroughs, 2004). Advisory comments from the U.S. Fish and Wildlife Service and the National Marine Fisheries Service identify potential problems created by dredging operations and suggest alternatives to minimize them.

Subsequently, the Sustainable Fisheries Act of 1996—a reauthorization of the original 1976 Fisheries Conservation and Management Act—established a process to protect fish habitats. Many aquatic organisms shift location at different life stages, making them vulnerable to habitat degradation in a variety of settings. To avoid this risk, the Corps of Engineers consults with the National Marine Fisheries Service and fisheries management councils when undertaking a project that could adversely affect essential habitat.

By the late 1970s, pressure had grown not only to regulate dredging but also to change the way it was funded. Many felt that the federal government should no longer assume the full cost of dredging, dams, and other large projects. Although the projects might be in the national interest, they also provided significant local benefits in the form of construction jobs and subsequent commercial activity. A funding formula that included local contributions was sorely needed. Without it, the adoption of comprehensive public works bills was not politically possible. In 1986 the Water Resources Development Act required that local entities pay ten to fifty percent of the cost for new dredging (Burroughs, 2005). Because channels, once dredged, begin to fill in again due to the natural transport of sediments, maintenance dredging must also be undertaken. Through the new law the federal government retained responsibility for maintenance dredging of federally authorized channels up to a forty-five–foot (13.7 meter) depth.

By shifting part of the responsibility for funding to local entities, the new law had important impacts on environmental protection. Under the 1992 amendments to the Water Resources Development Act, the federal government could pay up to seventy-five percent of the cost of environmentally enhanced dredged material disposal (Blume, 2002). Enhancements include the beneficial uses of adding sand to beaches where erosion is a problem or providing sediments for marsh restoration. Initially, only a token amount of funding was provided to meet this goal because not all agreed that the funding for environmental improvements was justified. Subsequent revisions of the law encouraged further consideration of environmentally enhanced disposal provided that the benefits to wetland restoration, shoreline erosion protection, or other activities outweighed the costs.

Over nearly two centuries the legal framework related to dredging underwent significant shifts in relation to environmental impacts, national interests, and the local share of costs. Prior to 1824 dredging was implemented and paid for by state and local entities (National Research Council, 1985b). From 1824 to 1986 the Corps of Engineers by law assumed responsibility for the deepening of federally approved channels, their maintenance, and the expenses of doing both. After 1986 the law changed again to increase local participation in funding and to explicitly recognize the need for funding environmental protection as a part of dredging operations.

Regulating the disposal of contaminated sediments

Safely disposing of contaminated sediment requires careful evaluation of the level of contamination and its environmental and health effects. Management systems designate contamination thresholds that trigger successively restrictive options in proportion to the level of pollution. When the regulatory system performs as ideally conceived, clean sediments require limited assessment as a precursor to a management decision. Conversely, sediments that are likely or known to be contaminated require the completion of additional expensive tests in advance of any decision about their disposal. This approach is described in detail in government manuals that identify regulatory procedures under the dumping provisions of MPRSA and CWA (EPA, 1991; EPA and U.S. Army Corps of Engineers, 1998). Harbor sediments from urban or industrial areas almost invariably require some form of bioaccumulation testing (box 5.1).

There is a continuum of sediment disposal techniques that provide higher levels of separation from marine systems for more toxic sediments. In extreme cases of contamination, underwater Superfund sites have been identified that require special care. In general, as the observed contamination levels go up, so do the costs of implementing acceptable solutions. With very low or no contamination levels, dredged sediments become valuable resources. Uses are determined by grain size, which determines the physical properties of the material. Sand and gravel deposits from beneath the sea find uses in conventional construction and in beach restoration. Clean silts or clays have been used in marsh restoration.

According to the Corps of Engineers, sediments with low levels of contaminants can be disposed at sea in many instances. To reduce the

---

Box 5.1. Bioaccumulation Testing

Because recent sediments from urban harbors almost invariably contain metals, synthetic organics, and other toxins, the disposal of dredged material requires special care. In many situations the regulations require laboratory measurement of biological impacts associated with dredged material. Sediments that have been proposed for dredging are placed in a laboratory environment with conditions as similar as possible to those found in nature to determine bioaccumulation as benthic organisms grow in the contaminated sediments. After ten or twenty-eight days tissues from the organisms are analyzed for metals and/or synthetic organic chemicals. This process assumes that if harmful levels of toxins are present in the sediments, then biological processes will deliver them to the tissues of the test organism. If levels observed in the tissue samples exceed allowable thresholds, then dredged material disposal plans will have to incorporate special handling for the contaminated sediments, which in some instances requires complete separation from the marine environment.

---

release of toxins to the environment some advocate the placement of clean fill on top of the contaminated dredged material (Kennish, 1991, 1997; Randall, 2004). This process, known as capping, reportedly works best where 1.6 feet (0.5 meter) or more of clean sediment is placed on top of the dredged material, and the cap is not disturbed by wave or current action. Caps are expected to limit release of dissolved contaminants from the dredged material and to prevent resuspension and transport of the contaminated particles. In some cases natural depressions in the seafloor are used. In other instances dredging deeper than the required channel depth creates a hole or cell where contaminated material may be dumped and subsequently buried with clean fill. In cases where the sediment contamination is so high that capping is not desirable, a secure landfill away from the coast has been identified as the only acceptable means of disposal.

Gridlock

Everyone who has ever been caught in a traffic jam recognizes that when intersections become congested, movement stops in all directions. Gridlock can also occur in sector-based coastal management. Shipping, dredging, environmental quality, fishing, and other needs compete much the same way cars seek to get through an intersection simultaneously. In dredging, gridlock can occur when a solution for disposal or reuse of sediments is selected. At that point different sectors within society review the decision from the perspective of their needs. As the diversity of values and the number of stakeholders promoting them increases, so too does the potential for gridlock. Projects can sit in limbo as their pros and cons are debated endlessly. Frequently they end up in court. To understand these phenomena we will summarize the situation in Oakland, California, and then use it and experiences at other ports to identify the key issues that contribute to gridlock.

Many cities have faced the competing demands of economic development and coastal environmental quality, but San Francisco Bay, and Oakland, in particular, exemplify the dilemma. In 1971 the Port of Oakland started planning to increase the channel depth from thirty-five to forty-two feet (10.7 to 12.8 meters), but nearly three decades were to pass due to conflicts over disposal of the dredged material before a final decision was reached. By the late 1980s, Oakland was struggling to keep up with the increasing size of ships through minor dredging operations, but with containerships calling only at high tide, and then only partially loaded, the port's future was uncertain (Kagan, 1991). Shippers found Washington State or Southern California more reliable. Port jobs in Oakland were poised to decline. Why not simply deepen the channel? There seemed to be no good way to deal with the resulting contaminated sediment without causing serious environmental damage.

Ultimately these issues were resolved through complex negotiations. Approximately twenty-seven years after the initial discussion and twelve years after federal funding of the project, the channel was deepened to forty-two feet (12.8 meters) (Kagan, 2001; Busch et al., 1998). Proponents and opponents had resolved their differences to a degree. Operationally this meant that technical solutions satisfied agency mandates, interest groups, and fears of scientific uncertainty. These technical solutions included use of the originally proposed bay site, an approved ocean disposal site, an on-land location for highly contaminated sediments, and a wetland restoration in the Sacramento River delta (figure 5.1).

Variations of the Oakland story have been repeated in ports throughout the country. Collectively these situations illustrate key issues that arise in sector-based management of dredged material disposal.

Inevitably the disposal of dredged material becomes a contest of values. Those who view shipping as a route to economic development demand that commerce not be restrained by disposal options. Those who view environmental quality as most important demand that contaminated sediments not affect marine life, habitats, swimmers, and other coastal activities.

Often these values seep into questions about what is known scientifically and how well it is known. What levels of contaminants cause serious problems? What are the environmental and health consequences of moving sediments to a new location? Unfortunately, the science isn't always so clear-cut: uncertainties abound about levels of contamination, effectiveness of containment for disposed contaminants, and costs to obtain certain levels of safety.

The Clean Water Act identifies contaminated sediments in multiple ways. For example, if laboratory testing shows bioaccumulation above the Food and Drug Administration standard for human consumption or at some small percentage of the acute toxicity, then the material is considered too contaminated for ocean disposal. Mapping which sediments fall into this category and removing them is conducted on a case-by-case basis. Compare these standards with the uniformly applied level of coliform bacteria permitted in pipe discharges from a sewage treatment plant. The latter are clear and unequivocal, whereas the former are difficult to discern and complicated to apply.

When differing values and scientific uncertainty combine, it is difficult to define clear standards and regulate accordingly. One person's precaution can be another individual's overregulation. The situation can easily gridlock with inconclusive regulatory and judicial decisions favoring one side and then the other with ever increasing demands for scientific certainty that obscure the underlying value conflict.

Our legal structure pits proponents of dredging against proponents of environmental protection, but fails to provide an effective structure for compromise and cohesive solutions. Under the law, the Corps and EPA are expected to resolve value differences among various interests that might occur in setting such standards. At times these two agencies have great difficulty in agreeing. Furthermore, other executive branch agencies are involved, as well as state and local governmental entities. Sector-based management has grown in such a way that different agencies with different legal mandates and constituencies, operating at different levels, often work at cross-purposes.

In Oakland, records show about a dozen circumstances in which one agency rejected the conclusion or action of another unit (Kagan, 1991). The Corps of Engineers, the Port of Oakland, and local interests proposed the dredging in response to the needs of the shipping industry. The U.S. Fish and Wildlife Service, the National Marine Fisheries Service, the state Department of Fish and Game, the federal EPA, the state water quality control agency, the California Coastal Commission, and the San Francisco Bay Conservation and Development Commission reviewed the impacts of the proposed dredging activity from the perspective of various laws they implement. Together with the Half Moon Bay Fishermen's Marketing Association, they opposed the placement of dredged material at a variety of locations. Without unequivocal standards, it's no wonder that individuals with different values will favor different courses of action.

When these interpretations diverge significantly, litigation results. In the end, if each sector demands that its needs be predominant, and the law has not identified which should succeed, then gridlock results. Adversarial legalism, an example of this, is characterized by a lack of authoritative determination of acceptable environmental risk and, for dredging, a tendency to require progressively more expensive disposal techniques (Kagan, 1991). Many court challenges of agency decisions and many years to reach a resolution characterize this form of gridlock. Adversarial legalism is caused by fragmentation of decision-making power across many agencies, demands for scientific certainty beyond what can be easily provided, and limited regulatory discretion. Agencies and the whole process can retreat into legalistic defensiveness, and unfortunately the decision process is subject to extortion by whichever interest holds the upper hand. There's neither a definitive rejection of dredging nor an environmentally optimal solution for disposal. Plus, this adversarial process eats up significant resources.

Enduring change?

In spite of nearly three decades of conflict Californians succeeded in fitting dredged material disposal through a complex set of values and an even more cumbersome institutional maze. Did they create enduring changes in processes or just negotiate out differences at a specific location? To consider these issues we will assess the Oakland situation in the context of national changes.

Several factors led to an eventual solution to the Oakland controversy, though deeper, systemic issues remain unresolved. First, as debate dragged on, California's economy declined, creating additional pressure to deepen the channel (Busch et al., 1998). Second, public hearings mandated by law were held only after the dredging plan had already been devised, causing some citizens, particularly those who cared about environmental consequences, to feel disenfranchised. To participate after important decisions had been made, stakeholders exploited sections of the laws that favored their interests and demonstrated that the whole process could be stopped. As a result new ways were devised to include public concerns earlier in the decision process. The Corps sponsored a Long Term Management Strategy group where dredging projects could be discussed. Third, some began to view the dredged material as not just waste but rather a material appropriate for what has become known as beneficial use (Kagan, 2001). Specifically, it was used to restore wildlife habitat along the shores of San Francisco Bay. Filling in coastal areas, if properly designed, became restoration of wetland habitat in the eyes of its proponents. Finally, the EPA located an ocean area where far more noxious substances had been dumped in the past and designated it as a new ocean site, further relieving the burden of finding disposal locations.

In addition to these changes in California, national reforms in the planning process paralleled the positive steps in Oakland (Juda and Burroughs, 2004; Kagan, 2001; Busch et al., 1998). The new approaches link local, regional, and national government and embrace a diversity of interests that had previously met in the courtroom.

The National Dredging Team, established by the U.S. Department of Transportation and several other agencies in the mid-1990s, has met for many years to provide recommendations on dredged material management and other topics that could be of value as individual ports propose specific projects. This federal interagency work group can plan, coordinate, and reduce scientific uncertainty for dredging decisions. Dredging teams at the port, state, or regional level can reduce the fragmentation driven by divergence in local interests. Although not all regions have embraced this approach, the concept remains available for those who wish to choose it.

Expanded participation in the decision processes came at a time when local authorities were also forced to take on greater responsibility for funding dredging projects. Presidents Carter and Reagan were unwilling to approve water projects bills under the iron triangle and pork funding formulas of the past, and by 1986 Congress agreed on a new approach to funding known as the Water Resources Development Act. Under the new arrangement, local sponsors pay between ten and fifty percent of dredging project costs, depending on the depth of the channel. Deeper channels require a greater local share. As in the past, the periodic redredging of channels to maintain their depths is paid by the federal government except when the channel depth exceeds forty-five feet (13.7 meters)—this triggers a local share of half of the maintenance dredging costs. The prospect of shouldering at least part of the costs discouraged local politicians from sponsoring questionable projects. In the end, the act encouraged Congress to make better investment decisions.

In its subsequent revisions the Water Resources Development Act also addressed the question of who should pay for environmentally enhanced projects. Previously, the Corps had focused on the lowest cost acceptable solution. But acceptability lay in the eye of the evaluator, and many local communities were not pleased with the results. In 1992 the law was revised so the federal government could provide seventy-five percent of the incremental cost of an environmentally beneficial solution. By 2000 the revised law opened the possibility for the dredged material to be marketed to government agencies and private parties. Dredging companies had long recognized the value of sand and gravel from rivers and the seafloor as an aggregate in a variety of applications. Not only would clean dredged material be used in construction but also the fine-grained material could be used in ways to enhance environmental quality, such as through marsh construction.

The enduring changes that occurred nationally during and after the Oakland controversy include incorporation of diverse stakeholders earlier in the process through dredging teams and requiring local participation in funding of dredging projects. These positive changes further empowered local communities to affect the future of their coasts. However, these changes in process do not resolve underlying value conflicts in society or their regular eruption in sector-based management, which pits economic development through dredging against environmental protection. Alternatives to sector-based management will be developed in the later parts of the book.

Summary

This chapter uncovered two types of problems. The first involves whether an adequate scientific and technical alternative can be found for the disposal or reuse of dredged material. The second problem emerges because sector-based management is unable to resolve differing values surrounding dredge and fill in a timely and effective manner. Here we have seen how a contest of wills among stakeholders can result in gridlock, as it did for decades in Oakland.

Although bigger ships and more efficient ports boost the national economy, they can also degrade the coastal environment. The deepening of channels for larger ships requires that places be found for the dredged material, some of which may be contaminated. This problem

raises important choices. If an acceptable solution for the dredged material cannot be found, then port and shipping expansion in an area will
cease. Conversely, making a poor dredging decision will irrevocably damage coastal environments.

The current approach to dredged material placement in the United
States relies on at least a dozen separate legal provisions (table 5.1) spread
across multiple jurisdictions (figure 5.3). Because dredging projects contribute to national economic growth, they are funded, at least in part, by
the federal government through the Corps of Engineers. However, other
law requires bioaccumulation testing of sediments, which may indicate
that an acceptable marine location cannot be found for the dredged material. If the project moves forward, the shipping sector benefits while
the environmental sector loses. Similar conflicts are repeated across many
pairings of laws in table 5.1. Furthermore, some interests have effectively
inserted themselves in the dredging iron triangle (figure 5.2), which allows special access to the decision process. In this setting, multiple agencies with different perspectives are expected to collaborate to produce an
agreement. With interests or sectors advocating different actions, selection of a binding solution, the key aspect of moving forward in the policy
process, can and has become gridlocked.

Nonetheless, both nationally and in the San Francisco Bay region a
number of constructive changes have occurred. In both settings dredging
teams created more opportunities for stakeholder participation. Environmentally preferable solutions became fundable, at least in part, by the
federal government through changes in the Water Resources Development Act. The combination of these changes can address issues like the
Oakland dredging dilemma, but leave unresolved the deeper divisions
among stakeholders that could easily reemerge because multiple laws and
values are at play.

Further dredging decision-making improvements could arise through
better quantification of environmental impacts and selection of a clearer
standard for sediment quality. Both would alleviate confusion in the decision process. If more definitive bioaccumulation standards were adopted,
decisions would be clearer cut and the number of legal challenges brought
to clarify the situation on a case-by-case basis could be reduced. Without such standards or other means of forming consensus, the adversarial
process grinds on.

In terms of the policy process as described in chapter 2, gridlock is the
inability to devise and agree to a solution that is broadly acceptable. It's
not too surprising that gridlock occurs because sector-based management

starts with the needs of individual, and often opposed, sectors rather than a broader common interest. In the case of dredged material disposal, sectors conflict and belatedly the administrative or judicial processes attempt to create solutions that most can accept. We will continue to probe the effectiveness of sector-based management by considering in the next chapter how well it has addressed conservation of wetlands.

6

Wetlands

Wetlands link land and sea as well as nature and society. Extending over large expanses, salt marshes and mangroves provide vital ecosystem services but have been profoundly damaged by human activity. Therefore, no approach to coastal governance is complete without a close look at our management of these regions.

To determine whether sector-based management is effective in this setting, we will examine coastal wetlands as natural systems that people value and use. Unfortunately, as human activities expand, the health of coastal marshes and mangroves seems to decline. Management becomes a balancing act between making use of the ecosystem and preserving it. Moreover, a fragmented system of laws and agencies governing wetlands makes program implementation difficult. These and other factors combine such that coastal wetlands continue to decline, albeit at a slower rate than in the past.

The nature of coastal wetlands

Many salt marshes and mangroves occur along the shores of the Gulf of Mexico in the southern United States. Salt marsh grasses dominate in the temperate latitudes and extend south into the Gulf. Unlike mangroves, they are able to survive freezing conditions in the winter, allowing them to grow throughout the East and West coasts and as far north as Alaska. Mangroves' specialized trees extend north from the tropics up into the Gulf (Mitsch and Gosselink, 2000; Day et al., 1989), stretching along southwestern Florida and southern Texas. Patches of mangrove are found in the Mississippi delta, but salt marsh predominates in that region of the coast. In fact, by one estimate forty percent of the coastal salt marsh in the lower forty-eight states lies in the Mississippi River delta region.

Whether grass or tree, wetland vegetation thrives in salty coastal waters where the ebb and flow of tides provide nutrients and remove wastes. Wetland plants have specialized techniques for dealing with salts, for growing in anoxic soils, and for reproducing in inundated environments.

In southwestern Florida, where mangroves predominate along the coast, three species are commonly found: black, white, and red mangrove (*Avicennia germinans, Laguncularia racemosa,* and *Rhizophoria mangle,* respectively) (Day et al., 1989). Fringe forests overlap the boundary between land and sea, shaping the location and type of coast. Organisms that take a significant role in designing their own environments are often referred to as *ecosystem engineers* (Mitsch and Gosselink, 2007). By changing materials from one form to another or by modifying themselves, they fashion the environment they inhabit. The mangroves of southwestern Florida fit in that category because they convert nutrients into plant materials, and as the plants grow, they affect water flow and other elements of the physical environment.

West and north in the lower Mississippi delta, salt marshes predominate along the coast. Typically, the elevation of the land surface determines which species of marsh grasses are present because water affects growing conditions (Mitsch and Gosselink, 2000). In this setting, smooth cordgrass (*Spartina alterniflora*) inhabits the low marsh closest to the creek or shore. Salt meadow cordgrass (*Spartina patens*) marks the elevated parts of the high marsh closest to the upland. Several plants fill in the assemblage and their presence is often determined by their tolerance of the level of salinity in the waters that contact the roots of the plant. Much like the mangroves, these plants are ecosystem engineers in the sense that with adequate mineral soil supply, the land-sea boundary may move seaward as a result of plant growth.

In addition to shaping the coast, wetlands provide a number of important ecological functions. They support algae that grow on and in the soil as well as on plant surfaces. Salt marsh plants provide shelter for other organisms, and the abundant plant detritus they shed becomes a major source of food for marsh inhabitants. In addition, the salt marsh, depending upon conditions, may serve as a source or sink for nutrients. Salt marshes and mangroves can export carbon in different forms. Conversely for other materials, temperate wetlands serve as a sink in certain situations and can sequester between twenty and thirty percent of the river flux of metals (Rozan and Benoit, 2001). In the Gulf of Mexico, detritus from the wetlands contributes to the food supply for commercially and recreationally harvested fish, while mangrove habitat supports more than one hundred species of birds.

The value of coastal wetlands

In recent years, there has been a debate about the value of ecosystems in general and of coastal wetlands in particular. Much of the discussion has focused on the services they provide. In broad terms, ecosystem services consist of "the conditions and processes through which natural ecosystems, and the species that make them up, sustain and fulfill human life" (Daily, 1997, 3). More specifically, ecosystem services can include water purification, oxygen supply, moderation of storm impacts, decomposition of wastes, sediment/nutrient transport/processing, support of human cultures, and aesthetics. In addition, wetlands enhance biodiversity through evolution and production (Ewel, 1997). Production includes wildlife, wood, and fiber that may be harvested or used for scientific, aesthetic, or symbolic purposes that usually do not require removal of the organisms. Wetlands cycle carbon, nitrogen, and sulfur. Finally, many people value the very existence of coastal wetlands: even if they do not live near or visit the coast, they want to ensure that this environment will survive in perpetuity.

Values operate at three scales: population, ecosystem, and biosphere (Mitsch and Gosselink, 2007). First at the population scale, harvests of timber, hay, birds, fish, shellfish, reptiles, and mammals benefit many individuals. In addition wetlands are home to many threatened and endangered species.

Some of these threatened birds were identified nearly two centuries ago through the work of John James Audubon. In 1831–1832 he traveled through Florida and recorded the rich diversity of bird life in the mangroves through a series of copper engravings (Siry, 1984). Many of the birds that captured Audubon's attention subsequently became highly valued for hats and other fashions—so much so that hunting threatened some species with extinction. In response, by 1886–1889 state societies named after Audubon had obtained thousands of pledges not to kill birds or wear their plumage. Eventually, governmental programs protected not only bird species but also their habitats. This early encounter linked human uses with wetland impacts and demonstrated that collective action both outside and inside government could and did protect the wetlands and their inhabitants.

Second, at the ecosystem scale wetlands protect against flooding and hurricane damage. They both store excess water and, due to their physical presence and vegetative covers, act to reduce the flow of storm surge inland. Under some conditions water percolating through wetlands will interact with soils and vegetation, improving water quality. In addition, many individuals value the aesthetics of undisturbed coastal wetlands.

In the Mississippi delta, direct destruction of wetlands grabbed national attention and emphasized the value of wetlands for storm surge attenuation. The combination of limited sediment supply to the delta surface, fluid withdrawal, and aggressive canal construction augmented erosion and relative sea level rise. As a result large areas of salt marsh disappeared. In 2005 when hurricanes Katrina and Rita came ashore, wetlands' value as storm buffers became clear. Katrina flooded New Orleans, and throughout the Gulf Coast more than 1,500 people died (Day et al., 2007). When a hurricane passes onto land it brings with it a storm surge of elevated water due to low atmospheric pressure at the center of the storm and associated winds. The measured storm surge southeast of New Orleans was twenty feet (six meters) (Day et al., 2007). Healthy salt marshes and mangroves are very important for storm surge attenuation.

The two hurricanes during 2005 allowed an interesting comparison. Most unfortunately, Katrina approached New Orleans on a path over open waters, degraded wetlands, and massive channel construction. Rita's path further to the west exposed it to a greater wetland area before reaching population centers. Observations along Rita's track showed a storm surge decline of 4.7 centimeters per kilometer of wetland traversed. In other cases, intact wetlands have provided attenuations of 7.9 centimeters per kilometer (Day et al., 2007). Rita's path over 18.6 miles (thirty kilometers) or more of wetlands meant that storm surge could be attenuated by more than three feet (one meter), a significant ecosystem service provided by the wetland landscape. With less wetland in its path, Katrina approached New Orleans with less storm surge attenuation. The result was more damage to the city than would have been the case with extensive healthy salt marshes. The tragic flooding of New Orleans illustrated the importance of healthy coastal wetlands and sparked numerous restoration initiatives (box 6.1).

Third, at the biosphere scale wetlands play an important role in cycling nitrogen, sulfur, and carbon. Healthy wetlands can reduce the flow

Box 6.1. Hurricane Katrina and the Marshes

In 2005, when Hurricane Katrina swept rapidly over the ocean, the salt marshes, and ultimately the city of New Orleans, few considered the role of the marshes. The horrific storm, loss of life, immense human suffering, and the fate of a flooded and uninhabitable city captured everyone's attention. But soon the relationship of those sad realities to the natural environment became apparent. Many decades of marsh loss, much of it related to human activity, had rendered the city more vulnerable than it might otherwise have been. Storm surge attenuation, an ecosystem service that was reduced by marsh destruction, could have limited the loss of life and damage to the city.

As striking as that reality may be, its salience to the policy process comes alive only if the observations are converted into meaningful action. Focusing events such as the hurricane are sudden, rare, and harmful (Birkland, 1997). They generate lots of public attention and can trigger action. Ultimately, if the focus is sustained and the follow-up is meaningful, significant change in society will correct, at least in part, the circumstances that led to the event.

Valuing coastal wetlands in terms of their ecosystem services for hurricane protection has been an ongoing discussion in coastal Louisiana, so there is a history of suggested actions that could follow the focusing event we know as Katrina. In 1990 the Coastal Wetlands Planning, Protection, and Restoration Act became a part of federal law, and through it, funding to the state of Louisiana has enabled the completion of more than seventy restoration projects. Initiatives under this and other programs have included everything from diversions of river water to the delta surface to the trapping of sediments using discarded Christmas trees. Projects have also included major geoengineering proposals that would redirect the Mississippi River and restore marshes where shipping channels or pipeline corridors have been created, and restoration use of many millions of cubic yards of dredged material that the Corps produces in the Gulf. Expanding the marsh between the city and the sea is not just an ecosystem services concept: it has substantial economic value. The hurricane protection services of wetlands in Louisiana are estimated to be $688 per acre per year ($1,700 per hectare per year). When all the area is considered and adjusted to present value, the amount approximates $28 billion (Costanza et al., 2008).

Katrina forced not only changes in amount of conventional restoration activity, but also, and most important, recognition of the degree to which past channel dredging has been damaging. Just over fifty years ago the Corps

of Engineers began dredging what became the Mississippi River Gulf Outlet and in the process destroyed more than 15,000 acres (6,070 hectares)
of wetlands. Hurricane Katrina approached New Orleans along a path that
severely flooded East New Orleans because of this channel and the loss of
the wetlands. In 2009 the first barge loads of rock were dumped to close
off this channel and begin the process of recreating wetlands. The extent to
which marshes lost to unwise dredging can be restored remains in doubt,
but recognition of the damage and this attempt to address it are hopeful
signs.

of nitrogen to coastal waters and limit the severity of dead zones caused
by excess nitrogen. Depending on how wetlands are managed, they may
store or release carbon and as a result play a role in climate change.

Uses and consequences

Making use of coastal wetlands can, not surprisingly, limit the services
they offer. As noted above, hunting can threaten bird survival and marsh
loss leaves cities more vulnerable to storm surges. These examples illustrate a few of the many ways that human actions, both direct and indirect,
affect wetlands' viability (Gedan et al., 2009). People depend on ecosystem services from wetlands and can simultaneously degrade the systems
and services as they procure them. Current management of wetlands is
directed not at the landscape but, for the most part, at the human activities on it. Therefore, it's vital to link laws that shape human activities and
the consequences of their discrete management interventions with the
fate of wetlands. The aggregate impact of separate decisions must be considered with respect to continued wetland vitality.

Furthermore, wetlands not only suffer from intensification of a single use but also from the *cumulative impacts* of different uses. The combined effect of multiple activities in a single geographic area requires
their assessment and limitation (Smith, 2006; Vestal and Rieser, 1995).
Unfortunately sector-based management has proven unable to rise to the
challenge. Consider for example the diversity of activities represented in
table 6.1 and the difficulties that would arise in orchestrating management of all of them. Only in rare instances does sector-based management
allow holistic assessment, and the results seldom have the power to limit
individual uses. Consequently, the inability of sector-based management
to address cumulative impacts results in significant wetland degradation.

Let's examine how impacts accumulate to the detriment of the wetland.

TABLE 6.1.
Human activities and modifications of coastal wetlands.

Category	Sample activities
Resource use	Extract oil, gas, minerals, groundwater, salt; harvest fish, wildlife, mangroves; agriculture
Conversion to dry land	Transportation corridors; industrial, urban, agricultural, and residential development; solid waste disposal
Conversion to open water	Shipping channels; aquaculture ponds; dams, ditches
Pollution discharge	Urban, industrial, and agricultural discharges of liquids and solid wastes
Indirect use	Fossil fuel burning and sea level rise; upstream damming of sediments; land subsidence from fluid extraction; hydrologic change
Natural change	Subsidence and relative sea level rise; storms; erosion
Shipping operations	Invasive species release

The Mississippi River and delta system is home to a very large area of the nation's wetlands and also where a great variety of impacts may be observed. Some are directed at the marsh itself, like dredging. Others are distant, like upstream dam construction or fossil fuel use. Dam construction upstream and levees in the delta limit the supply of sediments to the marsh surface. As a result the delta surface is starved of new sediments. At the same time fossil fuel use increases global warming and results in sea level rise. Without a robust supply of sediments, a rising sea level can overwhelm the wetland with a resulting loss of area. Furthermore, coastal wetlands have been a target of conversions that render them either drier for residential, transportation, or industrial infrastructure or wetter for ships, oil development equipment, aquaculture, or pipeline activity. In either case, wetland habitat is removed entirely or replaced with construction, such as an oil industry canal, that does not support salt marshes.

Not only do wetlands suffer from direct human activities, but they are also a part of the larger earth system that determines the relative sea level at a given area of the coast. By necessity wetlands are always found within three feet (one meter) or so of average sea level, so they are especially vulnerable to sea level rise. The capacity of salt marsh and mangrove vegetation to thrive under the influence of the tides is an important asset and a liability. When average sea level remains stable, tides deliver nutrients and remove wastes in a predictable manner over centuries. Plants do well and, with adequate sediment supply, the marsh or mangrove can grow seaward. But average sea level may change. In many low-lying coastal areas such as the Mississippi delta, the sea is rising with respect to the land. Known as relative sea level rise, this phenomenon has two causes. First, the land can move relative to the sea due to changes in the earth's crust, in a process known as isostasy (Carter, 1988). For example, interactions among the earth's plates may cause an area of the crust to rise, forming mountains. Conversely, the land surface of a river delta may sink as sediments depress the earth's crust and compact. Second, the sea can move relative to the land, which is known as a eustatic change. Eustatic rises in sea level are the result of adding water to the sea and warming the water in the sea. This additional water comes from glaciers that are melting because of climate change. Compounding the problem, ocean water expands as temperature rises, and as a result its volume increases ever so slightly. The combination of these factors causes sea level rise.

Sea level change and human uses combine to have a profound effect on the wetlands of Louisiana. A recent compilation of land loss in coastal Louisiana (figure 6.1) projects a net loss of 2,038 square miles (5,278 square kilometers) for the period 1956–2050 (Barras et al., 2004). This amounts to more than one football field of land lost to the sea each hour. This loss is due to a combination of relative sea level rise and direct human manipulation of the marsh surface through channels, levees, and other activities.

As we have seen, global changes and direct alterations by humans result in the loss of marshes. But other geologic forces also play a role. Deltas grow because rivers deliver sediments to them, particularly during floods, when the volume of sediment moving in the river is large. Water and sediment can spill over the edge of the channel and onto the delta surface. Furthermore, at the mouth of the Mississippi, sediments from the river accumulate in the Gulf in various river channel and marsh systems (Day et al., 2007). When a river changes direction, sediment supplies are reduced and waves, currents, and storms rework the sediments; the shape of the shoreline can change (Reed, 2002; Turner et al., 2006). Over time delta sediments compact as weight increases and fluids between the grains escape. Compaction lowers the surface. Furthermore, blocks of sediment can slide seaward, making the surface of the delta sink.

These geologic factors, when coupled with the eustatic changes mentioned earlier, account for a relative sea level rise of one centimeter per year in recent years (Day et al., 2007). For the delta to maintain its present

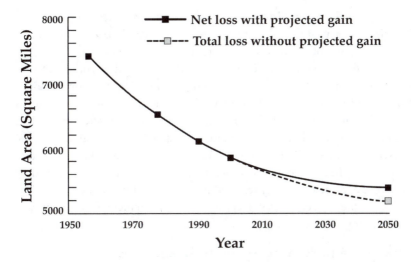

Figure 6.1. Land losses in coastal Louisiana. Although the vertical scale accentuates the process, a combination of sea level rise and anthropogenic activity has resulted in recent and projected future declines in land area. So far attempts to restore the delta have had minimal impacts on total land area. Data from Barras et al., 2004.

size, sediment supply and plant growth must keep pace with relative sea level rise. In some areas of the delta this is the case, while in many others, as documented by the land loss, the delta is not sustainable. Human activities such as levees, dredging, and oil pollution have worsened a difficult situation.

"No net loss"—a goal

The management of coastal wetlands is enormously challenging, as evidenced by their continuing disappearance. First, there are two environments: estuarine waters and adjacent coastal lands that influence them. Understanding the biophysical processes and relationships among land, sea, and wetlands is a complex undertaking made even more difficult when one has to transfer the science to a management regime. Second, U.S. legal and management traditions view most waters as public resources and most lands as privately owned resources. Although the natural system connects wetlands to both land and sea, the legal system, seemingly, does not. Third, in part for the reasons just mentioned, multiple values, laws, agencies, and interests are involved in decisions concerning wetlands. The web of laws is subject to multiple interpretations and prone to litigation. Finally, people's attitudes about wetlands have changed significantly.

Although wetlands used to be seen as noxious areas best suited for industrial use or waste disposal, they have more recently become valued as important parts of the natural ecosystem.

This change became evident in the 1980s as values shifted toward protection. In 1988 a group convened by The Conservation Foundation proposed that "no net loss" of wetlands should become the national goal (National Wetlands Policy Forum, 1988). Soon after, federal budget documents adopted the same language and subsequent presidents endorsed the concept. The idea is as straightforward as it seems: to protect all wetlands. In the event that wetlands were altered in one location, they would have to be created or restored in another to maintain the total. But although the objective was deceptively simple, achieving it has proven much more complex.

One wetland resource—multiple agencies

Even with knowledge of how the natural system functions, a clear appreciation of ecosystem services provided by wetlands, and a goal of no net loss, much remains to be done. Multiple laws across many agencies at three levels of government affect wetlands. The situation is fragmented. The antidote to fragmentation is a redesign that results in effective and seamless collaboration across many agencies and levels of government. That has not happened.

The executive branch agencies charged with protecting and restoring wetlands include the U.S. Environmental Protection Agency (EPA) and U.S. Fish and Wildlife Service (FWS), among others. However, the Corps of Engineers and the Department of Transportation are responsible for transportation and development, which can have negative consequences for wetlands. As we have seen before, agency missions conflict. Meanwhile Congress creates the rules of the game, and the courts resolve disputes concerning whether the executive agencies have appropriately interpreted the rules. Note that scientific information, both social and natural, is important in all of these venues.

Furthermore, scientists and managers view wetlands in different ways. Scientists want to classify wetlands for the purposes of research. Managers seek definitions that are meaningful for regulation and permits. Definitions affect actions. For the purposes of law and management, what is a wetland? This is an important question because regions classified as wetlands fall under governmental supervision in ways that limit certain uses. If an individual wishes to fill or drain an area of the landscape, that person will not want it classified as a wetland.

Federal agencies have defined wetlands in the context of distinctive missions and needs. Since the late 1800s, the FWS has had a role in the management of waterfowl (Lewis, 2001). In 1900 a new federal law prohibited the transportation of illegally captured animals across state lines. By the late part of the last century, an indirect control—the protection of habitat for waterfowl—became a well-established priority. To define appropriate wetlands for purchase the FWS used plant, soil, and saturation criteria. Once purchased, wetlands were to remain in their natural state.

Not too surprisingly, given the importance of water in this approach, other agencies have focused on it as the key element in their definitions. By the late 1970s the U.S. Army Corps of Engineers, which oversees dredging and filling operations, found wetlands to be where, under normal conditions, inundation or saturation of the surface produces hydrophytic vegetation (Lewis, 2001). In this approach, wetlands are delineated by where wetland plants live.

Because the legal and regulatory debate concerning wetlands does not distinguish inland from coastal wetlands, a third approach related to agriculture has also been important in structuring the definitions. In a mid-1980s definition, hydric soils and saturation/inundation that supports hydrophytic vegetation were determined as the appropriate means to locate wetlands in connection with farming activities.

Over the following years the debates about wetlands definitions have continued. Agencies charged with managing wetlands directly or activities dependent on wetlands attempted to clarify their respective purviews through regulation, guidance, and technical manuals. But alternative methods resulted in different determinations of what was and what was not a wetland. Those seeking to use the coastal or inland landscape for housing, industrial development, highways, or other purposes had a great stake in shaping the definition so their development prospects were not hindered by a wetland determination that circumscribed their plans.

Once defined, wetlands are protected through the Clean Water Act (Mitsch and Gosselink, 2007). As such they are subject to permitting processes under the dredge and fill provisions (Section 404) of the act. Litigation established that the navigable waters extend beyond those areas suitable for a ship or a boat to include additional tributaries. This system became known as waters of the United States (Lewis, 2001). Wetlands that abut relatively permanent nonnavigable tributaries were to be protected. Relatively permanent means three months or more of water flow per year. Another class of wetlands, according to the EPA and Corps understanding, would require the determination of a significant link between the wetland and the waters of the United States. The connection to other waters understood as navigable could be through significant chemical, physical, or biological impacts. In cases where a significant connection exists the wetland would fall under the control of the Clean Water Act provisions for protection.

Unfortunately, wetlands protection has turned out to be an area rich in litigation, and without clear legal instructions, anthropogenic wetland loss will continue. Not all wetlands are easily defined or for that matter equal under the law. For example, courts have focused on the connection of wetlands to adjacent waters or the nature of the habitat and its use by migratory birds. Very often, contentious issues reach the Supreme Court. The Court produces a new round of findings that, in turn, triggers new cases in a continuing cycle. In a recent case the Court and the agencies focused on adjacency and permanency of a wetland as a criterion for protection. Questions arose about how adjacent and how permanent a wetland should be to receive protection under the Clean Water Act. The agency interpretation of what the Court found provides, at least in concept, a way to define wetlands for protection, but will inevitably undergo further testing in the coming years.

Disparate values concerning wetlands and fragmented mechanisms for managing the resource have consequences. Since agency missions and definitions vary, wetland resources receive different treatment. Furthermore, with coastal land being limited, the pressure for wetland development remains high, making protections in the law the subject of continuing legal challenges. Definitive rules concerning the management of the resource lag, and protection of small or remote wetlands remains in question.

Management practices

Once an area is defined as a wetland, Section 404 of the Clean Water Act controls its use. To dredge or fill in the waters of the United States as well as most of the wetlands near them, one must have a permit from the U.S. Army Corps of Engineers (Mitsch and Gosselink, 2007). No discharge of dredge or fill material on a wetland is permitted if alternatives exist. To determine the fate of an individual proposal, a permit is filed with the Corps and it is evaluated with respect to fish and wildlife, conservation, aesthetics, flood damage protection, water supply and quality, navigation, and other factors. After this public process the application may be approved or denied.

Although the process seems straightforward, Section 404 of the Clean

Water Act allows the Secretary of the Army to issue permits in several ways. General permits cover broad categories of activities where minimal adverse effects are expected. There are nearly fifty active categories of general permits that include such things as docks, road crossings, utility lines, boat ramps, and the like. The district engineer may issue general permits on a state, regional, or nationwide basis. Projects that do not meet the requirements for a general permit are treated in the individual permit process. Generally, this is reserved for activities that require more analysis, time, and public notice. They tend to be more controversial and often require specific conditions. Finally, the law allows the state to assume responsibility for issuing permits provided that there is adequate coordination with the federal government. Should the Corps approve a permit for wetland alteration that the EPA does not believe is appropriate, the latter agency can appeal or veto the decision. Although this happens very infrequently, some believe that the possibility means the Corps has and will pursue its responsibilities most diligently.

Permit contents add further complexity because current practice includes a hierarchy of steps that go into offsetting wetland damage. To satisfy the no-net-loss directive, the regulatory system provides a prioritized mitigation sequence composed of three possibilities. First, the entity seeking to alter a wetland must demonstrate that they have attempted to *avoid* the change. Next, they need to show they have *minimized* the impacts. Finally, if the damage appears inevitable, then they need to provide a plan to *compensate* for the loss. Thus, under the law it is possible to destroy wetlands in one area if adequate compensation takes place somewhere else.

So, if damage appears inevitable due to growth in coastal areas, what processes may be used to compensate for it? Although the restoration and creation of wetlands has been a topic of scientific investigation for many years (Kusler and Kentula, 1990), the ability to predictably identify results and to formulate those processes into a regulatory system remains limited at best. In 2008, the rules were revised to clarify a hierarchy of alternatives to compensate for the loss of wetlands. The three alternatives include mitigation banks, in lieu fee mitigation, and mitigation in which the permittee is responsible for creation of new wetlands (Department of Defense and Environmental Protection Agency, 2008).

Wetland mitigation banks are a popular means of compensation. A bank consists of a wetland area that has been restored and protected under an agreement with the Corps or other regulatory agency and that provides compensation for the alteration of wetlands elsewhere. The entity managing the bank has an agreement with a regulatory agency that specifies a geographic location, legally sanctioned responsibilities concerning its management, an interagency oversight team, and a region that the bank may serve. If the bank is a successfully functioning natural wetland system, and the entity seeking to damage wetlands elsewhere purchases a share of the bank, then compensatory mitigation has taken place. Although this process is more certain than allowing the permittee to attempt to create or restore a wetland, many have pointed out that it is far from perfect.

The second preference in the hierarchy, in lieu fee mitigation, allows the applicant to restore, create, enhance, or preserve wetlands to offset the damage that is proposed should the permit be awarded. Under this approach a public agency or nonprofit is approved by regulatory agencies such as the Corps and EPA. The unit doing the compensating, such as a port, pays the public agency or nonprofit. Transfer of funds satisfies the mitigation requirement. The funds are pooled and in many instances used to create or restore wetlands. In some cases funds directed to public agencies have been used to meet the general budgetary needs of the organization. However, the goal is to require that at least one acre (0.4 hectare) of marsh be created at an ecologically suitable site for each acre of marsh that is destroyed. Unfortunately, sea level rise presents a formidable challenge to long-term continuity. In many areas of the coast sea level rise will force the landward migration of the environmentally ideal location of coastal wetlands. By 2005, there were thirty-eight approved in lieu fee mitigation programs in the United States (Environmental Law Institute, 2006). In one assessment the programs reviewed met only one quarter of the standards that were deemed to indicate success.

The third approach is to make the permittee responsible for the mitigation through restoration, establishment, enhancement, or preservation. The geographic locale may be adjacent to the site or frequently within the watershed but at a different location. Because permittees have limited experience with wetland preservation, many view this as the least desirable solution.

The coastal wetland program assessed

Given wetlands' value to society, their persistent destruction in the United States is troubling (figure 6.2). Since the 1970s, approximately 200,000 acres (80,937 hectares) of intertidal wetlands have been lost, limiting water purification and supply, flood control, biodiversity, and a variety of other services. In retrospect, we can see that the country prioritized transportation corridors, agriculture, mineral extraction, and residential and industrial development over preservation of wetlands. Wetland habitat shrank due to purposeful human intervention and in response to sea level rise. The proportions of this problem are large even if considerable debate remains concerning the details. One study indicates that from presettlement to the 1980s, fifty-three percent of U.S. wetlands, both coastal and inland, were lost (Mitsch and Gosselink, 2000). These losses of coastal and inland wetlands are highly variable, ranging from less than 0.1 percent in Alaska to as much as ninety-one percent of the wetlands in California.

Changes in water law in 1972 targeted dredge and fill activities. New laws were the basis for reversing a long history of wetland destruction. Since the 1970s the rate of coastal wetland loss in the United States has declined by most measures. Nonetheless, 29,000 acres (11,736 hectares) of intertidal wetlands disappeared between 1998 and 2004 (Dahl, 2006), indicating that achieving no net loss remains unlikely in coastal areas. One can take little comfort in the declining rate of loss because many areas, such as California, have lost almost all of their coastal wetlands.

Assessing the coastal wetland program extends beyond measuring the rate of loss. It raises some fundamental issues about management techniques and challenges. Aspects of current law and policy identify coastal

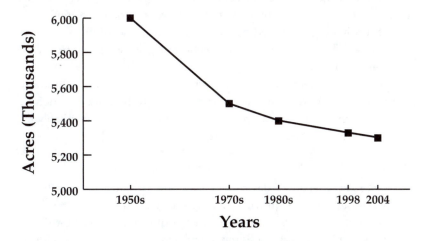

Figure 6.2. Intertidal wetland loss in the coterminous United States. Wetlands in estuarine and freshwater environments that are affected by tidal changes correspond with coastal areas particularly vulnerable to development pressures. This compilation shows the rate of loss slowing after the 1970s, but the "no net loss" goal remains elusive for intertidal systems due to a variety of factors. Data from Dahl, 2006.

wetlands as valued systems to be protected. From this perspective, wetlands programs are a conservation-minded form of sector-based management. Unfortunately, the programs face multiple challenges. Long delays in reaching decisions and loss of wetlands speak to a sector-based legal structure that has proven inadequate in resolving conflicting values. Developers and environmentalists appeal to elements of the regulatory structure that are sympathetic to their respective needs. This fragmentation is manifest in the Clean Water Act, Section 404, which assigns two agencies, the Corps and EPA, with different core missions to administer the program. The agencies understandably do have different missions and supporting interest groups, so it is not too surprising that collaborative work can be difficult. These conflicting interests and the inability to effectively manage for cumulative impact result in continuing destruction of intertidal wetlands. Were these challenges to be resolved, implementation of the wetlands program would still stretch from the federal government to state and local jurisdictions. Each link in that long chain offers its own potential for misunderstanding. Finally, the decision process itself is far more complex than the sewage example mentioned earlier. Some of the ambiguities in the process include the definition of the wetland, the permit category, and the governmental entity with ultimate authority. Although the sequence of considerations—avoid damage, minimize, compensate—is well established, it appears very difficult to implement. All of this has to be worked out for each wetland decision, and it's easy to see how advocates of wetland protection may feel excluded because of the complexity.

So the assessment of area loss and current program administrative mechanisms indicates that much more remains to be done to reach the goal of no net loss in coastal areas, and those initiatives will inevitably rely on innovations in the policy process.

Summary

Over the last several decades, society has come to value wetlands for the ecosystem services they provide. Salt marshes and mangrove systems provide a range of benefits, including water purification, habitat for diverse plants and animals, and flood and storm abatement, as well as biogeochemical cycling and aesthetics. Recognizing these services, the federal government set a goal of no net loss of wetlands in 1989. However, the continuing loss of intertidal wetlands, largely caused by human actions, demonstrates that management has not met this objective.

There are several reasons for the lack of success. National values remain conflicted; definitions of wetlands are contentious; governance is fragmented; and reliable mitigation has proven problematic. In most instances altering a wetland requires a mitigation proposal as part of the permit application. Mitigation consists of first avoiding and second minimizing damage to the wetland. The third step is to compensate for the loss. Compensation may be accomplished through, in order of preference, a wetland mitigation bank, an in lieu fee program, or direct responsibility by the permittee to restore or create equivalent wetland. Ensuring equivalence in structure and function in the restored or created system remains problematic. If damage appears inevitable and mitigation is appropriate in the eyes of the Corps of Engineers, a permit for the alteration of a wetland may be issued. In theory, this complex series of steps will achieve the no-net-loss goal. However, recent intertidal wetland loss shows this not to be the case.

Loss of wetlands and continuing litigation concerning permits makes clear that combining the often opposed interests of the Corps and the EPA has not worked well at the implementation stage of policy in this instance. Many are searching for alternatives. One is to proactively plan for a geographic region and then determine which uses in what areas are consistent with the overall plan. Spatial management for coastal lands and waters is an alternative described in the next chapter.

7

Managing Coastal and Ocean Spaces

In the previous chapters, we examined how sector-based management has been used to govern wastewater, oil dredging, and wetlands, with varying degrees of success. As we have seen, this approach is fundamentally reactive. A particular group or industry proposes a specific activity, such as dredging a harbor or disposing of sewage, and government responds by evaluating that activity and then issuing a permit if it is deemed acceptable. Unfortunately, the entity proposing the activity and the government body responding to the proposal rarely consider the cumulative effects of combined uses in a coastal land and/or sea area.

What if, instead, government began with objectives for a particular area of land or sea and then determined the suitability of activities within it? This approach, termed *spatial management*, is intended to reduce conflicts among uses. At its heart, spatial management is focused on orienting activities on the land and seascape and identifying preferred locations for specific uses.

Spatial management has operated in many contexts and in different forms over its long history. It has been practiced in geographic areas subject to different property regimes—private versus public—using local, state, or federal authorities. First, local government controls spatial management of land and affects activities on private property. Second, state government controls inshore waters, generally out to three miles (4.8 kilometers), and can zone that public space. Finally, federal agencies manage offshore waters—the area beyond three miles or in some cases three leagues.

Spatial management can start with a planning process to resolve competing demands for coastal or ocean space, or an individual use can be endorsed for a geographic area through legislation. In either case officials create a map of different zones in a geographic area, a description of activities appropriate for each zone—often backed by regulations—and a permit system to control those activities. Throughout the process, stakeholders may play a limited role—for example, by simply being informed of decisions at public meetings—or they may be accorded the power to resolve core issues. Regardless of who is granted decision-making authority, the key to spatial management is zoning. This approach provides an important alternative to sector-based management. *is what we have now*

To appreciate the problem created by sector-based management, we will explore the uses and types of conflicts that arise. We will then examine the Coastal Zone Management Act, which created programs for managing multiple uses, largely on land. This law established an important early precedent for spatial management. The chapter concludes with a consideration of spatial management for ocean waters, a topic of rapidly growing importance in the United States.

Uses of coastal lands and waters

The ocean and coastal policy described in the previous chapters reflects a piecemeal approach. As people recognized problems with sewage in coastal waters, dredging to deepen channels, and loss of wetlands, systems of governance resolved each issue separately. In fact, a vast number of sectors have been identified, and many have resulted in the creation of separate laws. In many instances, this single-mindedness of purpose resulted in significant success: sector-based management worked, at least in part.

However, these individually managed activities all take place in the same geographic space: coastal lands and waters. The sector-based process rests on an assumption that society can solve problems by regulating one use at a time. But as the number and intensity of uses increase, they begin to overlap. The health crisis created by disposing of sewage and harvesting shellfish in the same waters is one example of the many problems created by conflicting uses. A second big assumption in most sector-based approaches is that the solution to a problem in one sector will not become a new problem for another sector. A conflict of this nature arose with dredged material disposal. Dumping the dredged material in many areas of the marine environment harmed wildlife, fisheries, and aesthetics. In short, solving one problem simply created another. A different way of viewing this is that maximizing use within one sector does not necessarily produce an optimization across multiple sectors.

A third false assumption inherent in sector-based management is that society's values remain constant over time. When uses were small in number and limited in intensity, a sector-by-sector approach had great appeal. But as citizens began to add uses and increase their intensity, incorporating those new demands into traditional sector-based management proved exceedingly difficult. The shift in values resulted in the need for a more comprehensive management scheme for the coast.

The challenge of comprehensive management becomes clear when we examine the nature of the interactions among various uses (Ketchum, 1972). *Exclusive uses* preclude all others from the area in question. For example, a marsh on the shore of a bay may be converted to a container port through dredge and fill operations, or it may serve as a wildlife preserve, but it can't be both. The term "exclusive use" indicates that the requirements of one use are incompatible with other uses.

Compatible uses coexist with a minimal level of conflict in the same area—referred to as a *multiple use* setting. For instance, ships can traverse the same estuarine waters where effluent from sewage treatment plants has been discharged. Virtually no alterations of one use are required for the other use to occur in the same system, in the same geographic area, at the same time. These circumstances allow very different interests to be satisfied through the use of one region of the coast.

In fact multiple use dominates most situations along the coast. But not all uses are as compatible as shipping and waste disposal. To manage multiple use settings effectively, it is paramount to understand how various natural and social systems interact. For example, sustaining a coastal fishery, one use, may necessitate circumscribing wastewater discharge, habitat alteration, and dredging, in addition to limiting the fishery's harvest. Fitting these multiple activities together requires technological and managerial solutions to minimize the impact of one use on another.

Because coastal regions are finite and attract more uses than can be easily accommodated, managers may seek to identify *displaceable uses.* Restaurants, homes, and golf courses benefit from a beach view, but their physical operation does not require a waterfront. Conversely, container terminals, fish docks, shipyards, and marinas all demand waterfront facilities. In some cases, technological developments allow water-dependent activities to be moved, at least in part, away from the coast. For example, ports that handle liquid natural gas or petroleum may receive the fuel at an offshore location and then move it by pipeline across the shore to inland storage facilities. Similarly, a marina may reduce its impact on the coast by having boats stored in racks on land rather than at docks or moorings. To the extent that an activity can be displaced, it will require less costal land or water and may therefore become more compatible with other uses.

Managing multiple activities can be difficult if there is inadequate spatial and temporal information about how people are actually using coastal areas. Determining current use patterns is an important aspect of planning for the future, particularly if activities do or are likely to conflict. For example, building liquid natural gas terminals along the coast may exclude recreational activities. But if recreation has not been measured or documented, its significance may be discounted. Establishing and applying effective survey methods is a critical component of successful management (Dalton et al., 2010).

Conflicts

As we have seen, traditional institutions that govern the coast focus on individual uses or sectors. Often the rules that affect a single use are implemented by an organization such as the U.S. Environmental Protection Agency or U.S. Army Corps of Engineers. The earlier chapters of this book showed sector-based institutions in operation. In the end, sector-based management allocates resources, often with heightened conflict and unpredictable results.

Conflicts can arise in several different ways, as noted in table 7.1. They include the characteristics of the use, the actions of the participants who benefit from the activity or manage it, the information that participants have, the institutional structures that control activities, and the ultimate allocation or results of management (Brown et al., 2002). The extent to which a use is exclusive can also be a measure of the likelihood of conflict.

Some uses require the natural system to remain in relatively unaltered form, as illustrated by birds in wetlands. However, lands are typically in private hands. Private property owners alter natural systems for agriculture and home development and that in turn reduces or excludes certain birds. Resolving conflicts rooted in the different views of coastal resource users is a central charge for coastal management (Brown et al., 2002).

Societies resolve coastal conflicts through sets of rules referred to as

TABLE 7.1.
Coastal conflicts.

Sources of Conflict	Issues
Use characteristics	Direct or indirect overlaps in space used or environmental impacts resulting
Participants	Individuals, interest groups, or government agencies seek different outcomes
Information	Uncertain science communicated from the perspective of disparate values
Institutional structures	Fragmented legal and regulatory structure with poorly defined rights and responsibilities
Allocation	Competing demands for access, space, and/or environmental quality

institutions. Institutions include laws, regulations, and family or cultural guidance concerning behavior. Institutions determine which use has precedence in the event that more than one use is proposed for the same location at the same time. Organizations are the units that carry out the institutional guidance. Frequently they are government agencies, but they can also be organizations outside of government like trade associations or environmental groups.

Space-based management provides an alternative to sector-based institutions. In spatial management, the rules are focused on location of uses—certain zones for certain uses. The process used to define those zones, and the extent to which it is deemed equitable, are particularly important. If it is to be effective, the planning process must address each of the areas of conflict noted in table 7.1. Although technical experts can provide information and characteristics of uses, stakeholder involvement in the formative stages and a willingness to reassess institutions can very constructively preface the difficult challenge of reaching a just allocation of space and uses within it. The result is a proactive plan for a coastal area, which is enforced through permits that authorize uses. Ultimately geographic areas are matched up with preferred activities. A federal law passed in 1972 made it possible to allocate coastal space, as described in the next section.

The Coastal Zone Management Act

Change throughout the twentieth century laid the groundwork for spatial management. Americans in increasing numbers embraced the shore as a place for recreation, and in response the federal government added coastal lands and waters to the national park system. Furthermore, federal funding for estuarine studies and a national commission on the oceans emphasized the growing importance of the coast (Zile, 1974). In the 1960s the meaning of land in general and open space in particular had gained new importance on the national agenda, as evidenced by several laws concerning land use (Platt, 1996). The early years of the 1970s saw new requirements for environmental impact statements and initiatives to protect air and water quality. For a while, a national land use policy was considered through hundreds of bills in Congress, though one was never enacted.

In this climate a new national strategy for coastal lands and waters management came to fruition. It was the Coastal Zone Management Act of 1972. The law, originally ten pages in length, focuses on the coastal region as identified by each of the states that have voluntarily chosen to participate. All of the coastal states and territories, as well as all of the Great Lakes states except Illinois, have signed on. They, in turn, take action to plan for and manage activities along the coast subject to federal guidelines. Typically a state defines a terrestrial zone along coastal lands and a zone that encompasses state coastal waters. Uses are specified for the geographic areas—land and sea. This approach—of thinking regionally prior to focusing on specific parcels of land or water—establishes a spatial management scheme that designates zones for particular uses and provides guidance about how they will be conducted. Spatial management is implemented through the control that states and local governments exert over land use decisions and the extent to which states do likewise in coastal waters. Federally approved state plans include either local implementation, direct state-level land and water use control, or state review of plans or regulations (Platt, 1996). Actions taken by states in coastal zone management and by the federal government through the establishment of parks or offshore oil development areas, among many other programs (table 7.2), provide a background for the current discussions of marine spatial planning and management.

To participate, states generally adopt one of two basic frameworks (Born and Miller, 1988). In networked programs, the coastal state connects existing laws to form a fabric of activities that addresses coastal management needs, as has been done in Florida (box 7.1). This can be accomplished without new laws and through limited organizational change. Often the effort is led by a staff agency that coordinates across

TABLE 7.2.
Coastal and ocean programs with spatial dimensions.

Area	Authority	Purpose
Lands adjacent to marine and estuarine waters	Coastal Zone Management Act—State programs	Protect and develop coastal lands and waters
Coastal Barrier Resources System	Coastal Barrier Resources Act	Limit federal funding of infrastructure and insurance for coastal barriers
National Estuarine Research Reserve System	Coastal Zone Management Act	Acquisition/operation of estuarine areas for research
National Marine Sanctuary Program	Marine Pollution, Research, and Sanctuaries Act	Protection of biological and cultural materials in offshore waters
National Estuary Program	Clean Water Act	Selected coastal watersheds and bays managed to improve water quality
National parks and seashores	National Park Service Organic Act	Federal management for recreation and conservation
Marine Protected Areas	Executive order	Protection and use of resources in a national system of areas
Nonpoint source management	Clean Water Act, Section 319, and Coastal Zone Reauthorization Amendments, Section 6217	Alter land uses to limit pollution of coastal waters
National Flood Insurance Program	Flood Disaster Protection Act	Incentives and regulation to limit damage in flood-prone areas
Federal disaster assistance	Disaster Mitigation Act	Assistance to individuals and public entities in areas that have been flooded
Brownfields	Comprehensive Environmental Response, Compensation, and Liability Act	Assistance for development of contaminated areas

TABLE 7.2. *continued*

Area	Authority	Purpose
Offshore oil	Outer Continental Shelf Lands Act	Process to allow private firms to develop energy resources seaward of state waters
Ocean dumping	Marine Protection, Research, and Sanctuaries Act	Dumping of dredged material in ocean waters
Fisheries in federal waters	Magnuson-Stevens Fishery Conservation and Management Act	Limits fishing in specified geographic areas
Oil pollution	Oil Pollution Act of 1990	Specific remedies for areas affected by oil spills
Offshore ports	Deepwater Port Act	Mechanism to designate and operate offshore ports
Wildlife refuges	Migratory Bird Conservation Act	Protect migratory bird populations
Hydrokinetic energy	Energy Policy Act, Federal Power Act, Outer Continental Shelf Lands Act	Designation of sites for renewable energy equipment

units of state government. The alternative strategy is new legislation to empower a state organization to make decisions, as is the case in Rhode Island (box 7.1).

In designing and implementing a comprehensive program at the state level, government officials confront significant challenges. First and foremost is the fact that sectors or uses have traditionally been managed, for the most part, in separate units of government at each level of government (figure 7.1). This structure contains horizontal and vertical components (Sorenson, 1997; Kay and Alder, 2005). In the U.S. system federalism separates federal, state, and local governments that exemplify the vertical dimension (figure 7.1). Furthermore, because actions that shape human behavior related to the coast are increasingly located outside of government, private sector initiatives are a part of the vertical structure but beyond federalism.

Looking horizontally at the federal level reveals multiple executive branch entities that govern coastal activities. Not only are there executive,

Box 7.1. State Coastal Programs by Network or Legislation

State coastal programs meet the federal goals using different structures. In one approach, states connect a *network* of state laws that already exist, usually coordinate them through staff in or near the governor's office, and meet the objectives of the federal law for a successful state program. A new *legislative* act at the state level is the other alternative to gain approval for a coastal program. It usually results in the creation of a new organization to map and sanction specific uses. Two states illustrate these different approaches.

Floridians have implemented their coastal program through a network of existing laws. The Florida Coastal Management Program was approved in 1981. It networks twenty-three state laws and regulations and is implemented through fifteen agencies. The Florida Department of Environmental Protection administers the program to meet the requirements of the federal Coastal Zone Management Act. Florida's coastal zone includes the entire state and the adjacent state waters out to three miles or in some areas nine miles (14.5 kilometers). Among its many duties, the Florida State Clearinghouse reviews selected state and federal activities to confirm that they are consistent with the coastal management program. The clearinghouse distributes the application to appropriate governmental units, compiles their assessments, and informs the parties as to whether the application is consistent with state laws or not.

In Rhode Island a 1971 state law created the Coastal Resources Management Council (CRMC), a state agency that implements the federal Coastal Zone Management Act. The regulatory authority of this agency extends from three miles (4.8 kilometers) offshore to two hundred feet (sixty-one meters) inland from coastal features such as beaches, dunes, barrier islands, coastal wetlands, bluffs, rocky shores, and manmade shorelines. The sixteen-member council is appointed by elected officials and consists of members of the general public, coastal communities, and government officials. It is scheduled to meet twice a month. Approximately 1,100 applications are filed each year for homes, docks, subdivisions, and commercial and industrial developments. The staff resolves many requests, but the most significant developments are brought to a full hearing before the council. In addition the council participates in waterfront access determinations, workshops on emerging issues, and the creation of new regulations. In Rhode Island a special area management plan for the waters adjacent to the state has been used to identify geographic areas appropriate for wind energy development.

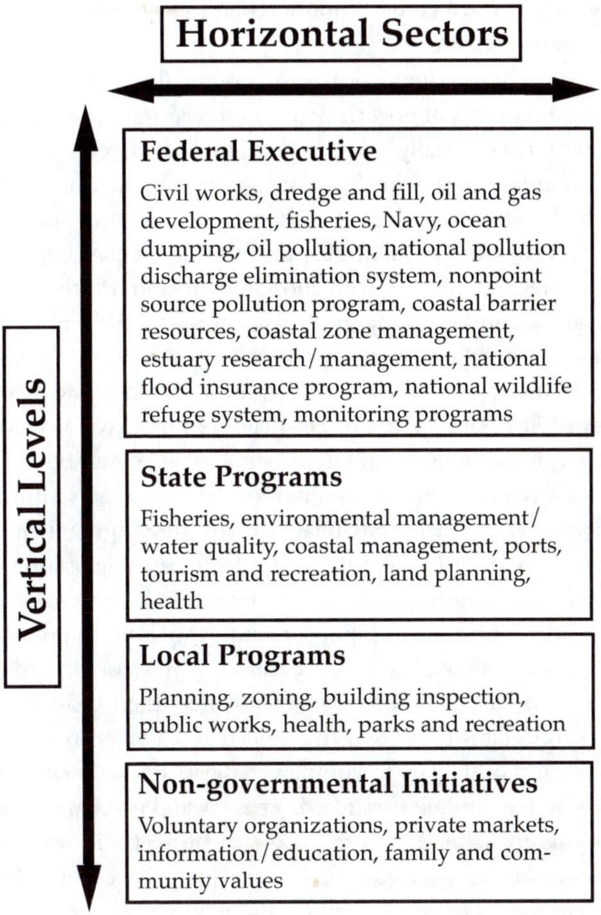

Horizontal Sectors

Vertical Levels

Federal Executive

Civil works, dredge and fill, oil and gas development, fisheries, Navy, ocean dumping, oil pollution, national pollution discharge elimination system, nonpoint source pollution program, coastal barrier resources, coastal zone management, estuary research/management, national flood insurance program, national wildlife refuge system, monitoring programs

State Programs

Fisheries, environmental management/ water quality, coastal management, ports, tourism and recreation, land planning, health

Local Programs

Planning, zoning, building inspection, public works, health, parks and recreation

Non-governmental Initiatives

Voluntary organizations, private markets, information/education, family and community values

Figure 7.1. Structure of coastal governance. Shaping human behavior in coastal regions involves three levels of government, hybrid organizations that operate among them, and initiatives operating outside of the direct control of government. At each level there are multiple programs focused on distinctive but often overlapping topics. The result is a fragmented structure requiring simultaneous collaboration across levels and topics.

legislative, and judicial units involved, but also within the executive branch coastal issues are spread across many agencies. Fragmentation of authority in waters off southern California is well illustrated by more than a dozen uses managed through multiple state and federal programs (Crowder et al., 2006). At times this fragmentation allows interests to shop for agencies most likely to support their needs, and it makes coherent management difficult.

Successful spatial management has the potential to link the horizontal and vertical dimensions of government. Approved state programs include a seaward boundary, usually three miles (4.8 kilometers) offshore, and an inland boundary based on biophysical or cultural features (Beatley et al., 2002). Among the obligations that states assume through a federally approved program are identification of areas for particular concern, access to beaches, and attention to shoreline erosion. Furthermore, state programs have become a testing ground for at least four important policy innovations in how society relates to coastal regions.

First, states interpreted the law to require that federal agency actions be consistent with state coastal plans (Davis, 2001; USCOP, 2004). As a result federal agencies were required to consider state interests before taking action that would affect land, water, or other natural resources at or near the coast. Federal decisions related to oil development in offshore waters are a primary example. Offshore oil spills damage state resources when the oil moves onshore. Even the routine development of offshore oil wells has effects onshore as support facilities are built to provide a base for the activities in federal waters. Therefore, states could comment on and at times veto federal actions that would affect their coastal zones.

Second, some states have used the special area management planning (SAMP) provision of the law to complete a detailed plan for a geographic area. SAMPs include policies, standards, criteria, and mechanisms to guide land/water use to achieve natural resource protection and reasonable coast-dependent economic growth. Special plans have been developed for coastal lands, coastal waters, and combinations of the two. Coastal plans rely on vegetative buffers, setbacks, storm water and septic regulations, dock regulations, and special use zones to shape human behavior so water quality and habitats are advanced (Davis, 2004). Coastal areas are frequently under siege by sprawling development. Among the many tools to address it are growth boundaries, infrastructure location, transportation planning, tax policy, and standardized development regulations, yet the SAMPs have yet to adopt many of these tools (Davis, 2004). Currently, a number of states have completed plans for managing their ocean waters and others are in the process of doing so.

Third, as states have planned for future uses, the recurring desire to increase access to the shore has emerged. Access to the coast varies by state. Typically, the area landward of the high water mark is private, which allows the public to pass along the wet beach area (Davis, 2001b; Beatley et al., 2002). However, coasts change due to erosion and deposition. Add to this variability differences in state law, and management of this zone is complicated. The annual increase in the number of access points to the nation's shorelines signals success for one element of the coastal program (Government Accountability Office, 2008a). Depending on the amenities (e.g., parking, trash collection) at the access point, each may provide the public with an effective means to enjoy the shore. By fee-simple purchase the local or state government may enhance access. An alternative is to purchase an easement or the right to use land for a specific purpose.

In addition states have joined with the federal government to create estuarine research reserves, a final innovation. The reserves serve as field laboratories where research can be carried out to learn how natural processes and human activities affect estuaries. More than two dozen research reserves have been created through the coastal act.

Other space-based coastal management programs

Although coastal zone management extends along almost every inch of ocean-facing and Great Lakes coastline in this country, it is not the only space-based program. Additional programs have been developed at the federal, state, and local levels of government. These programs target specific geographic regions, and they often advance a particular or exclusive use. Many of the early spatial management designations for marine waters amounted to staking claims for exclusive uses of certain geographic areas. Unlike coastal zone management, which targets both protection and development, these other programs advance the needs of one sector. More than two dozen federal programs of this type exist (table 7.2).

Programs established to protect geographic regions on land and sea include the national parks/seashores, coastal barrier resources, estuarine research reserves, and marine sanctuaries, among others. In each case the program identifies a designated portion of land and/or sea with a specified objective for it. These programs emphasize protection, recreational use, and research, among other goals for the designated areas. In response to an executive order federal agencies have recently identified more than two hundred marine protected areas in a national system, which includes approximately ten percent of U.S. waters between zero and two hundred miles (322 kilometers) offshore (www.mpa.gov).

Other programs identify areas for the purpose of resource extraction, waste disposal, and a variety of additional uses. For example, under the ocean dumping law, areas of the seafloor have been mapped and designated for disposal of dredged material. Additional programs respond to a region affected by a specific event. Flood insurance, disaster assistance, and oil pollution response programs fit this type of regional activity.

Spatial management techniques

The shift from regulation of uses to holistic management of geographic areas is built on a change in technique. One has to decide proactively which activities to prefer at what locations. Solutions require consensus among many parties. Legislative guidance about what is appropriate helps. The transition from goals to actions may be accomplished in several ways. Table 7.3 identifies tools for spatial management.

First and foremost is the legislative route to determining the use of a region. Legislative clarity is a powerful antidote to fragmentation, especially when the law defines a use and identifies a geographic region for it. For example, federal legislators can and have identified the location of marine sanctuaries. Similarly, the president has the power to establish marine protected areas through an executive order under the Antiquities Act. In both cases political actors identify the boundaries of geographic areas and the purposes for the regions.

Second and more commonly, law creates administrative processes that allow federal agencies to identify geographic areas for specific uses. For example, federal law established administrative procedures to create and operate estuarine research reserves.

Third, zoning provides another means to govern a specific area of land or sea (box 7.2). Zoning relies on the spatial separation and control of incompatible uses (Platt, 1996). Traffic lanes for ships going in different directions are just one of many examples.

Fourth, public entities can acquire coastal property to shape its long-term use to meet locally or nationally identified goals. National parks/seashores have been created using this approach. Fee-simple property acquisition by state or local government can do likewise. To fund this, communities have used a real estate transfer tax of a few percent of the value of the sale or a surcharge on property taxes (Beatley et al., 2002). The land banks that are funded by these revenues purchase coastal lands for recreation, conservation, hazard reduction, and other public purposes.

Fifth, development rights for private lands could be separated from the land and sold separately as a means of continuing the existing use. For example, by purchasing the development rights of a seafront farm, a land trust can ensure that condominiums will not be built on the farmlands. Furthermore, it's possible for government to insist that a property owner

TABLE 7.3.
Selected techniques for spatial management.

Technique	Operation	Example
Legislation	Congress designates a use for a geographic area of land or sea	Ocean areas designated as sanctuaries
Presidential discretion	Marine national monument	Papahanaumokuakea Marine National Monument, Hawaii
Administrative	Executive agency classifies federal waters for specific use	Dumping or oil development
Zoning	Mapped areas with uses specified by regulation	Zoning of state waters
Setback	Distance from coastal feature within which development is prohibited	Many coastal state programs
Fee-simple acquisition	Purchase of coastal area and all associated rights	Some national seashore lands
Purchase of development rights	Public entity acquires legal entitlements to improve land and chooses to leave it undeveloped	Farm lands adjacent to coast to maintain open land in perpetuity
Tax incentives	Taxing levels adjusted to encourage certain uses	Reduced property tax for some working waterfronts in Maine
Public infrastructure	Withhold public funding of infrastructure for undeveloped areas	No bridges to undeveloped barrier islands

who wishes to develop lands must purchase a certain number of development rights from others prior to gaining approval for development of a specific parcel. The transfer of development rights tends to concentrate activity and can reduce sprawl.

Sixth, states and coastal communities can use their taxing powers and choices they make about spending to shape the nature of coastal development (Beatley et al., 2002). Through differential taxation, certain uses may be encouraged. Reducing taxes on land that is kept open is one possibility. Working waterfronts, the homes of traditional marine industries, may also merit special tax status if water-dependent uses such as boatyards, fish

Box 7.2. Zoning

In the early part of the last century congestion in urban areas led to a push for greater public control of privately owned lands to avoid nuisances, protect health, and enhance safety (Platt, 1996). Implementation of zoning requires a planning board or commission to propose uses for zones, approval of zones by an elected local government, a permit system, and a zoning board of appeals where landowners may go to seek flexibility. Zoning can regulate the use of private land by specifying the density of development and the dimensions of buildings. A local zoning ordinance will include a map with zones for different uses identified and text describing the nature of the uses.

Zoning, an example of regional or area-based management, differs from sector-based management in several ways. It often provides detailed information about what may be anticipated in geographic areas and on specific parcels. Requirements for sector-based decisions frequently emanate from the federal government, whereas control of zoning decisions is held locally in most instances. Sector-based decisions focus on the acceptability of a single use, but regional decisions focus on the future of a portion of the land or sea with cognizance of its potential for multiple uses. And finally, a central part of the decision document is a map. Proactive regionally based management of the coast by local entities is the hallmark of this approach.

Setbacks, commonly implemented as a part of zoning, require structures to be built a specified distance from the edge of a parcel. When the edge of the parcel is the sea or the beach, specifying a setback can protect the dunes and provide a margin of safety from sea level rise and storm surge incursions that might destroy houses too close to the sea. Additional practices include techniques to provide incentives for more efficient use of land or to concentrate development while leaving other lands open.

docks, and cargo terminals are to be favored over displaceable uses such as condominiums, hotels, and restaurants.

Some have recognized that inhabiting coastal areas can be particularly costly after a major storm strikes the coast. Mapping vulnerable areas and identifying obligations of their inhabitants both prior to and after storm damage occurs constitutes a sound government policy. Special benefit assessments raise funds for these eventualities through charges to property owners who will derive benefits but also incur potential liabilities from the location of their properties. Similarly, local impact fees allow communities to collect funds that are used to offset subsequent costs of risky development.

Government can also influence development in hazardous zones by choosing not to provide publicly funded infrastructure—for example, roads, water supplies, and sewage treatment—that will encourage development in hazardous areas. If the original investment is made, then after major storms government-supported rebuilding inadvertently encourages additional development (Bagstad et al., 2007). Through the Coastal Barrier Resources Act the federal government has strongly discouraged development of certain parts of the coast by designating these units and eliminating federal subsidies for those areas (Salvesen, 2005). However, in some instances local communities have paid for infrastructure to facilitate development. As a result the act has only slowed coastal development in some areas.

Evaluation of state programs

Spatial planning and management has changed the way decisions are made. But has the Coastal Zone Management Act worked? Through the act, Congress proposed to "preserve, protect, develop, and, where possible, to restore or enhance, the resources of the Nation's coastal zone for this and succeeding generations" (Coastal Zone Management Act, Section 303). These ambiguous goals must be reconciled with rapid population growth along the coast. Development that spreads housing across the landscape, separates it from jobs and services, and requires many highways is sprawl. Tabulations at the county scale portray an ominous picture. Between 1970 and 1989 forty-seven percent of the housing units permitted in the United States were in coastal counties (Culliton et al., 1992). More recent compilations find that this trend is continuing and assert that by 2025 a land area roughly the size of Wyoming will be converted to residential and commercial use, mostly along the coast (Pew Oceans Commission, 2003). In this setting the act's call for restoration, enhancement, preservation, and protection of resources confronts extreme pressures for development. Many states have chosen to define their official coastal zones as the veneer of land facing coastal waters. As a result sprawling development continues just inland. Better metrics for identifying coastal sprawl trajectories are available (Crawford, 2007), and the need for more effective coastal planning is apparent (Norton, 2005; Tang, 2008). It could focus on rapid development just inland from the oceanfront, reconsider the balance between economic development and environmental protection, and monitor more effectively.

State management has been plagued by society's conflicted values concerning the coast and, as a consequence, a lack of standards and actions to meet environmental goals. In the absence of specific targets and standards, it remains difficult to calibrate the states' success at protecting coastal environments. To address this problem analysts have designated core objectives that include resource protection, access, and urban/port areas (Good et al., 1999; Hershman et al., 1999). They have assessed the importance of core areas in each state, identified management tools, and considered results. Although state programs were deemed effective, Hershman et al. (1999) noted limited information on outcomes, lack of indicators of success, and the absence of a performance evaluation system as weaknesses. In response to the need to more effectively assess progress, the National Oceanic and Atmospheric Administration created a measurement system, which includes environmental features (water quality, habitat, hazards), uses (public access, development), and governmental activities (financial measures, government coordination). In spite of these innovations one recent assessment calls for further progress (General Accountability Office, 2008a).

Over time revisions of the act have provided additional substantive guidance, which could be the basis for establishing indicators. The changes in the law include expectations for preservation or restoration of specific areas such as shellfish beds, the redevelopment of urban waterfronts, shoreline stabilization, and other activities. Another revision of the law in 1990 encouraged states to protect wetlands, enhance access, reduce exposure to hazards, establish special area management plans, locate energy facilities, and control cumulative and secondary impacts. Federal funding has been made available for many of these initiatives, and those states that have received funding could be assessed with respect to the results obtained.

Alternatively, state implementation could be evaluated in terms of how effective the processes are as opposed to whether the results match the goals of the act. In that context a successful program is one that has devised improved means for resolving conflicts among users of coastal resources. Owens (1992) found that over one five-year period thirty-nine percent of national funding was devoted to improving governmental decision making and twenty-eight percent went to natural resource protection. Because decision-making improvements deal with conflict reduction at least in part, focusing on the sources of conflict is an important first step. State implementation could be viewed positively to the extent that it produces more timely and predictable results (Knecht et al.,

1996) and to the extent it uses consistent criteria for reaching decisions and results in less litigation after they are announced.

Spatial planning and management of ocean waters

Federal waters, the zone from three to two hundred miles (322 kilometers) offshore, are a focus for a renewed effort in spatial management. In these areas federal authority is preeminent, and the proliferation of single-use initiatives increasingly results in overlap and conflict. Commission reports have highlighted both the importance of and potential for spatial management for watersheds to the two hundred–mile line or exclusively in federal waters. Pew Oceans Commission (2003) proposed zoning to consider a full range of uses, reduce conflicts, and enhance marine conservation. The U.S. Commission on Ocean Policy (2004) identified the need for coordinated governance of offshore waters and proposed the creation of regional governance councils that would help policy makers address conflicts among uses.

The present management situation for offshore waters is not satisfactory for a number of reasons (Ehler, 2008). Sector-based regulation with little effort to anticipate conflicts has resulted in a growing burden of cumulative impacts where individual uses intensify, and different types of uses combine to stress part or all of the coastal environment. Current frameworks in the United States seldom mandate planning across all activities in a marine area, and in most instances ocean regions lack a common vision of goals for the future. Without a framework for assigning future uses, one finds (i) an absence of managed connections among offshore activities and onshore communities, (ii) limited proactive conservation, (iii) a lack of investment certainty for developers, and (iv) ineffective connection among governmental authorities (Douvere, 2008). In the end activities inevitably overlap and conflicts can build.

A planning process that leads to a zoning map, regulations, and permit procedures to control performance of human activities is the heart of implementation for spatial management, particularly in federal waters (Crowder et al., 2006; Young et al., 2007; Douvere and Ehler, 2009). Many government programs designate geographic areas for specific activities or uses (table 7.2), but management of ocean space lacks a comprehensive vision. Without a plan for the region as a whole, development can follow the pattern used in the Wild West, in which users who acted quickly staked claims and obtained the greatest benefits. For a regional plan to be taken seriously, many believe that statutory authority and enforcement mechanisms are mandatory. If this were to be the case, then one would need to involve stakeholders in constructive ways to reach common goals for the plan and the zones identified. Spatial management is a tool, and the purpose of the plan can range from protection to development, depending on how the stakeholders see their common interest. In fact many look to experience with coastal zone management, state coastal waters plans, and other space-based programs to establish the process elements that would be valuable in this setting.

In recognition of multiple and often separate initiatives in coastal and marine spatial planning, federal agencies have proposed a framework to span their multiple responsibilities (Ocean Policy Task Force, 2009). Under the proposal nine regional planning bodies would be created to cover coastal and marine areas as well as the Great Lakes. Federal agencies, state governments, and stakeholders would prepare development agreements for the region that would consider alternative uses and trade-offs as well as cumulative impacts. With astute implementation regional plans could become very influential in directing future activities.

Summary

So far we have discussed two styles of coastal management. Under one approach, as presented in earlier chapters, one can regulate the use or sector and allow the users to decide on its location. Or as shown in this chapter, one can focus on where uses fit in the landscape or seascape through a spatial management approach. Being proactive by locating uses can reduce conflict by establishing precedence and by creating processes so individual decisions can be reached in concert with a larger plan. The Coastal Zone Management Act and laws that established national seashores, sanctuaries, research reserves, dumping areas, and oil development, among other uses, represent a body of practice related to spatial planning and management (table 7.2).

As we have covered it here, spatial management exists in three different contexts. Most coastal lands are in private ownership, and planning for their uses is accomplished primarily through local zoning. By sensitizing decisions related to local land use adjacent to the coast, the Coastal Zone Management Act plays an important role in shaping results. Second, state government controls some coastal lands and almost all coastal waters. As a result zoning of state waters has become an effective way to signal preferred uses. The federal government also participates in spatial management of coastal lands and inshore waters through the Coastal Barrier Resources Act, estuarine reserves, national seashores, and wildlife refuges, among other programs. Third, the federal government designates areas of federal offshore waters for uses such as sanctuaries, offshore energy ports, energy developments, dumping sites, and a variety of other activities. Taken together, these spatial management initiatives include about eighteen programs (table 7.2).

The opportunity to proactively consider uses for a specific geographic area was a major advance in coastal management. States that chose to participate in the federally sponsored Coastal Zone Management program were encouraged to produce management programs with maps to indicate areas where uses for coastal waters and adjacent shore lands would be acceptable consonant with the overall national policy to protect and develop the coastal zone. When viewed from this perspective coastal management is a multiple use management program. Coastal areas may be identified for preservation, protection, and restoration. Barrier islands, sea grass beds, and wetlands have all been managed from this perspective. In addition the law indicates that the coast may be managed for development. In this context cities, transportation systems, housing developments, and restaurants may all make a claim on coastal space by virtue of the way the law is constructed and implemented. With funding from the federal government states have restored wetlands, opened access points, and built public docks, among many other accomplishments. In addition the Coastal Zone Management Act has encouraged innovative practices. Federal approvals for offshore energy systems or new shipping facilities must be consistent with state plans for the coast. Within state programs, special area management plans can provide more precise direction for specific uses of coastal lands and waters.

Spatial management clearly enhanced the nation's ability to manage conflict in coastal areas. Like any policy innovation, it will require continued evaluation and enhancement. Analysts have struggled to identify goals, performance standards, adequate data, and levels of success for state programs. Some have even raised the question of whether substantive goals, such as improvement of environmental quality, or process goals, such as more predictable decisions, should be the target for evaluation. In the end, after decades of implementation, the ecological health of some coastal waters lags and coastal lands are subject to ever increasing sprawling development. These realities run contrary to what many hold as the need for preservation, restoration, and enhancement of coastal resources, but they reflect the nation's conflicted attitudes toward protection and development. Many have proposed ecosystem-based management, the subject of the next chapter, as a means to enhance and focus coastal management for the future.

8

Ecosystem Governance

Coastal areas incorporate land and sea as well as social and ecological systems. The sector-based and spatial management practices assessed earlier are unable to fully synthesize and manage across coastal uses in an effective manner. The former misses most of the links. The latter accommodates multiple uses but often fails to advance ecosystem health. Two national commissions have criticized this current state of affairs and each proposes ecosystem-based management as a solution (Pew Oceans Commission, 2003; U.S. Commission on Ocean Policy, 2004).

This chapter identifies the diverse opportunities for ecosystem-based management in coastal areas. The linkage between ecosystems and social systems is illustrated by considering the use and impacts of fertilizer in farming. Fertilization in the midwestern United States damages water quality in the Gulf of Mexico. Ecosystem thinking goes far to address problems of this type.

Inevitably the rate and style of adoption of ecosystem-based management will vary. Slow or incremental change consists of small departures from existing procedures that allow managers to test new approaches. More abrupt changes involve significantly different steps that are legitimized through new laws or other authoritative means. Fragmented governmental systems, environmental decline, and growing demands for better performance make the coast particularly ripe for these changes.

Nitrogen links between land/sea and society/nature

In coastal areas, social systems (households, farms, fisheries, markets, schools) and natural systems (nutrients, tides, runoff, plants, animals) are located in the same geographic region and are intimately connected. Effective management recognizes these links as well as the limits of the combined social/ecological system.

Ecosystems are made up of biological communities and their physical habitat, as well as people. These systems are defined by flows of materials and energy in bounded geographic regions. Systems with greater biological diversity, or biodiversity, are more likely to remain stable when disturbances arise (Schmitz, 2007; Cotgreave and Forseth, 2002). For example, if there are multiple food sources for an animal to draw on, then food substitution can occur. Because ecosystem productivity, stability, and other desirable features are related to biological diversity, it attracts special attention in management. Furthermore, research has demonstrated that the degradation, fragmentation, or destruction of habitat reduces diversity.

The movement of water influences organisms in marine systems. As rivers flow to the sea they exchange materials with the atmosphere and land, tightly linking terrestrial and marine systems (Crossland et al., 2005). The shape of the seafloor in estuaries and sounds coupled with water flow, tides, and winds determine how long the average water molecule stays in the embayment. This retention time determines the character of chemical exchanges. Long retention times can lead to environmental problems.

In this setting nitrogen plays a particularly important role. It is used to fertilize agricultural lands and gets into the waters that run off from them. It connects land to sea and links social and ecological systems. It is a necessary component of proteins, chlorophyll, and nucleic acids—all required for life. Most of the time, nitrogen is a limiting nutrient in marine systems, which means that if the supply is restricted, plant growth will be inhibited. Conversely, in excess it produces far too many plants and can result in low oxygen conditions in the water. Nitrogen flows among land, air, water, and sediments (figure 8.1), and occurs in a variety of different forms. Organisms, including humans, affect its forms and flows.

Human activity dramatically increases the flow of nitrogen to coastal waters, resulting in profound changes in marine environments. Sewage, fertilizer on crops, and burning of fossil fuels all contribute nitrogen to

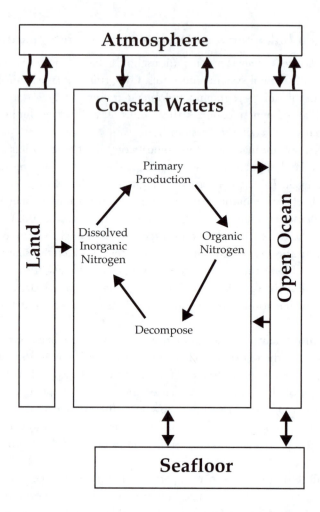

Figure 8.1. Nitrogen flows. Each of the rectangles holds nitrogen and the arrows signify flow of it among and within compartments. Human activities affect the flows of nitrogen and in aggregate have increased nitrogen in coastal waters.

coastal lands and waters. The transfer of reactive nitrogen from rivers to oceans may have grown three- to fourfold due to human activity. Excess nitrogen unlocks rapid phytoplankton growth, which leads to respiration and decay, causing low oxygen in coastal waters. The resulting anoxic or hypoxic zones are marked by much lower levels of oxygen than would normally be expected (Rabalais and Gilbert, 2009). When dissolved oxygen in the water column drops to less than two milligrams per liter, the waters are referred to as *hypoxic*. When there is virtually no oxygen available, they are *anoxic*. These areas are known as dead zones because many animals commonly found in coastal waters cannot survive there.

The consequences of nitrogen loading are well known. At first, increased nitrogen in coastal waters appears beneficial because it allows the growth of more phytoplankton and expansion of some fisheries. But phytoplankton becomes a burden on the oxygen budget of the coastal area. When alive and not photosynthesizing at night, phytoplankton consume oxygen. When dead they become a food source for aerobic bacteria, which require oxygen as they decompose the algae. As a result, oxygen levels decline. In summer solar heating and calm winds stratify the water column and intensify the problem. Therefore, deep waters, which do not mix with surface zones and atmospheric oxygen, become hypoxic.

In recent years hypoxic waters in the northern Gulf of Mexico have averaged 5,212 square miles (13,500 square kilometers) from mid-May through mid-September (Rabalais and Gilbert, 2009). The size of the hypoxic zone has been related to the nitrate load the Mississippi River delivered over the two months prior to the sampling. Nitrate load from the river is mostly determined by concentrations in waters that drain lands rich in agricultural activities. Because this nitrogen flows from farm fields rather than from pipes, it is called a nonpoint source. So humans using fertilizer on crops connect ocean phenomena, hypoxia, to farming far inland. The extent, duration, and intensity of hypoxia in this area of the Gulf have been increasing since the 1970s.

Reduction of oxygen will have direct consequences for all marine organisms that require high levels of it to survive. Over time, the composition of species in the sediments shifts to those that can tolerate the low oxygen conditions. Animals that can escape will do so when oxygen levels fall to near hypoxic conditions (Rabalais and Gilbert, 2009). At even lower levels of oxygen, animals that live in the mud at the bottom of the sea attempt to leave the sediments and often die. As conditions become anoxic, benthic species diversity declines linearly with oxygen decline.

Increasing nutrient loads also affect fisheries (Rabalais and Gilbert, 2009). When coastal waters move from the low to mid range of nitrogen loading, fishery production and yield increases. At higher loadings fisheries tend to collapse as hypoxic conditions develop. Another trend noted is that the species of fish harvested shift in response to nitrogen increases from those that feed on the bottom to those that live in the water column and feed on plankton.

The multiple factors influencing the dead zone are illustrated in figure

8.2. Agricultural and wastewater disposal practices and management of the river's wetlands, all to a significant extent under the direct control of people, affect the dead zone. They do this by changing nitrogen flows. Climate, which controls wind and precipitation, is superimposed on the other factors. It determines the rate and timing of nitrogen delivery to the Gulf, and the extent to which the waters of the Gulf mix and remain oxygenated. These factors can combine and result in serious damage to fisheries harvests.

This review of causes for the Gulf of Mexico dead zone demonstrates

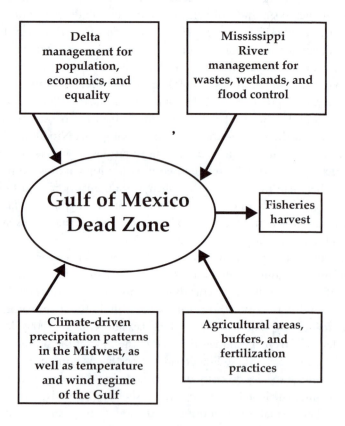

Figure 8.2. Causes of the dead zone. Nitrogen enrichment of the Gulf of Mexico adjacent to the mouth of the Mississippi River causes phytoplankton blooms and ultimately low oxygen in the waters. Anthropogenic nitrogen loads to the Gulf are determined by fertilizer use, effluent water discharge from sewage treatment, and a variety of other factors. When large areas of the Gulf have low or no dissolved oxygen in the water, higher organisms suffer.

that human-mediated flows of nitrogen produce dramatic and unfortunately detrimental results. Ecosystem science provides a clear understanding of how this linked human/natural system works. However, past management initiatives have been focused on discrete parts of the system and lack coordination. In short, fragmented, sector-based management has limited utility. By diagnosing the situation in ecosystem science terms, it becomes very clear that the more holistic management approach known as ecosystem governance or ecosystem-based management would do much to address this and other similar problems.

Ecosystem-based management in concept

To appreciate how ecosystem-based management might benefit the Gulf of Mexico and other threatened areas, it is worth considering how experts have conceptualized this distinctive form of governance (table 8.1). The U.S. Commission on Ocean Policy represents many interests and provides a national perspective. The commission declared the need to manage all components of the ecosystem—including people—collectively. This principle has widespread support, but is not currently reflected in most governance activities.

Nonetheless, the potential for ecosystem-based management is great and various groups have detailed what it would entail, as shown in the second section ("Group") of table 8.1. The groups cited there believe strongly in ecosystem-based management; their proposed policies address general purposes or desired states of affairs. Collectively the statements establish a goal of healthy, productive, resilient ecosystems able to provide services people need and want. Institutions with the capacity to manage holistically using the principles of ecosystem health, sustainability, and precaution are advocated. Such institutions, if present, would be particularly helpful in resolving management of issues related to the dead zone.

The concluding quotes in table 8.1 give selected analytical perspectives on ecosystem-based management. The authors emphasize a common goal under which multiple sectors of coastal activity may be managed in an integrated fashion using natural boundaries and operating at a landscape scale. Collaborative planning built on public participation and equity should lead to flexible and adaptive program implementation. For ecosystem-based management to be successful the authors cited in the "Analytical" section of table 8.1 expect it will have to account for cumulative impacts, incorporate precaution, and provide trade-offs among services. As more experience is gained with these concepts, they will inevitably be refined.

TABLE 8.1.
Explanations of ecosystem-based management.

Perspective	Explanation
National	"U.S. ocean and coastal resources should be managed to reflect the relationships among all ecosystem components, including humans and nonhuman species and the environments in which they live." USCOP, 2004, 62.
Group	"National ocean policy and governance must be realigned to reflect and apply principles of ecosystem health and integrity, sustainability and precaution. We must . . . organize institutions and forums capable of managing on an ecosystem basis." Pew Oceans Commission, 2003, x.
	"An integrated approach to management that considers the entire ecosystem, including humans. The goal of ecosystem-based management is to maintain an ecosystem in a healthy, productive, and resilient condition so that it can provide the services humans want and need." McLeod et al., 2005.
	"In general, EBM is a broad approach, involving the management of species, other natural commodities, and humans as components of the larger ecosystem." Arkema et al., 2006, 525.
Analytical	"1. EBM focuses on the ability of the ecosystem to continuously provide . . . services . . . and includes . . . humans.
	2. Natural boundaries are more relevant.
	3. Sectors of human activity . . . require some level of management integration.
	4. Accounting for cumulative impacts and necessary trade-offs among services 5. Making decisions under uncertainty." Rosenberg and Sandifer, 2009, 14.
	"First and foremost, EBM involves addressing problems at a landscape or regional scale. . . . Second, EBM entails collaborative planning, in which public officials, private stakeholders, and scientists assemble voluntarily to seek consensus. . . . Third, EBM relies heavily on flexible, adaptive implementation of planning goals." Layzer, 2008, 22–23.
	"Principles . . . need to be incorporated into a regime for . . . management . . . in an ecosystem context: integrated management, public participation, equity, precaution, economic incentives, and adaptive management." Juda, 1999, 99–106.
	"A comprehensive approach to protecting the structural integrity and natural functioning of large geographic regions in perpetuity. Sustainable human economies should be integrated into overall ecosystem capabilities." Burroughs and Clark, 1995, 649.

Degree of change

How much change is really required to implement ecosystem-based management successfully? Here we'll consider three approaches or degrees of change. One approach would be to maintain the *conventional management* system, characterized by sectoral management, and simply try to improve its techniques to meet the new ecosystem goals. Unfortunately, the record suggests that this strategy would be difficult. In spite of many enhancements over the years, important measures of environmental health such as water quality are stable or declining. In fact, the increasing size of the Gulf dead zone makes clear that orchestration of fragmented government initiatives has not been adequate to control hypoxia and the impacts associated with it. There is also the matter of intent. Some purported transformations are mere rhetoric, rather than a substantive change in policy. By simply declaring current practices a form of ecosystem management, officials can avoid making needed changes.

A second approach is to undertake *incremental* change. This strategy involves changing parts of the existing policy system in small ways and then evaluating the consequences before contemplating additional changes (Lindblom, 1959). The idea is that by "muddling through" officials can keep personal risk low and still transform the system—at least in part. The technique is not fully rational because managers do not specify all values and policy alternatives before selecting the most appropriate. Rather, analysts agree on plausible actions, but do not explicitly note the policy objective or indicate that they have selected the best means to reach it. In this ambiguous situation some elements of ecosystem-based management may find a home. The policy solution is selected by considering experience with small policy changes that have been made in the past. An important test for an incremental solution is whether it has moved forward without overwhelming objections. By muddling through, only part of the goal can be achieved, which means that the process must be repeated endlessly. In an incremental change, officials could utilize ecosystem thinking within the confines of existing legal structures and routines to enhance results. Almost all examples of current ecosystem-based management fall under incremental change.

Incremental change has reshaped coastal and ocean management in the past. The arrangements for offshore oil development, originally established in the 1950s, were altered in the 1970s (Juda, 1993). Public attitudes about the values of marine waters had shifted and the U.S. legal regime reflected this change. The National Environmental Policy Act, the Coastal Zone Management Act, and the revised Outer Continental Shelf Lands Act instructed government officials to consider the environmental consequences of decisions. The growing importance of environmental impacts was confirmed through judicial decisions and together with changes in the law altered the collection and use of environmental data (Burroughs, 1981). After the transformation the government was increasingly charged with anticipating the environmental impacts of offshore oil and taking action to avoid them by suspending part or all of certain developments.

A third possibility is that change becomes revolutionary—that is, both rapid and fundamental. *Fundamental change* becomes particularly important when the characteristics of the problem demand bold solutions or a shift in goals results in needs that are beyond the reach of incremental change (Birkland, 2005; Cortner and Moote, 1999). Responding to the Great Depression, landing a human on the moon, and protecting equal rights required fundamental changes in policy. Coasts and oceans are receiving similar attention by many today. The chair of the Pew Oceans Commission stated that their group found the ocean in crisis and advocated for "a fundamental change in this nation's posture toward its oceans," noting that "reforms are essential" (Pew Oceans Commission, 2003, i). The early 1970s were a time of rapid and fundamental changes in environmental policy. Ecosystem-based management could inspire similar advances in the second decade of the twenty-first century.

Policy elements

Whether change is fundamental or just incremental, adopting ecosystem-based management will alter various elements of policy. The people involved, the tools used to implement solutions, and the government agencies that employ those tools can all be affected. Change can be made in many places. It is important to ask which policy elements get changed and how (Schneider and Ingram, 1997; Schneider and Sidney, 2009). In this section, we will consider how targets, agents, and tools could be affected by the introduction of ecosystem management (figure 8.3).

Policies are created to change the behavior of particular individuals, groups, or organizations, often referred to as "target groups" or simply "targets." New policies involve new target groups or revised expectations for those currently involved. For example, shifting to ecosystem-based management of the Mississippi River and Gulf of Mexico will require engaging farmers to improve coastal water quality. The coordinated

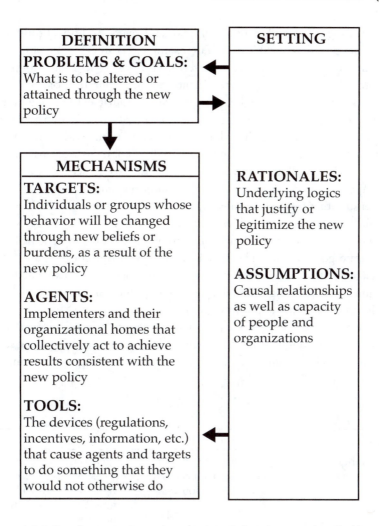

Figure 8.3. Policy change: Setting and mechanisms. Policy change as described by Schneider and Ingram (1997) is applied to ecosystem-based management in this figure. To practice ecosystem-based management, agents will use tools in innovative ways to change the behavior of target populations.

management of farmers and fishers as well as their respective governmental agencies will become necessary.

Just as ecosystem-based management may involve new target groups, it may also require new tools to influence their actions (table 8.2). To return to the previous example, farmers' use of fertilizer (which can damage water quality) could be influenced by changing agricultural subsidies or creating forest buffers between fields and rivers. Additional tools may also be considered (table 8.2). For example, because sewage discharge (point source) as well as excess fertilizer from agriculture (nonpoint source) is responsible for water quality decline, utilization of new tools such as cap and trade may become particularly valuable. To reduce overall pollution loading, trades among the sources may be executed in a manner that allows the least costly pollution removal option, usually the sewage treatment plant, to be used and supported by compensation from other parties whose pollution may be more expensive to reduce.

Agents, commonly government organizations, are empowered by law to ensure that tools are applied in a manner to achieve the goals of the policy. Agents also create new tools as required. Agents for sewage treatment are located in the federal Environmental Protection Agency and the state governments. The U.S. Department of Agriculture and its associated state entities influence farming practices. An ecosystem focus requires orchestrating multiple agents among different governmental entities to consistently apply appropriate tools.

Increasingly it is becoming clear that ecosystem-based management can benefit through agents from outside of government using tools, such as markets. This conversion of ecosystem-based management from the

TABLE 8.2.
Policy tools.

Type	Description	Examples
Authority	Compel particular behavior by law or through access to or denial of resources	Regulations, taxes, services, modified private rights, or frameworks for economic activity, licenses
Hortatory	Persuasion of individuals or groups to behave consistently with the new policy	Public campaigns, informal negotiation
Inducements/ sanctions	Cause voluntary or coerced actions	Subsidies, fines
Capacity-building	Technical assistance, education, training, or information that enables individuals and groups	Agency budgets, provision of information services
Learning	Creation of understanding related to specific aspects of a policy problem	Census, survey, opinion poll

purview of government alone to the responsibility of diverse agents in society is a major change. To signify the involvement of agents in and, more important, beyond the government, many refer to it as *ecosystem governance*.

Ecosystem-based management rests on the principle that real solutions involve the full spectrum of social and ecological systems. By involving new target groups, employing new tools, and incorporating agents throughout the society, this approach seeks to address the root causes of problems. The following sections illustrate the practice of incremental change and the possibilities for fundamental alterations to advance ecosystem governance in coastal areas.

Incremental change: Marine sanctuaries

Using an ecosystem management approach to reshape aspects of an existing program is an example of incremental change. The Marine Sanctuaries Program can be viewed from this perspective. In 1972 the Marine Protection, Research, and Sanctuaries Act was passed to both use marine resources and protect natural assemblages of organisms and historical sites (Brax, 2002; Chandler and Gillelan, 2004). Thirteen national marine sanctuaries have been established covering over 14,000 square nautical miles (48,018 square kilometers) of the sea and totaling almost one percent of eligible area (Chandler and Gillelan, 2004). The growth of ocean area in sanctuaries has occurred in a few short periods of rapid increase (figure 8.4).

At the time the law was passed, some anticipated that fishing, oil production, and gravel mining would be compatible with sanctuary status. Others viewed the objective of marine sanctuaries to be comparable with wilderness areas on land, and as a result extractive uses would be prohibited from sanctuaries. With these large questions of intent still looming, there has been no expansion of the sanctuary system in recent years (figure 8.4).

However, over time scientific findings concerning the environmental benefits of limiting certain uses became more widely accepted. In the broader scheme of marine protected areas, of which sanctuaries are just a small part, a number of generally recognized environmental benefits have been noted as levels of protection have increased (Lubchenco et al., 2003). Marine reserves connote geographic areas of the ocean that are completely protected from extractive and destructive uses. Benefits to natural systems inside reserves include increases in the abundance, diversity, and productivity of marine organisms, which is further improved

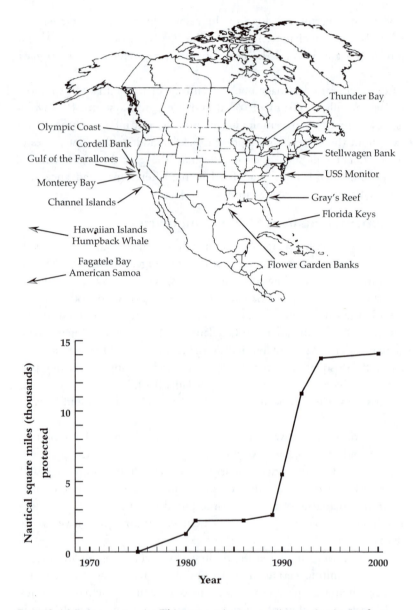

Figure 8.4. Marine sanctuaries. Thirteen marine sanctuaries ranging in size from 0.75 square nautical miles (2.6 square kilometers) (Monitor) to 4,023 square nautical miles (13,799 square kilometers) (Monterey Bay) have been designated. Ocean area encompassed by marine sanctuaries expanded rapidly around 1990 but has remained stable since. This tabulation does not include national monuments, which have proceeded under different authorization. Data from Chandler and Gillelan, 2004.

by larger size reserves and more complete levels of protection (National Center for Ecological Analysis and Synthesis, 2001). Outside the reserve boundaries there is some evidence that size and abundance of exploited species increase and that larval export replenishes regional populations. In this context networks of reserves could offset harvests, buffer against environmental variability, and provide protection for marine communities. Furthermore, the relationships among social systems and protected areas are receiving increasing attention in many coastal areas around the world (Christie et al., 2009). In sum, reserves could advance the resilience of biological systems (see box 8.1). Resilient populations and systems return to their previous state after disturbance. Resilience is a different target from seeking to restore the system to an optimum related to some baseline in the past.

One way to change public policy to reflect the growing scientific consensus about marine protected areas is to make a series of small alterations or incremental changes. Federal managers, a target group of actors,

---

Box 8.1. Resilience

Coastal regions are shaped by natural variations as well as by human stresses. Unfortunately, most anthropomorphic changes diminish an area's ability to rebound after natural stresses. One approach to management is to promote resilient natural systems that can withstand shocks.

In its most basic form resilience is the capacity of a linked human and natural system to absorb disturbance while at the same time retaining its basic structure and function (Walker and Salt, 2006). Measures of structure include such elements as standing crop biomass, species population density, and species richness. Measures of function include the rate and manner of nutrient cycling through the system or the rate of growth of plants or animals within it. Furthermore, a resilient system would return to similar groups of organisms feeding on their customary prey in a shorter time than other less resilient systems. In this setting a coastal manager might strive to create conditions where a disturbance such as a flood, hurricane, or oil spill could alter a coastal system, but in time the system would return to its previous function and state. In this setting a management failure would occur when the disturbance results in the system crossing a threshold and settling into a different state than the one it was in before. Very different populations of organisms define the new state.

could reshape objectives for existing sanctuaries and establish new ones. Scientists could be asked to prioritize additional protection measures, assess ecological linkages between sanctuaries and other ocean waters, and identify areas where extractive use would be prohibited. In addition scientists could structure monitoring programs and identify gaps in protection. Users of ocean resources, a primary target group, could be subject to new restrictions on activities in the sanctuary. Over time fishermen and others could be excluded or their activities limited. Conversely, whale watching or scuba diving to observe, not harvest organisms, could be encouraged within strict constraints on the nature of those activities.

With a change in policy also comes a shift in tools or techniques. In sanctuaries the prohibition of certain activities such as oil development and the regulation of other activities through permits have reshaped the behavior of users. For example, shipping routes that transit a sanctuary have been altered to reduce the number of whale strikes by ships.

Incremental change through existing programs can alter use in significant ways. However, some argue that incremental change may not move as rapidly or as effectively as circumstances require. Failure of incremental change to meet the needs of society is marked by litigation and discredited officials. At times, management failures gain enough public attention to become points of contention between political candidates. As controversy builds, government officials are less and less able to control the situation. If the need for change is widely acknowledged, fundamental change may result.

Fundamental change: Ecosystem services

What would a fundamental shift to ecosystem-based management look like? In this section we will consider the rationale for such a change, the policy elements involved, and an example of a proposed change of this magnitude.

Rapid and dramatic policy transformation is not unprecedented. For example, the Federal Water Pollution Control Act Amendments of 1972, commonly known as the Clean Water Act, represented a profound shift from reliance on voluntary pollution-control measures to a "command and control" approach. To protect recreation and fisheries, the new law set up a permitting system to control discharge of effluent from pipes, with treatment requirements based on technological feasibility. The act specified discharge limits for individual contaminants and created a monitoring and enforcement system to ensure compliance. Ecosystem-based management targets human behaviors that jeopardize social and ecological system sustainability, involves various governmental and non-governmental actors, and, when implemented, will involve a mixture of tools (table 8.2) and compliance mechanisms.

When pursuing change of this magnitude, it is important to consider the principles driving it. The explanations of ecosystem-based management in table 8.1 establish a clear direction. In addition, others focusing on sustainability, an element of ecosystem-based management, have proposed four principles to aid in implementation (Costanza et al., 1998). First, stakeholders should be involved in formulating and implementing policies, and those policies should be ecologically sustainable and socially equitable. Second, institutional scales for decision making should match ecological inputs. Third, potentially damaging activities should be approached with caution, and there should be ample opportunity to adapt and improve policies. Finally, Costanza et al. (1998) recognized that sustainable governance of oceans rests on full allocation of social and ecological costs and benefits. If markets are used, they will have to be adjusted to reflect full costs.

Changing to ecosystem-based management requires a shift in how we conceive the process of reaching decisions. In constitutive decision making, basic allocations of authority and control are made (Lasswell, 1971; Clark, 2002). The ideal constitutive decision process for ecosystem-based management will give precedence to the most widely shared common interests and produce adequate authority to ensure effective implementation. The reliance on stakeholders in the planning process and proposals for adaptive management exemplify constitutive changes.

The central challenge of ecosystem-based management is to consider all factors that affect ecological systems and to manage activities so as to sustain the services provided (Levin and Lubchenco, 2008). Ecosystem services are defined as the "conditions and processes through which natural ecosystems . . . sustain and fulfill human life" (Daily, 1997, 3). There are four categories of ecosystem services (UNEP-Millennium Ecosystem Assessment, 2005). The products or goods obtained from ecosystems are known as provisioning services. In coastal environments they include fisheries, mariculture, genetic diversity, medicines, transportation, minerals, and energy from wind, tides, and waves. Ecosystems also provide regulating services by controlling climate through carbon storage and land cover, water quality through decomposition, and natural hazards through protective features such as marshes and reefs. Ecosystems also provide spiritual enrichment and aesthetic and recreational values, which are known as cultural services. Finally, the indirect and long-term benefits that are the basis for the production of all other ecosystem services are known as supporting services. Water or nutrient cycling and photosynthesis are examples.

Services of an estuarine system in the northeastern United States have been enumerated (Farber et al., 2006). They include regulation of gas (carbon dioxide, methane), disturbances (storm surge, flood), water, and nutrients. Humans rely on the recreational, aesthetic, spiritual, and historic services of the estuary. Food production, soil retention, and genetic resources are additional services the system provides to people. Each service is tied to an ecosystem function. Human activities affect functions of ecosystems. As a result adjusting human behavior to be more compatible with ecosystem functions better ensures continuity of services.

To what extent do ecosystem services provide a means to deliver key attributes of ecosystem-based management? Several investigators have laid out a conceptual basis of ecosystem-based management (Slocombe, 1998; Yaffee, 1999; Layzer, 2008; McLeod and Leslie, 2009; and table 8.1 here), and the Millennium Ecosystem Assessment (United Nations Environment Program, 2006), among others, proposed that ecosystem services are an effective means to convert concepts into practices. Because services are frequently beyond the regulatory jurisdiction of agencies, their implementation will almost certainly require use of new tools such as inducements and learning (table 8.2). Rules that support ecosystem services initiatives can rest on tools such as markets, tradable pollution permits, government ownership, government regulations, incentive payments, voluntary payments, and other means (Ruhl et al., 2007; Brauman et al., 2007). Ecosystem services require thought and action based on natural systems, not political jurisdictions. Working at the regional scale will almost certainly lead to better understanding of cumulative impacts and need to act so as to not jeopardize the ecosystem services at stake.

If we adopt ecosystem services as an organizing principle, there will be changes in the policy that results and the means to implement it. Some target populations of individuals or groups will benefit. Environmental scientists, for example, are instrumental in creating the new policies for the coast and in assuming important positions to carry them out. Employment and research will expand among those seeking to manage their own activities under the new ecosystem paradigm. Some, such as those who recreate or sport fish, may see benefits. Conversely, extractive users may be burdened. By focusing on long-term sustainable uses, implementation of ecosystem-based management will likely limit certain fishing activities and stop mining or oil development in areas where other ecosystem services are preferred. New or transformed governmental organizations will manage ecosystem services. Skills of governmental officials and purviews of their organizational homes will span multiple issues while requiring specific actions to sustain services.

Ecosystem service districts are one way to achieve this new goal (Heal et al., 2001; Lant et al., 2008). The United States has many regional organizations that manage geographic areas for specific purposes. State law or local initiative can create a district to manage erosion, water supply, or floods. These serve as prototypes for ecosystem service districts, which can be linked in ways that allow their geographic jurisdictions to match ecosystem properties, thus ensuring effective oversight. An ecosystem service district is a governmental entity managing a geographic region and empowered to coordinate, zone, and tax. Hypothetically the ecosystem service district would select the least costly means of providing a service. For example, New York City faced a trade-off between managing its watershed to protect drinking water quality and installing water treatment. By establishing a prototypical ecosystem service district surrounding the reservoirs, the city could and did benefit from the ability of ecosystem processes to purify water in lieu of technology investments to achieve the same results (Heal et al., 2001). Sorting out the advantages and disadvantages of different proposals becomes more complicated as more services and values are considered, but the objective remains to produce the maximum possible value.

Creating a new system of targets, agents, and tools around the concept of ecosystem services will be a big challenge. Ecosystem services have not been incorporated in law (Ruhl et al., 2007), and ultimately legislatures are responsible for creating the mandates for ecosystem-based management initiatives (Rosenberg and Sandifer, 2009). In summarizing existing legislative authority for ecosystem-based management, Searles Jones and Ganey (2009) noted the need to act decisively to shift existing institutions. Thus, although prototypes for ecosystem services mechanisms are currently in play, an overarching federal policy mandating them is not in place. Such a policy would have an unequivocal mandate, revised elements, and unambiguous decision rules and authority to manage conflicts and trade-offs while using decision-making structures scaled to ecosystem boundaries.

The concept of ecosystem services is not without liabilities. Managing ecosystems solely on the basis of the monetary advantages they provide could promote the view that "nature is only worth conserving when it is, or can be made, profitable" (McCauley, 2006, 28). Given this pitfall, proponents must design tools and organize agents with great care to ensure that the broadest reach of ecosystem functions and biodiversity is protected. Otherwise the initiative may result in minimum gains to selected services and potentially harm to others (Daily and Matson, 2008). In spite of these issues, ecosystem services provide a new model for coastal and ocean regions, which may presage a fundamental shift in coastal governance. If effectively implemented, this new approach could provide significant gains.

Summary

Ecosystem-based management recognizes that human economies and social systems need to fit within ecosystems; it alters processes of decision making to encourage collaboration and equity; and it relies on flexible implementation. In spite of a logic well attuned to the times and endorsement by many natural scientists, others question whether it is compelling. That is, do people use these principles in making decisions about the coast today? Although a final answer is unlikely in the near term, cases such as nitrogen enrichment of coastal waters indicate that concepts related to ecosystem-based management have growing utility in resolving coastal management issues.

Changing national policy to incorporate ecosystem considerations will involve activities both within and beyond government. Ecosystem governance, which includes both governmental and private actions, draws on traditional and new policy tools to promote behavior consistent with the long-term health of social and natural systems. Tools include rules, incentives, education, technical assistance, learning, and other techniques to shape human behavior (table 8.2).

Change may be incremental or fundamental. Many agree that incremental advances under existing law, as exemplified by marine sanctuaries, are desirable. The current state of incremental change will be assessed further for the watershed and the fishery in the next two chapters. Others observe that if ecosystem governance is to be successful, fundamental changes are required. Ecosystem service districts focus management on the value of natural environments in providing for human needs and represent a type of fundamental change that could occur. Continued transformation of governance, whether incremental or fundamental, will follow shifts in the attitudes and needs of citizens. The challenge for those interested in the coast will be to understand the nature of the new directions and, if desired, create governance systems to make them realities.[9]

9

Watersheds and Bays

As we saw in the previous chapter, a central goal of ecosystem management is to bridge divides—between individual sectors and between human and natural systems. This holistic approach could be particularly effective for watersheds: areas that defy artificial boundaries between land and sea, as well as people and nature. Because rivers flow to the ocean, carrying along pollutants from agriculture, industry, and other activities taking place on land, human actions in the watershed determine many of the conditions at the coast. So it seems logical to manage the watershed and coastal bays as a single unit. Unfortunately, administrative obstacles stand in the way. In this chapter, we will explore those obstacles, how watersheds have traditionally been managed, and how an ecosystem-based approach could improve management of connected landscapes and seascapes.

Evolution of river basin management

The first European explorers of North America moved inland along river corridors, and settlements developed at the landward extent of navigation. Later, rivers supplied water for growing cities, and manufacturing grew from waterpower. Rivers for direct water use, for navigation, and for economic development were essential for the growth of the country. It's not surprising then, that government has long been focused on individual activities within watersheds. But over time, policies have shifted in response to society's changing values.

143

From the early years of the nation to about 1900, rivers fueled economic development carried out by the private sector. John Wesley Powell proposed that the right to waters be linked to lands and that drainage basins be used as the unit for management (White 1969; Sabatier 2005b). Through these observations Powell anticipated many of the ongoing discussions about the relationship of land and water. Early on, the U.S. Army Corps of Engineers assisted private interests through structural improvements to navigation systems. In response to floods along the Mississippi River during the 1870s, the Corps also began building levees to protect communities on the river.

By the early years of the twentieth century, government had moved away from its exclusive focus on private economic activity to a more public-spirited engagement with river basins. Progressives pushed for watersheds to be managed for the greatest good of the greatest number of Americans (Sabatier et al., 2005b). Increasingly, citizens expected government programs to be administered by technically trained but neutral officials. The development of water resources for multiple purposes emerged through creation of federal dams to control floods, supply municipal and irrigation water, produce electric power, and ultimately provide recreational opportunities (Goldfarb, 1994). Growing cities such as New York, Denver, and Los Angeles controlled rivers and created reservoirs at quite a distance from urban areas to ensure adequate water supplies.

For the purposes of management, rivers were seen as single units extending from headwaters to coasts. A watershed, also known as a catchment, is the geographic area from which surface or groundwater draws its supply of water. Divides separate watersheds and are normally marked by high ground. Within these clearly bounded geographic units human uses are integrated through water systems.

By the Great Depression in the 1930s, river management had become synonymous with planning and managing for the broad economic development of a region, which was usually defined as the watershed (Wengert, 1985). Publicly funded infrastructure such as dams and dredged channels were seen as effective means of catalyzing private economic activity in manufacturing and shipping. In this context management incorporates activities throughout the drainage basin and involves other resources in addition to water (Barrow, 1998). For example, the federal government created the Tennessee Valley Authority in 1933 to provide economic opportunities through electricity generation, flood control, navigation, and fertilizer production. The management unit for this river-based economic development zone includes most of Tennessee, parts of Alabama,

Mississippi, and Kentucky and very small areas in three other states. With judicious management of the rivers and watersheds, the Tennessee Valley Authority would reduce poverty and improve the environment. Of course, such advances require management across sectors, jurisdictions, and agencies so development can take place. Unfortunately, that has not been replicated in many other settings.

By the 1950s river development had emerged as single or multipurpose activities (White, 1969). Municipal, district, or federal government agencies constructed channels, dams, sewage treatment plants, and other facilities for single purposes. Single-agency, single-purpose construction tended to be readily justified in the economic framework of the time, did not require consideration of alternative means, and found solid support by well defined constituencies. In addition, private single-purpose construction provided rural water supply, irrigation, and hydroelectric power, but used a wider range of technologies and focused on economic criteria irrespective of the impact on the landscape or society.

Multipurpose facilities became an attractive alternative. Dams were constructed for the combined benefits of water supply, hydroelectricity, and flood control. White (1969) has characterized water programs by purpose, means, and agency responsible. For example, expanding navigation (single purpose) through dredging (means) has been carried out by the Corps of Engineers (agency) for well over a century. Alternatively the goal of reducing floods, a single purpose, might be carried out by agencies using multiple means such as dams upstream and levees downstream. Public managers could also undertake activities like wetland creation as the means to meet multiple objectives such as flood control and wildlife habitat protection. When using the term *multiple* it's important to recognize that it may apply to purposes as well as means.

The means just noted were structural. That is, they include controls of water flow (channels, dams, diversion structures, treatment plants, and hydroelectric plants), all of which can be built through governmental programs or private initiatives. It's possible that means may be nonstructural, such as markets, zoning, regulation, incentives, and insurance. Instead of building levees, one might consider incentives to encourage people to move out of particularly dangerous areas of the floodplain. In some cases structural controls were encouraging people to inhabit floodplains where damage would be particularly great if the structures failed.

Changes in federal legislation in the 1970s overtly signaled a split that had been growing in the previous decade. Abruptly, water quality was given precedence over other concerns as the organizing principle for federal policy. Passage of the National Environmental Policy Act, among others, is evidence of the change. Furthermore, through revisions of water legislation, the means of improving water quality was based on each piped discharge meeting a standard that limited the contaminants in it. With this change came the diminution of coordination across watersheds (National Research Council, 1999). The government eliminated federal funding for many river basin management programs in the 1980s. The president had created a new and powerful organization, the Environmental Protection Agency (EPA), in 1970. In addition interaction of the government with citizens concerning watersheds changed (Sabatier et al., 2005b). Federal funding allowed states to increase their capacities to understand technical issues associated with water pollution, expand their ability to build projects, and create the means to respond to public interests more effectively. Earlier eras had strong federal domination; subsequently state and local government came to the forefront.

The decline of watershed management was short lived. During the 1990s it rapidly became clear that meeting environmental objectives would require a return to regional management. For example, the decline of salmon was recognized to result from destruction of habitat in the watershed through logging, dams, and development. In addition the focus of pollution control had shifted to runoff from diffuse land use activities known as nonpoint sources. Management of salmon or of nonpoint sources as well as other issues requires a watershed perspective if it is to be successful in protecting river and coastal waters.

Understanding the role of watersheds can be pursued from two perspectives. First, and most commonly, the land–sea connection is specified through the hydrologic cycle. Scientists recognize that in the hydrologic cycle water evaporated by solar energy falls on the surface of the earth and moves through many pathways to the sea (Gregersen et al., 2007). Along the way, processes, many of which are influenced by human activity, affect the quantity and quality of the flows, which may be above or below ground. As a result landscapes, and human uses of them, affect coasts through the quantity and quality of water delivered.

A second perspective is based on human uses. The value of this second approach becomes clear when one considers that management seeks to change human behavior. Representative watershed uses are shown in figure 9.1. The left column of the figure shows interests present in watersheds and coasts. If significant activity is associated with an interest it is shown by an asterisk, and if it has a strong connection to the coast a solid line will connect it to the coastal symbol. Watershed interests with

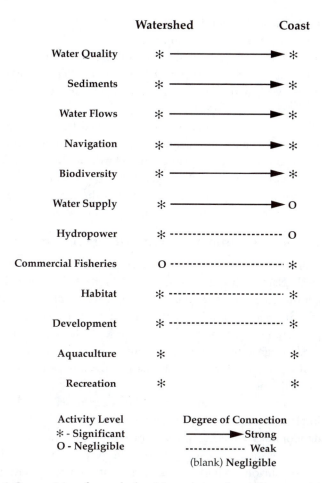

	Watershed	Coast
Water Quality	* ⟶	*
Sediments	* ⟶	*
Water Flows	* ⟶	*
Navigation	* ⟶	*
Biodiversity	* ⟶	*
Water Supply	* ⟶	O
Hydropower	* -------	O
Commercial Fisheries	O -------	*
Habitat	* -------	*
Development	* -------	*
Aquaculture	*	*
Recreation	*	*

Activity Level	Degree of Connection
* - Significant	⟶ Strong
O - Negligible	------- Weak
	(blank) **Negligible**

Figure 9.1. Connectivity of watershed activity and coastal uses. Human activities on the lands and rivers affect water quantity and quality, which can affect uses of estuaries and oceans. As a result managing watersheds and coastal waters as a single unit can provide many benefits.

at least one asterisk and a strong watershed–coast connection are the top targets for management if water quality in coastal bays is to be protected. For example, landscape decisions affect sediment supply to rivers. River management affects the supply of sediments to the coast and influences its final resting place. In four cases the dashed lines indicate lesser levels of connection. Among them, hydropower is pursued inland where the conditions favor it and has limited connection to conditions at the coast. In contrast water supply can result in significant removals. Excessive water withdrawals, particularly in the West, deprive bays of a supply of freshwater and in some instances have eliminated freshwater that flows to estuaries and oceans altogether. Because six uses in figure 9.1 strongly connect the watershed with the coast, one can easily appreciate that management of the watershed and the coast as a single unit would be highly beneficial.

Whether watershed-coastal systems are viewed from the perspective of the hydrologic cycle or human uses, the need for comprehensive management remains obvious and large. The rebirth of river basin management in this context will be the topic of the rest of this chapter. A key element of this challenge lies in orchestrating the disparate activities of federal agencies when they operate in a single watershed.

River/watershed management: An agency profile

Although land, water, and air are connected through natural processes, the biophysical relationships are not necessarily reflected in federal agency collaborations. Agencies tend to focus on uses. Sector-based management dominates. In fact, combining natural resource management and economic development, a feature of the Tennessee Valley Authority, fell out of favor. Although some elements of holistic management may be gathered in an agency or through a program across more than one agency, examples of this are limited.

However, natural processes integrate the effects of separate federal programs implemented in a watershed, whether their coordination has been planned for or not. Problems can arise when the organizations are operating in a single watershed at cross-purposes. One way to define the integration challenge involves identifying government agency responsibilities.

Selected agency responsibilities for water and watershed management are profiled in table 9.1. The number of federal agencies and the overlapping and potentially conflicting responsibilities exemplify fragmentation within the executive branch of government. The Bureau of Land Management, Forest Service, and National Park Service hold and manage land, mostly in the western United States. The former two supervise extraction of timber, forage, minerals, and oil. The latter focuses on conservation and recreational uses. All of these federal landowners manage land and water in concert with the uses they promote.

Licensing for or actual production of hydropower occurs through the auspices of the Federal Energy Regulatory Commission and the Bureau of Reclamation. Because the latter operates facilities, it is also a major supplier of water. By assisting private landowners with their selection and

TABLE 9.1.
Federal agency watershed activities. Sources: Office of Federal Register, 2008; Goldfarb, 1994; and agency Web sites.

Agency	Purpose/Mission	Means/Program examples
Army Corps of Engineers	Engineering services to strengthen security and the economy while reducing risk from disasters	Reservoir construction, civil works program, dredge-and-fill permit program
Bureau of Land Management	Protection, development, and use of lands and resources under principles of multiple use and sustained yield	Watershed management to protect soil and enhance water quality
Bureau of Reclamation	Water supplier and producer of hydroelectric power	Dam maintenance and hydropower production
Environmental Protection Agency	Coordinated effort to keep the nation's waters clean and safe	National Pollution Discharge Elimination System, nonpoint source control
Federal Energy Regulatory Commission	Hydropower project location	Licensing
Fish and Wildlife Service	Conservation of fish, wildlife, and habitat	National wildlife refuge system, endangered species program
Forest Service	Sustainable, multiple use of land to meet the diverse needs of people	Permit program for timber sales
National Park Service	Conserving natural and cultural resources of the park system for this and future generations	National parks and seashores
Natural Resources Conservation Service	Help private landowners develop and carry out voluntary efforts to conserve natural resources	Environmental Quality Incentive Program, Small Watersheds Program, Conservation Reserve Program, Wetlands Reserve Program

manipulation of fertilizer and vegetation on the landscape, the Natural Resources Conservation Service can affect sediment and nitrogen loads in rivers. The Fish and Wildlife Service through the Endangered Species Act has a particular interest because of its mandate to ensure the survival of species that require habitats with adequate water quality and quantity. In aggregate, decisions made by these agencies can have a large impact on freshwater quality, timing, and volume at the coast.

Throughout the watershed the U.S. Army Corps of Engineers, through its Civil Works program, constructs dams and modifies channels. Through its dredge and fill permit program, it shapes where and how navigational improvements occur. Many of these decisions, and often the most controversial ones, are in coastal areas. Modifying the shape of the watershed and the coast can alter flows within it and reduce flood risk, but often with significant impact on other natural processes and values. Conflicts arise. For example, the Fish and Wildlife Service focuses on organisms and their habitats throughout watersheds and coasts. It both controls land directly through the national wildlife refuge system and seeks protection for endangered species with consequences for development plans. To the extent that water volume or quality determine the fate of an organism, the Fish and Wildlife Service will make decisions that affect watersheds and water. Thus, one can see that a navigation improvement that affects habitat or water quality could conflict with protection of species and result in conflict between two federal agencies with different missions.

Finally, the EPA is responsible for keeping waters clean and operates regulatory programs throughout watersheds. Its decisions related to permits for discharges upstream, as well as those in the coastal areas, largely determine coastal water quality. Given its preeminence, the activities of the EPA will be considered in greater detail in the next section.

Managing the landscape to preserve/restore bays

Contaminated waters that flow across and below the landscape, known as nonpoint sources, damage water quality in bays. For the most part they have escaped effective control. In the U.S. regulatory system, the conveyance determines much of the logic of control. Wastewaters that are discharged through pipes, as described in chapter 3, must meet a technology-based standard of treatment. The discharger must install and properly operate technology to remove the most troublesome aspects of the contaminant before discharge. Otherwise, no permit to discharge is granted, or violation of it leads to penalties. To evaluate the overall effectiveness of the program, one may consider the number and stringency of the permits issued, the amount of contaminants removed from the wastewaters prior to discharge, and other parameters. Clarity of purpose, discrete technological solutions, clear authority, and effective means of implementation make most point source control programs a success when viewed in terms of the contaminants trapped through treatment.

But many of the pollutants that get to coastal waters do not flow through pipes. If the goal remains high water quality and pipe discharges are controlled but water quality trends are not improving, then consideration of other sources becomes paramount (Burroughs, 2003). Current management programs categorize nonpoint sources by different types of human activities—agriculture, forestry, hydromodification, habitat alteration including wetlands changes, marinas, mining, roads, and urbanization.

To gain an appreciation for the importance of nonpoint sources, assume we have a well-functioning point source control program for a bay. However, the level of certain contaminants in the bay remains high. Remember that the basis for setting the level of discharge in a point source control program is technology. By specifying a certain level of technology for each piped discharge, as required by the Clean Water Act, we are assuming that limiting discharges from point sources will result in the water being fishable and swimmable. In our hypothetical bay this is not the case. What has gone wrong? One possibility is an incorrect assumption that all pollutants flow through pipes. Pollutants could also reach the bay through surface runoff, groundwater, and the air. Without effluent limitations for nonpoint sources the landscape activities could become the main reason that a water body fails to meet expectations. Furthermore, the larger the nonpoint source load relative to the point source load, the more important control of nonpoint sources will become in the quest to obtain high-quality coastal waters.

The Clean Water Act addresses nonpoint source pollution through several provisions. In Section 208 states were financially supported and given wide latitude to develop regional plans. The resulting geographically specific plans identified pollution sources and controls, including changes in land use to limit discharges of pollutants (Anderson, 1999). Unfortunately, the plans were not implemented (Adler, 1995), and this approach failed to improve coastal water quality.

Under Section 319 of the 1987 amendments to the act, states are required to report on waters that do not meet intended uses and create best management practices for controlling the activities that result in pollution. Best management practices for storm water include modifying the plans for developed landscapes so evapotranspiration, infiltration, and detention will reduce peak flow, total volume, and pollution delivered to receiving waters. However, state participation was voluntary, and states were not compelled to penalize nonpoint source polluters who failed to change practices (Johnson, 1999). Without clear authority, detailed monitoring, and enforcement powers, this section of the law produced limited results (Ruhl, 2000; Anderson, 1999).

The reauthorization of the Coastal Zone Management Act in 2000 offered an opportunity to create a nonpoint source control program that would benefit coastal waters in particular. Under Section 6217, states in the coastal program of the federal government are required to control nonpoint sources through enforceable policies to change land uses. State plans must indicate how control of activities that produce nonpoint source pollution will be carried out. Implementation is anticipated to occur over a period of fifteen years.

Finally, Section 303 of the Clean Water Act requires states with impaired waters to calculate a total maximum daily load (TMDL) of the pollutants that may be tolerated while still pursuing the intended uses (Healy, 1997; Houck, 2002). Knowing the acceptable flow of a given pollutant is only a first step in this process. Next, the waste load allocation apportions the sources. Unfortunately, this program has weak authority to regulate; specific contaminant loads are difficult to determine; and a variety of legal issues have arisen concerning allocation of the loads (Ruhl, 2000). Furthermore, attempts to clarify processes under the program through regulatory changes have been controversial. Managing the landscape to meet objectives for coastal waters has been the biggest challenge for Chesapeake Bay water quality, the topic of the next section.

Watershed management for the Chesapeake Bay

Regional solutions for watersheds and coastal areas occur when the involved parties agree on the need to resolve an environmental problem and believe that a comprehensive management system will ultimately benefit them. Because problems related to bay waters span multiple political jurisdictions, problems with use of the environment quickly become issues that require new, more comprehensive administrative structures.

For more than two centuries states abutting the Chesapeake have negotiated regional arrangements to advance their interests. In a 1785 compact Virginia gave free access to the bay for ships headed to Maryland and both states stipulated that their citizens could navigate the Potomac (Capper et al., 1983). By the early twentieth century pollution affecting

oysters had been a significant concern for a number of years. The U.S.
Congress authorized a study of it, and with the assistance of health officials from both states, reports on the Potomac and the bay were published
in 1916. Years later in 1963 the Public Health Service initiated a project
that spanned water quality issues for the Susquehanna River and the bay.
It noted the need for a basin-wide framework for water quality management decisions and called attention to enrichment of bay waters as a
source of the problems (Capper et al., 1983). These discussions resulted in
the formation in 1940 and revision in 1970 of the Interstate Commission
on the Potomac River Basin and the creation in 1970 of the Susquehanna River Basin Compact through federal law.

More recently with the passage of a major change in federal water
pollution control legislation in 1972, the current era for collaboration
concerning the Chesapeake began. In it environmental scientists define
watershed/bay problems that require changes in administrative systems
if they are to be resolved. The combination of environmental problems
driving institutional and organizational change exemplifies incremental
change using the principles of ecosystem-based management.

In 1975 Congress directed the EPA to conduct an extensive study of
Chesapeake Bay, which initiated a series of actions concerning the water
body (table 9.2). At the time many felt that a better understanding of the
natural system could establish a foundation for cleaning up the bay. Heavy
rains and subsequent flooding in the summer of 1972 had raised awareness about the need to assess factors such as the impact of sediments on
submerged aquatic vegetation (Boesch and Goldman, 2009). The results
of the seven-year EPA study emphasized links between human activities

TABLE 9.2.
Selected governmental organizations and actions for Chesapeake Bay.

Scientific studies of the Bay, 1975 (Environmental Protection Agency)
Chesapeake Bay Commission, 1980 (primarily state legislators)
Chesapeake Bay Agreement, 1983 (watershed/bay organizational structure)
Chesapeake Executive Council, 1983 (primarily governors)
Clean Water Act Amendments, 1987 (Chesapeake Bay Program in federal
law)
Chesapeake Bay Agreement, 1987 (restoration of bay and forty percent re-
duction of nutrients)
Chesapeake Bay Agreement, 1992 (coordinated management strategies for
tributaries)
Chesapeake Bay Agreement, 2000 (specific restoration targets)
Presidential Executive Order, 2009 (coordination of seven federal agencies)

and the health of bay systems. Furthermore, the scientific studies laid out problems that seemed to require a new governance structure for effective resolution.

In 1978 the Maryland–Virginia Chesapeake Bay Legislative Advisory Commission reinvigorated a bi-state approach to the bay (Chesapeake Bay Commission, www.chesbay.va.state.us). Negotiations between the states over fisheries had extended back many decades. However, this committee signaled that although the mechanism might be similar, the objective was expanded to environmental quality. The Legislative Advisory Commission recommended the formation of the Chesapeake Bay Commission, which was established in 1980. In 1985 Pennsylvania joined Virginia and Maryland on the commission and with that change each state had five state legislators serving in addition to citizens and state government officials. The commission advises the legislative branches in the states and serves as the legislative arm of the EPA Chesapeake Bay Program.

In 1983 the governors of Maryland, Virginia, and Pennsylvania, the mayor of the District of Columbia, the chair of the Chesapeake Bay Commission, and the administrator of EPA signed a Chesapeake Bay Agreement. Because recently completed scientific studies of the bay had shown a decline in the living resources, observers felt that cooperation among EPA and the states was necessary to fully address pollutants entering the bay. The agreement became the foundation of a new structure that allowed multiple governmental entities to collaboratively address bay/watershed environmental problems. The agreement established the Chesapeake Executive Council to oversee activities to improve water quality and living resources of the bay (Chesapeake Executive Council, www.chesapeakebay.net/exec.htm). The 1983 agreement also created an implementation committee and called for a liaison office, which is known as the Chesapeake Bay Program, at the EPA facility in Annapolis, Maryland (www.chesapeakebay.net). Following the 1983 agreement numerous state initiatives were undertaken to manage land and resources in concert with the regional objectives (Costanza and Greer, 1995).

Upon reflection, this administrative arrangement for coordinated management of the watershed and the bay is enormously complex. At the federal level those departments or agencies operating primarily on land (Agriculture, Interior), in coastal lands and waters (EPA, Defense, Homeland Security, Transportation) and primarily in coastal waters (Commerce) will need to be coordinated. This horizontal division of bay and watershed management obligations is further complicated by the vertical dimension, which involves states, counties, and local governments. By the year 2000 Virginia, Maryland, Pennsylvania, and the District of Columbia were state-level participants and brought with them innumerable county and local governments. Furthermore, an organizational entity operating across state legislatures, the Chesapeake Bay Commission, and another that involves the states and the EPA, the Chesapeake Executive Council, had been established. So at a minimum, coordinated management on a watershed/bay scale involves seven units at the federal level, four at the state level, two cross-state and federal coordinating entities, and innumerable county and local governments. The ability to act—even in a limited form—would require substantial political will and great skill on the part of the administrators. Nonetheless, important actions were forthcoming.

Over time, the Chesapeake Executive Council became committed to restoring and protecting the bay, and by 1987 selected eight goals to do so. At this point the parties had begun the process of identifying activities to restore the bay. By supporting a comprehensive approach toward the management of the bay system and by providing for increased citizen participation, the signatories adopted an approach and a process that used some of the principles of ecosystem-based management. Furthermore, by seeking to manage human population growth and land development while restoring living resources and habitats in the bay, they firmly connected land and sea. Most dramatically they sought to implement "a basin-wide strategy to equitably achieve by the year 2000 at least a forty percent reduction of the nitrogen and phosphorous entering the main stem of the Chesapeake Bay" as the means of reducing hypoxia (Chesapeake Bay Agreement, 1987). This controversial objective, which in retrospect was not implemented, required a robust program to meet bay water quality objectives by altering activities on land.

In 1987 the EPA Chesapeake Bay Program was authorized through changes in the Clean Water Act that ensure annual consideration for federal funds. In specific the law directed that EPA continue the Chesapeake Bay Program to coordinate efforts to improve water quality with specific attention to sediments and nutrients as well as other contaminants. This action by Congress further legitimized and empowered the solutions that the stakeholders from the bay and its watersheds had selected. Grants to states would be a primary way of delivering the program.

In 1992 the Chesapeake Bay Agreement was amended to focus on tributaries to the bay as a means of meeting the nitrogen and phosphorous reductions proposed in 1987 and to use the distribution of submerged aquatic vegetation as an initial measure of progress. Tributary strategies would identify the means to reduce nutrient and sediment loads to the bay through use of best management practices (Hassett et al., 2005). Preferred practices include forest buffers, changes in agriculture, and retention/purification of storm water. In agriculture fertilization practices can be altered; cover crops can be planted; and planting may occur with minimal soil disturbance. Furthermore, signatories identified air deposition of nitrogen as an additional factor that should be considered.

The 2000 agreement affirmed previous goals and in some cases identified actions required to meet them. The signatories sought a ten-fold increase in the native oyster population, restoration of anadromous fish passages in currently blocked rivers, and restoration of the crab fishery. They reemphasized land-use practices by setting goals for permanently preserving from development twenty percent of the land area in the watershed and reducing sprawl by thirty percent through a variety of means. To enable many to enjoy the bay they proposed to expand the number of public access points by thirty percent.

Most recently in 2009 President Obama ordered seven federal agencies to conduct their activities consistent with objectives for the watershed. This follows the 1994 ecosystem management agreement among federal agencies that promoted coordination of research and data in a Chesapeake Bay management partnership. In an executive order the president created a Federal Leadership Committee for the Chesapeake Bay to oversee the development of programs and their implementation. Although the initiative is structured to better coordinate existing initiatives, it includes adaptive management principles and decision support for ecosystem management. In adaptive management, solutions are implemented and evaluated as a basis for determining the best course of future action. Others have advanced these same ideas as key principles in ecosystem-based management.

As we have seen, Chesapeake Bay policy has been redesigned several times. But have these revisions led to success? One evaluation divided the early years of the program into key issue identification followed by establishment of a multistate-federal cooperative program that by 1992 had resulted in an expansion of goals and commitments to restore the bay (Hennessey, 1994). At the time the program was viewed favorably, but agreements about a desired course of action, although important outputs of the policy process, are only one part of program implementation. A truly successful program must also include means to change human behavior and must record real changes in the natural and social environments.

Monitoring change has been particularly important with respect to oxygen levels in bottom waters of the bay. To reduce hypoxia, action must be taken throughout the watershed and airshed. So this one measure becomes a way to evaluate both the ability of the Chesapeake Bay Commission to influence human behavior and the extent to which the low oxygen problem has been resolved. Data collected on water quality, habitat, and organisms have been used to establish trends and inform observers about the status of similar programs (Leschine et al., 2003). The results for the Chesapeake have not been good: agriculture continues to be a significant source of excess nitrogen. Ernst (2003) found that in the decades after the nutrient problem was originally noted and attributed to nonpoint sources, agricultural interests have hamstrung efforts to address what he refers to as the bay's primary environmental hazard. This finding amplifies other critiques that found limited restoration of dissolved oxygen levels, crabs, oysters, and other bay systems. Subsequent evaluations have pointed to a lack of coordination, particularly between management of agriculture and suburban development (Government Accountability Office, 2008b; EPA, 2006, 2007). Agriculture and urbanization of the watershed, targets of the tributaries approach in the 1992 agreement, have proven particularly difficult to address because of lack of political will. As a result the bay remains in an apparently stable, yet degraded state (Boesch and Goldman, 2009).

Ecosystem management for watersheds and bays

The Chesapeake Bay experience illustrates the shortcomings of current management of watersheds and coasts: specifically, a lack of integration, coordination, and full consideration of natural processes. Based in the natural sciences, ecosystem-based management is gaining significant national attention as a compelling way to improve techniques and results for linked social and natural systems. But to work, it will need to be effectively incorporated in the policy process, as we will discuss in this section.

Most policy discussions start with the definition of a problem, that is, a divergence between current conditions and goals (table 9.3) (Burroughs, 2003). The divergence is initially recognized in environmental terms, but that frequently leads to a realization that new institutions are necessary to resolve the issue. In the case of the Chesapeake, there is a great gulf between current conditions (poor water quality and declining harvests) and the goal of a healthy, productive, and resilient water body. By prioritizing the functioning of natural systems, ecosystem-based management has the potential to help close the gap.

TABLE 9.3.
Ecosystem-based management and the policy process.

Stage of the Policy Process	Ecosystem-based Perspective
Problem/Goal	Seek healthy, productive, resilient ecosystem
	Protect/restore ecosystem services
	Sustainable human uses
Solution	Stakeholder involvement
	Collaborative planning
	Regional scale with ecosystem boundaries
	Resilience
	Assess cumulative impacts
Selection	Collaborative decision making
	Prefer precaution
Implementation	Coordination across agencies and jurisdictions
	Application of new tools
Evaluation	Monitoring before and after
	Adaptive
	Stakeholder collaboration

As we saw in chapter 2, the second stage in the policy process is the design of solutions that use tools to change human behavior (tables 2.1 and 8.2). Although in the past watershed management has often been characterized by a top-down, agency-only, command and control approach, ecosystem-based management empowers stakeholders to participate in policy design. Stakeholders bring the human dimensions to the environmental issue being considered. Shared knowledge in design and collective will in implementation are viewed by many as a route to far more effective programs (Sabatier et al., 2005a).

Ecosystem-based management principles also affect the content of solutions. Because the scale of solutions is at the ecosystem level, boundaries that match the natural system as opposed to the political system are important. Political boundaries arbitrarily divide environmental and social systems, which makes integrated management difficult. Watersheds managed in concert with associated coastal areas permit the design and implementation of unified policies for nutrients, water flow, economic development, and sediments.

Proponents of ecosystem-based management believe that new policy should be vetted in terms of how resilient the resulting social/ecological system is likely to be. By resilient, designers mean that the resulting coupled watershed and coastal system will be better able to absorb disturbance and retain its basic structure and function. Following this principle, measures would be targeted on those human activities that amplify disturbance and affect basic ecosystem functions.

Resilient solutions address cumulative impacts. Cumulative impacts can come about in two ways. First, without a limit, the number of legally sanctioned users (septic systems, fishermen, etc.) of an ecosystem may grow so that, although each is operating legally, the aggregate impact is not tolerable. Second, it's possible that different types of uses, each in compliance, may have their effects combined through a natural or social process. Failure can occur because the stresses from different sources affect a single part or process of the ecosystem. To address these problems of aggregation, government has at times limited the number of fishing licenses or house lots. However, translating a scientific understanding of cumulative impacts into effective management across sectors has proven nearly intractable (McLeod and Leslie, 2009).

At the selection stage, a solution from among those proposed is adopted. Ideally, those in authority follow the rational model of public policy and select a solution that is consistent with the "facts" as presented. But often "values" also affect the choice. Elaborate and, some would argue, failed government structures have been established to incorporate societal values into the selection process. However, in collaborative stakeholder processes individuals managed by or otherwise interested in the new policy are empowered to directly apply their values to selection of the solution. To the extent that these values reflect society's common interests, the decision will be relatively uncontroversial. To the extent that the policy solution only serves the needs of a few but affects many, opposition and lawsuits will arise. Collaborative processes, if they include diverse interests, can reduce conflict during and after selection of a new policy. In addition, note that the extent to which societal values are consistent with ecosystem-based management is the extent to which the new approach is likely to be adopted by Congress, federal agency decision makers, or local officials. Proponents hope that advances in understanding, crises, and deft leadership will open the way for selection that more consistently favors ecosystem-based management.

Selection can also be precautionary in that collaborators may seek a policy of lowest risk for a specific attribute. Precaution recognizes that complexities in the behavior of ecosystems can result in surprises—scientific and social predictions are not always accurate (Moore and Russell, 2009). Effective management compensates for scientific uncertainty by taking specific actions to reduce the risk of faulty solutions, often by further limiting human uses.

In the Chesapeake, stakeholder collaborations have had a profound impact. Involving interests and government officials allows collaboration for policy design that crosses jurisdictional and agency boundaries and as a result matches the watershed and bay region. To the extent that these stakeholders are meaningfully involved in policy selection, their values are present in the final policy. As both targets and agents of the policy, they will consider their own interests in determining policy preferences. For example, agricultural interests in the Chesapeake region may limit government control of fertilization practices and seek deeper cuts in sewage treatment plant discharges of nitrogen. Bay water quality could improve, but the burden of making it happen would be shifted. Management of the policy design process under these circumstances requires careful attention.

The fourth stage, implementation, requires the application of resources, usually people and funding, to use tools selected and produce the results intended. In command and control regulation, implementation was restricted to required technologies, permits, and clearly defined responsibilities. By contrast, ecosystem-based management considers all components of the system (including humans), operates at a landscape/seascape regional scale, and adapts techniques as more information becomes available.

Ecosystem-based management principles encourage managers to try tools that have been infrequently used in the past. For example, the traditional solution to watershed and coastal water quality has been regulation of pipe discharges. This tool relies on authority, which can work well if effectively marshaled. However, many of the issues in coastal and watershed management do not rest on unequivocal legal authorities. Two alternatives arise. One is to change the legal authorities. Because this is difficult most discussions center on the second alternative, which is the application of new tools within current legal constructs. For example, estuary programs use information and persuasion to attempt to change individual behavior. Trading or other processes that allow lower cost reduction of pollutants have been used. In fact, each of the tools described in table 8.2 may be considered. However, policies that rest on weak tools or limited enforcement are unlikely to be successful.

Evaluation, the final stage in the policy process, can focus on changes in the process used to create new policy, outputs that reflect changes in the governance structure, and outcomes that measure the effects on social and ecological systems. Constructive process changes could include evidence of stakeholder collaboration and adaptive implementation. For example, in estuaries where significant federal investments have been made in collaborative approaches, stakeholders' opinions have changed (Burroughs, 1999; Lubell, 2005). Although disagreements are not eliminated, the costs of information, bargaining, monitoring, and enforcement can be reduced as stakeholders gain confidence in the process.

Effective program outputs include management at a landscape scale; use of scientific and planning information; coordination across jurisdictions and agencies with consistent results; creation of higher levels of trust; and willingness to exceed legal requirements (Layzer, 2008). For the Chesapeake, outputs are most clearly shown in the agreements that the Executive Council has reached.

Measures that have been used to demonstrate the outcome in the Chesapeake include water quality (dissolved oxygen, clarity, chlorophyll a, chemical contaminants), habitat (bay grasses, bottom habitat, phytoplankton, wetlands), and fish and shellfish (blue crabs, striped bass, oysters, shad, menhaden). If monitoring shows remaining gaps between current conditions and goals (as is the case in the Chesapeake), then the policy is failing to deliver the results anticipated. Adaptive management recognizes the inevitable need to change management strategies in response to shortcomings (Lee, 1999). Proponents of ecosystem-based management argue that flexibility—a willingness to change course in response to new information—is critical to creating healthier watersheds and coasts. So adaptive management using ecosystem governance principles will connect gaps between goals and observed outcomes in social and natural systems with continued policy innovation to address shortcomings. However, closing the gaps tests political will that is often lacking in the Chesapeake and many other watershed/bay systems. In these settings adaptive management works only if commonly shared goals are apparent and tools for effective implementation are adopted.

Summary

When watersheds and coasts are viewed as single units, a number of management initiatives are far more effective. The connectivity of watersheds and coasts may be viewed from the perspective of the hydrologic cycle and from the uses we make of the systems. In the former the flows of water and changes in water quality inform managers about which issues require attention. In the latter the uses that emerge as most important to society more readily attract attention. Managing the landscape to achieve desired water quantity and quality throughout the watershed and coast has become a primary task of governance.

Although the logic of comprehensive management is compelling, the organizations and initiatives are fragmented. The reality is that disparate government programs once implemented in a specific watershed will be integrated through flows of water and human activities. One should plan across all the agencies and jurisdictions so implementation does not inadvertently damage social or ecological systems. That requires understanding agency mandates and laws while seeking constructive change to a more comprehensive governance system. At least nine federal entities are involved, which causes overlaps and conflicts. Furthermore, when those elements of water quality affected by land use are singled out, the application of multiple federal initiatives have resulted in limited success to date.

Chesapeake Bay has been the testing ground for overcoming these difficulties. Improving the environmental quality of coastal waters will require management of land uses such as suburban development and agriculture. States in the watershed have formed a Chesapeake Bay Commission composed principally of state legislators and a Chesapeake Executive Council dominated by governors. These innovative organizational structures extend governance to the ecosystem scale and involve political units that are empowered to implement programs within that geographic range. They have made considerable progress in problem definition and planning, but are facing major difficulties in program execution as evidenced by gaps between goals and current conditions in the bay.

Ecosystem-based management principles show great promise in overcoming fragmentation of federal agency responsibilities, ambiguities in legislation, and difficulties in implementation. By relating ecosystem-based management to each stage of the policy process, its distinctive contributions become apparent. This new approach not only sets ecologically meaningful goals in concert with human uses by identifying ecosystem services and other means, it also extends the management objectives across regions whose dimensions match natural systems. Designing alternative solutions relies upon collaboration among stakeholders. Solutions encompass watersheds and associated coastal waters, address cumulative impacts, and provide opportunities for increasing system resilience. In ecosystem management, stakeholders participate in selecting the preferred solution and value the extent to which precaution is included. Implementation increasingly relies on new tools to create changes in human uses and the environment. Ultimately proponents of ecosystem management will monitor the results of the programs and use adaptive changes to improve program results.[10]

10

Fisheries

Fishing is one of the oldest uses of the sea. Until the 1990s commercial harvest steadily increased in the United States because of advances in technology and the growing appetite of a larger population for seafood. Now, this is no longer the case. The switch from apparently ever-increasing abundance to a plateau, or at times decline, has proven particularly difficult. Both understanding the biological system—given its dramatic fluctuation from year to year—and having the basis for a management system that is respectful of natural limits, individual livelihoods, and coastal communities has proven challenging in many geographic regions. A combination of lower populations for some stocks and regulated reductions in fishing effort has resulted in declining harvest. Future management will need to reconcile the desire for harvest with the capability of the natural system. Ecosystem management integrates human needs within ecological systems and provides new perspectives for fisheries management. This chapter describes ecosystem approaches for fisheries and explains how governance either is or might change to accommodate them.

Expansion of U.S. Fisheries

Commercial landings tell one story of the U.S. fisheries. They represent the tonnage of fish harvested and ultimately sold, a number that has been expanding over much of the past century (figure 10.1). In the late 1920s, the U.S. marine catch of fish and shellfish in aggregate amounted to about three billion pounds per year. After peaking in the early 1990s, the

Figure 10.1. U.S. catch of fish and shellfish, 1921–2006. Harvest increased approximately fivefold until the early 1990s and has remained stable since, but at a somewhat reduced level from the peak. Annual data compiled from Fisheries of the United States, Department of Commerce, and Department of the Interior.

commercial harvest now hovers around 9.5 billion pounds per year. That is a threefold increase and a success for those who eat or sell fish.

Several factors influence this expansion. First, harvesting new target species results in greater landings. Off New England, monkfish, which had been discarded because of a lack of market, now find their way into chowder and other recipes. With this market monkfish became a new target species.

Second, expanding the geographic range for fishing has increased harvest. Some species that were originally found close to shore are caught offshore using larger vessels. Over time, nations claimed two hundred–mile (322-kilometer) exclusive economic zones adjacent to their coasts and established clear expectations about expansion of fisheries offshore. Also during the period shown in figure 10.1, fishing in the newly added states of Alaska and Hawaii increased total harvest for the country.

Third, technological improvements in fishing equipment, in transportation, and in preservation of the catch produced more food from the sea for larger numbers of people. Technology included new ways to locate the position of the vessels, new means to find fish, and new equipment to harvest them. Electronic devices for navigation and fish location coupled with hydraulic systems to replace manual labor increased the volume of fish that were found and handled on a vessel. Alternatives for preserving the fish and expanding capacity to rapidly move fish to new inland markets fueled even more activity. For example, when freezing of fish at sea supplanted chilling them using ice, the marketing possibilities expanded greatly. Fish could be kept for much longer periods of time, released when prices favored, and distributed over long distances.

Finally, by increasing time at sea and horsepower of vessels, more effort went into fishing. For those vessels that harvest fish by pulling a net through the water increasing the horsepower of the engine means that the net can sweep through a greater volume of water in a set time. Furthermore, spending additional hours or days at sea could also increase the harvest. If more fish are to be had, it's likely that horsepower or effort increases will yield them. Taking all these factors into consideration, many fisheries have expanded until recently.

Biological limits to the fishery

Can this expansion of the U.S. fisheries resume? Has it already peaked? The fisheries are part of a larger biological system. Solar energy and nutrients are restricted in the ocean, and the rate at which they can be amassed and moved through food webs to nourish populations of desirable species is set by properties of the natural system. Clearly there is a top end. Biologists express this as carrying capacity, which is the maximum population in a region given the available amount of resources necessary for survival and replacement reproduction. Expansion of commercial fish catch through increasing geographic area, technology, and effort can move harvest to or beyond the capacity of the biological system to produce.

This issue of how much fishing is too much has been with us for well over a century. At the end of the nineteenth century one European view was that overfishing would cease in response to a diminished population of fish long before permanent damage was done. As late as 1960 in the United States, observers optimistically looked forward to substantially increasing the world's food supply through use of the seas (Cowen, 1960). Together these observations would lead one to believe the fisheries would be self-regulating and could expand substantially. However, things turned out to be more complex.

By the late 1960s, observers considered fisheries in the context of the biological systems that supported them. This approach was to identify a potential total harvest for the world ocean based on primary production and trophic efficiency (Ryther, 1969). The former measures the amount of plant growth in the ocean. Simplifying assumptions about the operation of oceanic food webs allowed a calculation of the trophic efficiency with which the primary production or phytoplankton growth was transferred to higher species or trophic levels that were harvested by humans. By focusing on a measured amount of primary production throughout the ocean and the efficiency in transferring it to harvested species, one could project how much commercial harvest might be available. Part of the annual growth of the target species was not to be harvested so that the organisms would be able to reproduce, survive environmental fluctuations, and serve as food for other organisms. The remaining annual growth of the target species would be available for harvest. Using this rationale, a worldwide annual limit of 110 million metric tons (242.5 billion pounds) was estimated (Ryther, 1969). According to the Food and Agricultural Organization (2005), reported worldwide marine harvests have fluctuated at about 80 million metric tons (176 billion pounds) over the recent decade. Others have modified this estimate to include fish and invertebrates that are caught and returned to the sea, commonly dead, and those caught and brought ashore but not reported. Including these additional categories, the amount that has been killed exceeds 100 million metric tons (220 billion pounds) each year since 1985 (Pauly and Watson, 2003). The latter estimate makes global activity perilously close to the estimated global biological limit.

Some traditional measures of fishing activity for individual species provide insights into limits. If humans seek to extract ever more fish from the sea, what signals are available to indicate that a fishery is or could become in trouble? Catch per unit effort (CPUE), if accurately measured, provides one way of establishing a baseline (box 10.1). If one towed the same net with the same horsepower vessel through the same volume of water, then effort or volume of water fished would not change from one year to the next. Assuming that the net accurately sampled the fish in the sea, then one could compare the catch from year to year. If the population of fish is stable, then the same effort from year to year should produce the same catch. With a declining population then the same effort should produce less catch. Ideally CPUE can signal the health of the fishery.

The National Marine Fisheries Service (NMFS) regularly tows at many stations on Georges Bank, located east of Massachusetts in the north Atlantic Ocean. In the late 1960s, the mean catch of cod per tow was about twenty-two pounds (ten kilograms) (Mayo and O'Brien, 2006). For many years since 1990 it has been below eleven pounds (five kilograms) per standardized tow. A decline in CPUE usually indicates a

Box 10.1. What's Your Baseline?

Coastal systems and organisms continually change. One year a favorite fishing spot is productive, the next year not. Average water temperature from one July to the next varies. The shape and location of the shoreline at a beach changes over time. Each of us remembers a set of environmental conditions that were present at a time in the past, which can be considered a baseline.

Scientists do the same but use quantitative measurements of conditions at multiple times. Monitoring change from baselines and determining causes provides new understanding of how the natural environment works. This has been particularly important in the management of fisheries where the abundance or harvest of a species has been recorded over many years. However, individuals can establish a baseline to focus on different time periods and in so doing become a victim of the shifting baseline syndrome (Pauly, 1995). Specifically, a fisheries scientist could establish a baseline for stock size and species composition at the start of her career and use it to evaluate change. With a declining fishery each new generation of scientists will start with a baseline indicative of a different time period. Not only does the baseline shift, but also the decline in the coastal system is gradually accommodated in the perceptions of the individuals assessing it.

Kelp beds illustrate shifting baselines in action for an ecosystem (Dayton et al., 1998; Jackson et al., 2001). Historically, human harvest has removed sea otters and fishes that consume sea urchins. As sea urchin populations expand in absence of predators, they consume kelp and deforest areas, producing sea urchin barrens. Although plants may return due in part to harvesting urchins, the Steller's sea cow, which probably affected kelp ecosystems through grazing, has been extinct for decades. With vast shifts in a coastal ecosystem such as kelp beds, the identification of a baseline using recently collected ecological data will tell only a part of the story.

reduction in the number and/or size of fish in the sea. When CPUE and biomass decline significantly, reducing the effort directed at the affected organism is prudent.

Biomass measurements are routinely used to assess fisheries. NMFS identifies stocks that have a biomass level below thresholds established in management plans as overfished (National Marine Fisheries Service, 2008). In late 2009 twenty-four percent of the assessed stocks or stock complexes were overfished (NOAA Fish Stock Sustainability Index,

2009). One-third of the national stocks deemed to be overfished are found off the northeastern United States.

Fisheries both globally and within many areas of the United States face limits. In many instances when declines are noted and suitable actions are taken, recovery is possible. Patterns for individual species vary greatly. Some, such as the Atlantic halibut, were in decline by the Civil War and remain depleted, while others, such as the Atlantic striped bass and Pacific halibut, have been recovered for years. Repeated sampling has established trends in biomass, which are used to assess the health of the system. Dips in biomass signal that current practice is approaching or exceeding the ability of the biological system to produce at the current level.

Fisheries management

Because many U.S. fisheries expanded to the point of reaching biological limits, fisheries management became a necessity. Without management, overfishing could result in plummeting populations of some fish, over-investment in fishing equipment, and decline of coastal communities as fishing ceases to be productive. The policy process, as described in chapter 2, provides a framework to assess elements of fisheries management. Figure 10.2 presents the stages model of the policy process in a fisheries context.

In the 1970s many noted a decline of certain fisheries, marine environments that supported them, and the coastal communities that rely on the fisheries. Along the East Coast, industrial fleets, largely from Eastern Europe, caught large amounts of fish. The Fishery Conservation and Management Act of 1976 phased out foreign fishing and created a management system for the U.S. fisheries. The law established a federal fisheries zone and the means to practice conservation within it so that U.S. citizens could use fishery resources on a continuing basis. The law provided new rules or institutions to control the relations among individuals and the environment (Jentoft, 2004). Sustainability for a fishery, or harvesting today in a manner that will allow future generations of people the same opportunity, became a central theme. In recent years social goals, including employment but extending to other aspects, have been added to the objective of long-term health for the biological community. Under that law fisheries management councils (FMCs) create plans for fisheries with the assistance of and ultimate review by the federal Department of Commerce and its NMFS (box 10.2)

The councils and the NMFS play prominent roles in addressing U.S. fisheries problems. The councils create management plans and the NMFS

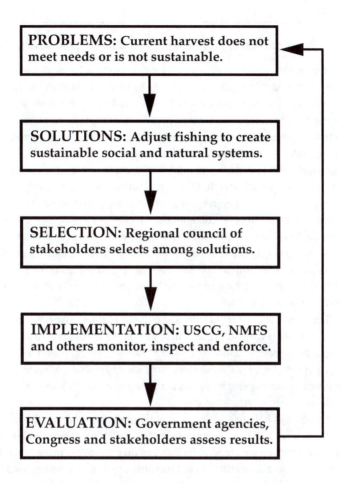

Figure 10.2. U.S. fisheries management in a policy process context. The actions that fisheries management councils take to manage fisheries may be assessed using stages in the policy process.

and others provide information and implement the plans when approved. Biological, and increasingly social, data are collected with the intent of shaping fisheries decisions. The information could be important in both creating policy and establishing its effectiveness. How healthy is the harvested population and associated habitat? What are the situations of fishers and communities dependent on the resource? The councils, which are responsible for geographic areas along the coast, include stakeholders as well as government officials. They produce fisheries management plans (FMPs), which specify how fishing will be conducted. The councils create

---

Box 10.2. Fishery Conservation and Management Act

In 1976 the U.S. government asserted control over the fisheries from three to two hundred miles (4.8–322 kilometers) offshore through the Fishery Conservation and Management Act. The law has been revised several times since. Fisheries management plans produced by councils established under the act are expected to "promote domestic commercial and recreational fishing under sound conservation and management principles" (Section 2[b]). Under the law managers moved to exclude foreign fishing vessels and began conservation efforts (Young, 1982). As U.S. capacity to fish grew, aided in part by government programs, the allocation of fish among domestic interests became contentious. National standards clarified intent by requiring councils to prevent overfishing and to achieve optimum yield while minimizing bycatch. Councils created plans to manage individual stocks as units and where possible consider relationships among stocks. Further, the standards called attention to the importance of fishing to livelihoods and to communities.

These tasks and others became the purview of a new management unit, fisheries management councils. The councils were established for eight geographic regions around the United States and charged with preparing management plans for fisheries primarily located outside of state waters but inside of the seaward boundary of the two hundred–mile exclusive economic zone.

The councils both use scientific information from and produce management plans subject to review by the NMFS. Prior to implementation of a plan, the NMFS creates federal regulations that ultimately make it binding on fishers. Some argue that in concert with congressional delegations the councils have become more powerful than the Secretary of Commerce, who by law has the power to approve or reject plans from the councils. Furthermore, stakeholders who question the process may appeal to the Secretary of Commerce or litigate. As a result the process has been gradually opened to many stakeholders beyond the commercial fishing industry.

---

solutions and select a preferred management option. This includes setting a biologically acceptable limit to harvest and adjusting fishing practices to meet the limit.

In fisheries management a limited number of government actions dominate. If a stock is overfished, then restrictions appear in management plans. The councils can propose that the government directly regulate fishing activities by limiting time, area, gear, harvest, or targeted species, among other possibilities. A mix of these actions, enforced through monitoring and sanctions, forms the core of the regulatory approach. The government has changed the system from open access, which meant that most anyone could fish, to a system that requires commercial fishers to have permits to participate.

Not all fisheries management is or will be a government activity. Governance practices for fisheries include ecolabeling and education. The former relies on knowledgeable consumers to purchase fish that have been harvested in an environmentally sustainable manner (Roheim, 2008). A third party such as the Marine Stewardship Council certifies the sustainable fishing practice and adds its label to the product. Market pressure forces larger numbers of fishers to meet the environmental standards if they wish to sell their product. In a similar manner, education of consumers about the status of fish stocks or the nature of fishing practices may result in purchasing decisions that favor sustainability. Many fish consumers carry cards with them that identify the environmentally preferable fish to eat at restaurants or to purchase in markets.

In contrast with governance processes just mentioned, implementation under the Fishery Conservation and Management Act proceeds with enforcement techniques used by NMFS and the U.S. Coast Guard, as well as others. At this point in the policy process, the fishers who were stakeholders in the creation of the policy become the targets in its implementation. Although the FMP can be developed in a consensual manner, its implementation takes on a different tone. Monitoring the location and activity of fishing vessels has been implemented in a variety of ways. The Coast Guard performs inspections at sea, and the NMFS monitors sale of fish and other activities related to the federal fishery onshore. Fishers can be fined, lose licenses, and forfeit catch, among other sanctions.

Ideally one would monitor the biological and social systems to determine if the policy, once implemented, has met the goals specified. This is the evaluation step shown in figure 10.2. The Fish Stock Sustainability Index and other means have been used to evaluate the biological results of management practices. Regrettably, little systematic analysis has been done to assess the results of fisheries management on social systems. Specifically, understanding the social benefits of biologically restored stocks, if widely apparent, would be a powerful incentive for fishing communities to fully engage in the restoration of fisheries. Evaluation can take many forms, but the most influential are those that are commissioned or collected by Congress and used to revise the law. For example, the

U.S. Commission on Ocean Policy (2004) recommended changes to the designation of essential fish habitats and to bycatch reduction plans so that decisions are based on ecosystem properties, not individual species. Furthermore, the commission noted that managing impacts of fishery plans on fishers and communities is a necessary part of the ecosystem-based approach.

The councils

FMCs deserve a close look because they determine rules for the fishery. The councils decide who gets to fish and how much. The membership of the councils, their relationship to NMFS, and means of clarifying duties through the national standards in the law have been contentious in recent years.

By law the councils include voting members selected by the Secretary of Commerce and drawn from individuals with knowledge of or experience in management, conservation, or harvest. State or federal officials directly involved in fisheries management supplement them. Nonvoting members represent other federal agencies affected by fishery decisions. Council membership is a hybrid of regulatory officials and nongovernmental stakeholders. Council members appoint advisory groups and are assisted by a professional staff of government employees.

One of the innovations of the 1976 law was to directly involve the fishers in decisions by making it possible to appoint them to the councils. Among the charges to the council is to create plans that stop overfishing. Thus, through this process fishers can become self-regulators. Comprehensively viewing the law and the potential roles of fishers in carrying the law out shows that they could participate as stakeholders or agents in plan design and as targets when the plan is implemented.

Furthermore, in plan design and implementation, the fishers' knowledge about the environment would be beneficial, which is another reason for their participation. However, others found flaws in this approach and have blamed representation of commercial and recreational users on the councils for declines in certain fisheries (Okey, 2003; Eagle et al., 2003). The source of this problem, some suggest, is that when asked to limit total catch and allocate among fishers through the plans, the councils were likely to increase harvest beyond what was biologically appropriate as a means of satisfying constituencies. Self-interest, presumed by some at the time of the law's creation to be a powerful incentive for conservation, has been reinterpreted as the source of the overfishing problem.

Through the council process, the Scientific and Statistical Committee of each council, as well as other advisory bodies and the public, assist in setting objectives for the following fishing year. The NMFS fisheries science centers around the country provide fish stock assessments that may be used to determine allowable biological catches (Eagle and Thompson, 2003). For overharvested fisheries, councils are charged with creating plans that will restore a stock to a prescribed level. In recent years the focus on biological data has been augmented by new information on the social and economic aspects of fishing.

Coastal areas depend on fishing in a variety of ways. As a result data collection and council deliberations have expanded from biology to economics and now to impacts on the human communities that depend upon fishing. Fish are food; harvesting and processing them provides employment; and they form the cultural connections that sustain many communities. In this context a fisheries-dependent community may be viewed as a population of individuals that relies on the fishing industry for its continued economic, social, and cultural success (Brookfield et al., 2005).

National standards are a part of the act and serve to clarify the intent of the law and guide the councils concerning which of the data should be given most weight in preparing plans. Separate standards identify conservation, defined as prevention of overfishing and rebuilding of stocks, and sustained participation of fishing communities (standards 1 and 8). Because aggressive conservation will curtail current harvest, some interpreted it to limit community participation in the fisheries. However, case law interprets conservation of the biological resources as the most important goal (Bagley, 2003). Intent was further clarified through the 2006 revisions of the law. They mandate an end to overfishing by 2011 through the use of annual catch limits in FMPs.

Concern about these tensions between community health and fish populations has taken many forms. The community development quota, initiated in 1992, is one manifestation. Through it approximately ten percent of the Bering Sea groundfish are managed to promote fisheries-related economic development for communities in western Alaska (Ginter, 1995). More recently social impact analysis and means to address social consequences of actions taken by FMCs have received attention as mandated by revisions of the Fishery Conservation and Management Act.

Fisheries management as ecosystem governance

If fisheries management were to become ecosystem governance, what would it entail? Would stakeholders approve? How might it emerge?

These are not idle questions because the Pew and U.S. ocean commissions speak of ecosystem-based management as a means to improve current situations. Traditional fisheries management starts with a species or stock and considers reproductive success, growth, and associated biological factors (Link, 2002a, b). Recognition that there are multiple species in a given ocean area expands the science to include predation, competition, and other factors. Ultimately biodiversity, habitat, and climate expand the realm of considerations to include the ecological community and its environment.

However, for ecosystem-based fisheries management, one considers uses and incorporates social systems as well as biological ones in the planning process. What is the logic for including people as part of the ecosystem? Quite simply, meeting goals of a sustainable natural system requires changes in human behavior. People are central to management. They design the management actions. They respond to the directives or choose not to. As agents, they determine the status of the ecosystem. For some people in these regions, direct use of natural resources constitutes a principal means for livelihood. Almost all agree that people are a part of the fisheries ecosystem and that biological sustainability is required, but the specifics of just how these needs, ecosystems, and livelihoods are to be integrated vary. Ultimately, it is through managing human actions affecting anthropogenically stressed natural systems that sustainability may arise.

Ecosystem-based management has been repeatedly proposed, defined, and at times applied to fisheries (Pikitch et al., 2004; Garcia and Cochrane, 2005; Fluharty, 2005; Parsons, 2005; Arkema et al., 2006; Field and Francis, 2006; Francis et al., 2007; Marasco et al., 2007). Social dimensions of the ecosystem approach include explicit incorporation of humans and recognition that, as stakeholders, their needs must be a part of management. Often such needs are expressed through reliance on ecosystem goods and services such as food, water quality, tourism, and recreation.

Biophysical dimensions of the ecosystem approach to management include minimizing risk of irreversible change and achieving ecological health while recognizing the complexity and variability of marine food webs and habitats. Often this takes the form of protecting biological diversity, which is a measure of species within a habitat or across a seascape.

Management using an ecosystem approach requires the integration of social needs with biological capabilities. Many propose adaptive approaches wherein a logical policy is implemented with minimal risk to biological systems. Monitoring this approach allows adjustments in human use based on the new information.

To clarify the differences between traditional fisheries management and the ecosystem approach, it's instructive to compare elements of each (table 10.1). In traditional fisheries management, the goal is to maximize yield from individual species. The ecosystem approach looks more broadly and recognizes that livelihoods and human communities depend on healthy ecological systems and that those biological communities are in decline in many cases. Specific goals in this context could include food security, livelihoods, access, equity, economic efficiency, resource rehabilitation, and ecosystem integrity (Garcia and Cochrane, 2005).

In traditional fisheries management designing alternatives and adopting solutions has revolved around maximum sustainable yield (MSY), or variations of it, for individual species. This MSY or theoretical maximum harvest that can be sustained from year to year is calculated with primary attention to biological features of the system. However, the law introduces the idea of modifying the MSY to an "optimum" that includes relevant economic, social, or ecological factors.

As a result FMPs created by the councils start with biological data and frequently impose limitations on effort, harvest, or gear to meet biologically specified ends. Three steps accomplish the task (Babcock and Pikitch, 2004). First, biological reference points that include biomass, fishing mortality rate, and other factors are established. Fishing mortality is the amount of organisms removed during fishing operations as opposed to via natural causes. Second, observing performance indicators identifies when a fish stock is out of compliance with the biological

TABLE 10.1.
Elements of fishery management.

	Traditional	Ecosystem-based
Problem	Focus on single species harvest	Focus on sustainable systems
Ideal solution	Optimum fish harvest	Health of social and natural systems
Implementation	Regulations by government	Stakeholder management plans; new instruments and implementing entities
Evaluation	Harvest within maximum sustainable yield	Coastal systems that are socially and biologically sustainable

reference points and, for example, overfished. Third, certain values of the performance indicator trigger a management response, such as a reduction in fishing mortality or harvest.

The principles of ideal ecosystem-based management of fisheries incorporate an expanded set of considerations. The change includes both a more complete consideration of the trophic interactions and the incorporation of livelihoods and communities. By considering bycatch—nontargeted organisms that are captured—or climate change, individual fishery plans have demonstrated capability to incorporate ecosystem considerations. Furthermore, initiatives of researchers to understand the role of communities or of nongovernmental organizations to participate on behalf of fishers demonstrate how social considerations are entering fisheries planning.

The NMFS and the USCG, through inspections, fines, and other means, implement fishery plans approved by the Secretary of Commerce. In contrast ecosystem-based management relies upon more consensual methods that empower stakeholders to act in the collective interest of the fishery. By including additional incentives, this new form can gain higher acceptance but at the cost of speed and decisiveness. Once a consensus is reached, fishers and local entities are expected to assume a greater role in enforcement. To some extent councils are a stakeholder process and represent an ecosystem-based approach. However, the results of their activities measured in terms of recovered stocks are variable and indicate that for some regions much more work needs to be done. In short, some argue that the councils are not restoring fisheries at the rate that is necessary. Others observe that even at the current rate, the social consequences for communities and livelihoods are far too great.

These evaluations make clear the variety of goals being considered. For traditional management it is harvest within a biological limit. Ecosystem-based approaches anticipate harvest levels will be limited so as to provide sustainable activity, but they operate with much broader horizons. Sustainability is both a social and natural phenomenon, so biological solutions must be put forward in a manner that limits social impacts.

But to date, evaluation shows that ecosystem-based fisheries management is only sparsely represented in actual plans of the councils. Significant changes will need to occur to incorporate robust, broadly defined ecosystem considerations in fisheries management. So the ways in which people decide to incorporate new ideas in fishery planning and management become important. As presented in the following sections, the change may be incremental or abrupt.

Incremental change

Incremental change, the concept that management can shift through a series of small readjustments, can be observed in three ways. First, government agencies can support research related to ecosystem-based management. A second measure is the extent to which the FMP process encourages ecosystem-based management concepts in the preparation of plans. Finally, the tools or instruments adopted can be assessed with respect to the extent that they are likely to support ecosystem-based management outcomes. Each of these measures is explored further below.

First, consider the possibility of expanding research beyond the impacts of harvest on single species of fish to include broader natural processes and the social phenomena related to them. One example illustrates the progression (Marasco et al., 2007). In it fisheries-pertinent research expands from population biology, the mainstay of fisheries science, to community ecology, an analysis that embraces interactions among species in a region. Not only are target species considered but also their prey. For example, the population of menhaden, the prey, influences bluefish and striped bass numbers. In a further expansion of the research purview, environmental impacts and/or the effects of fishing on other species through bycatch and habitat alteration could be analyzed. Finally, one might assess all of the above as a precursor to setting the total allowable catch (TAC).

Furthermore, because all fisheries include people, social dimensions should be included in research. Fisheries meet social needs and share coastal waters with other users. Consider the possibility that a manufacturing activity employs lots of people but also discharges contaminated water to the coast (Parsons, 2005). The pollution reduces fish yield. In this context ultimate decisions would require an understanding of the natural system to define impacts and means of controlling them. In addition, an analysis of the social factors is needed to develop a program to reduce the noxious discharges or choose to favor manufacturing over fishing and the consequences of the choice on livelihoods. Further, one may look at the economic, social, and cultural health of the individuals and communities dependent on the fishery.

A second area to examine for indication of incremental change is the extent to which FMPs further ecosystem-based management. Stakeholders have latitude in framing the content of fisheries plans and in revising them if they fail. Direct experience with the fishery and data concerning the status of the marine environment allow constant comparison of expectations and performance. The councils are ideally positioned to implement a practice-based approach to ecosystem management (Brunner and Clark, 1997). From that perspective they can learn, correct, and improve the plan to better match social perspectives with ecosystem requirements.

Given the latitude that council members have in plan design, what aspects of ecosystem-based management might they incorporate? Many proposals for including ecosystem considerations in fisheries plans have been put forward (Ecosystems Principles Advisory Panel, 1999; Fluharty, 2005; Field and Francis, 2006; Marasco et al., 2007). Delineating ecosystem boundaries, modeling the food web, and developing indices of ecosystem health have been suggested. Biological measures of ecosystem health include diversity and biomass. Within a region, total removals of fish and their impacts on biomass, trophic structure, and habitat augment ecosystem measures. In addition social measures of ecosystem health focus on the needs of people and include well-being (Pollnac et al., 2006). Well-being is the degree to which an individual, family, or community can be characterized as sound, functional, happy, and prosperous. It contrasts with economic measures that, for example, focus on income.

Ultimately ecosystem-based management requires an assessment or modeling of the ecological, human, and institutional interactions with attention to the stability of social and natural systems. Such social-ecological assessments become operational if council plans tie them to catch objectives and their impacts on other species, biomass, trophic structure, livelihoods, and community health, among other factors. However, although scholars and some environmental groups have identified opportunities for ecosystem governance principles to be incorporated in the plans, other stakeholders have been reluctant to move in that direction.

A third area to examine for incremental change is the extent to which policy tools or instruments are used to advance ecosystem-based management. In traditional fisheries management, tools were focused on biological systems and fish yields from them. Operating a fishery within a TAC can be accomplished by controlling inputs or outputs. Inputs include areas, times, and gears fished, among other factors that, if restricted, could reduce harvest. However, the threat of a fishery closing in an unpredictable manner results in a race among fishers to land as much as possible as quickly as possible. Flooding the market with fish drives down prices and can affect quality of product as well as safety aboard the vessels.

Recognition that some instruments have negative consequences has led to an alternative approach. One can work backward by identifying fisheries where recovery of populations has occurred due to declining exploitation rates and then ask which tools were most influential (Hilborn, 2007; Worm et al., 2009). Local characteristics shape which tools will be most effective, but some generalizations apply. TAC was the most commonly used tool in successful fishery rebuilding efforts. Attention to just how it is implemented is particularly important given the race to fish example just mentioned. Gear restrictions to increase selectivity and reduce bycatch, closed areas, comanagement, and assigning catch shares to fishers or communities have also been deemed influential.

Closed areas deserve special attention. Eliminating fishing in certain areas, which may be marine protected areas or essential fish habitats, can result in resurgence of target populations. If the closed area is temporarily opened or if organisms move from the protected area to other locations, fishers can harvest them. Evidence showing how this would work in detail is presently lacking for many species, but benefits of its application in tropical environments are encouraging (Roberts, 2007; Christie et al., 2009). In the United States temporarily opening formerly closed areas for sea scallop harvest has resulted in a resurgence of that fishery.

Establishing and applying indices related to the ecosystem is another tool. When an index departs from the desired range of values, action to correct the situation is undertaken. This is analogous to establishing biomass or spawning stock biomass targets for single species and reducing fishing if the biomass falls too low. Ecosystem indices include factors such as species composition. Alternatively they may focus on special environments such as eelgrass or coral systems (Done and Reichelt, 1998; Food and Agriculture Organization, 2003; Babcock and Pikitch, 2004). Furthermore, because ecosystems include people, indices related to human needs are equally important. For example, a quantitative index that measures well-being at the community level could be applied to assess the effectiveness of a management action just as easily as a biological measure (Pollnac et al., 2006). Because many recognize "no fish, no fishery," human well-being is tied to the biological health of the fishery. With that in mind robust biological and social indices become a powerful tool to assess the trade-offs implied by different management alternatives.

Opportunities for incremental change also exist in single-species plans by connecting them and keeping multiple species above reference points (Mace, 2001; Babcock and Pikitch, 2004). An example of this is bycatch. Concentrating on bycatch reduction in a single-species plan, a common practice now, assists in meeting ecosystem-based management goals by stabilizing populations.

Finally, traditional governmental tools such as taxes and subsidies can find new purpose in ecosystem-based management of fisheries. Decisions about who gets to participate in the fishery, what they get to harvest, and how much are central parts of fisheries management. If access is uninhibited, overharvest can result and populations of target species decline. As harvest is restricted to meet biological objectives, communities and families suffer. An ecosystem approach can benefit from looking beyond the immediate limitation of harvest to the possibilities of linking it to tools such as subsidies, services, and taxes to encourage results for communities that are consistent with sustainability—biological and human. The extent to which these tools could advance ecosystem-based management objectives has not been fully explored.

Fundamental change

Some have argued that the incremental changes are insufficient. By adopting a different goal, starting with a new premise, and restructuring means or creating new ones, the approach can shift in fundamental instead of incremental ways. Paradigm shifts in public policy originate from the top by creating a new way to view the relationship of society to natural resources, by establishing new burdens, and by making the expectations universal through law or custom. Revising the water pollution law in 1972 is an example of a paradigm shift. Moving fisheries from open to regulated access in 1976 is another example. The new fisheries law reshaped harvest by encouraging adoption of techniques such as TAC, trip limits, and overall capacity reduction as part of management (Field and Francis, 2006). The pending shift to ecosystem-based management of fisheries will represent an equally large change.

Ownership determines use. The Fishery Conservation and Management Act makes clear that the government through the councils manages fisheries in the three to two hundred–mile (4.8 to 322-kilometer) coastal zone adjacent to the country. However, the public through the councils controls the objectives and processes in management. To date many considering fundamental change have focused on needs related to natural systems. Some have proposed that minimizing damage to coastal ecosystems would provide more ecosystem services (Jackson et al., 2001). They focus on how fishing and other stresses have impoverished the biological communities. They further argue that enhancing ecosystem properties such as forage fish populations or total biomass will result in more stable coastal systems (Pikitch et al., 2004). In fact some suggest that one could measure the effectiveness of fisheries management by monitoring the biomass left for predators rather than the spawning biomass of the target species in the fishery (Mangel and Levin, 2005). In these management approaches, the focus shifts from single-species yields to ecosystem function and the health of nontarget species (Tudela and Short, 2005). Each of these shifts implies that the public will redirect some of the productivity away from extractive use and toward other values. In some instances this reapportionment could have positive spillovers on fishery productivity, while in other cases fishing limits would be detrimental to livelihoods.

If broadly accepted, these new values would change the way access to resources is granted or withheld. Macinko and Bromley (2002) proposed that access could be specified by a change in the law. In 1976 the law incorporated several standards about how conservation and management should be pursued with respect to science, management, cost, and other parameters. Revisions of the law have added standards and could do so again in the future to clarify who has access in a limited entry fishery and how they obtain it.

The future of fisheries can also be shaped by more general governance changes for coasts. The U.S. Commission on Ocean Policy (2004) proposed regional ocean councils. Their purview would be ecosystem units instead of political jurisdictions, and, as a consequence, management of the region would include multiple uses for the area through techniques such as zoning. The commission identified several examples of existing regional units, and their activities may serve as a useful guide. Organizing topics included endangered species, hypoxia, water quality and quantity, climate change, and bay health. A legal regime for managing coastal and ocean space would place the fishery as but one user and require heightened coordination among agencies.

Who decides?

Many recent changes signal a shift in power from the central government to actors closer to the resource. Comanagement, community-based management, and privatization exemplify the trend. In comanagement the government grants a role for users in the management of the fisheries (Pomeroy and Berkes, 1997; Noble, 2000). The FMCs initiated in 1976 are a form of comanagement. Through comanagement communities have greater access to and involvement in decisions. This can increase program legitimacy.

Jentoft and McCay (1995) assessed the level of community involvement by using Arnstein's (1969) ladder of citizen participation. The ladder explicitly recognizes that involvement may come with little or no control, such as when the users are informed of the decision and perhaps asked to comment. Conversely at the top of the ladder, the stakeholders make the decisions (Berkes, 1994). Plummer and FitzGibbon (2004) extended this concept by adding the dimensions of who is involved in the management regime and what processes for management are selected. In fisheries, power sharing can result in producer organizations assuming responsibility for management functions. In seeking to create conditions where the properties of the fishery shape the governing system, Jentoft (2007) identified the need to contextualize, coordinate, learn, and safeguard. In many instances local stakeholders are best equipped to pursue each of these.

Further empowerment of the community through a more or less complete transfer of government authority is known as community-based management for control and management of natural resources (Tacconi, 2007). This process reverses top-down management and creates a community-led process (Brown et al., 2002). In this context one would have to alter the FMCs to maintain sovereignty but remove state and federal voting participation and review.

A third possibility is to privatize the ownership of the fishery. Individual transferable quotas are an example because they can transfer ownership from the public to private entities often on the basis of fishing history. Leasing is an alternative way to accomplish a similar end but maintain a higher level of government control. Privatization includes increasing the role of private enterprises, which may be for-profit businesses or non-profit service agencies. Privatization takes several forms (von Weizsacker et al., 2005). In the fishery there are proposals to transfer public assets and portions of their management to private entities. Forms of privatization range from weak to strong, depending upon the degree of empowerment of the private entity and the management function privatized. For example, in self-management users may fund their own management system within a framework established by government, and they may enforce the system they design (Hughey et al., 2000). Some self-management systems have been designed so that the public retains ownership.

Transfer of ownership to private entities and the transfer of management of public resources to private parties are separate changes that can be joined through sector-based approaches. The Magnuson-Stevens Fishery Conservation and Management Reauthorization Act of 2006 for fisheries opened this possibility. In sector management a portion of the fishery is transferred to a group of individuals in a fishing community or a regional fishery association for their collective benefit and management.

The privilege or share of the potential harvest transferred could be expressed as a percentage of the TAC for the fishery. Apportioning the fishery would consist of reserving a percentage of the TAC for the sector at the start of the season. In theory each privilege holder would know in advance how many pounds of fish they could harvest based on a formula that divides fish among the group. The group could enforce regulations related to the fishery and ensure that the sector's harvest was within the agreed upon limit.

Privatization associated with self-management is not without significant risk (Lemos and Agrawal, 2006). Hybrid governance consists of arrangements between state agencies and communities, between state agencies and businesses, between businesses and nongovernmental organizations/communities, and combinations of all three. As the state recedes, those new actors with greater access are likely to derive greater benefits. Consequently, market-oriented approaches may favor corporate gains over equity and community participation. In the U.S. fisheries, historical harvest, employment, investment, and dependence, as well as social and cultural factors, have been proposed to ensure a fair allocation. Careful attention to who is empowered, to what extent, and for what fisheries management functions becomes of paramount importance.

Summary

Harvest in U.S. fisheries has increased threefold since the early part of the last century. Advances in technology, increases in fishing effort, expanded geographic areas, and new markets for species that were previously discarded have all contributed. However, this expansion has stopped as many fisheries experience population declines and regulations restrict harvest. In late 2009 twenty-four percent of the assessed stocks or stock complexes in the United States were overfished and about one-third of the overfished stocks were located in the Northeast.

Eight regional FMCs for federal waters are charged with developing controls that balance human expectations for harvest with biological realities concerning what can be safely removed. Stakeholders in councils include commercial and recreational fishers, among others. The councils consider information about the fishery, assess alternative management plans, and select a preferred approach. If the Secretary of Commerce approves their proposal, it sets the rules for the fishery. Usually the plans are focused on a single species or a small groups of species.

Exclusive attention to single-species harvest levels, while positive, ignores relationships with other species, the marine environment, and social systems, which are all important elements of ecosystem-based management. Fisheries link the natural system with the social system. Human needs for food result in fishing that in turn affects the populations of fish. If overfishing degrades the biological system, then livelihoods and communities are affected. The challenge for fisheries management is to adjust human behavior so that natural and social systems prosper. The linkage of social and biophysical systems frames the concept of ecosystem-based management for fisheries. In this setting people are not only a part of the ecosystem but also prime movers in creating a sustainable future.

Ecosystem-based fisheries management, or as it is also called, an ecosystem approach to fisheries, requires new thinking about the role and means of management. Incremental change is coming about in at least three ways. First, research has expanded about processes in social and natural systems as well as their primary linkages to better understand ecosystem-based opportunities. Second, the expectations for FMPs have been expanded to include ecosystem principles. Third, on occasion conventional tools of fisheries management have been expanded to incorporate ecosystem considerations. Most fisheries that have recovered have implemented a TAC program. In addition modification of single-species plans, creation of protected areas, and development of indices have all been used for rebuilding fisheries and do advance ecosystem considerations. In addition the creation of regional ocean councils could extend ecosystem management principles over many uses including and beyond fishing.

New stakeholders and processes are empowered through comanagement, community-based management, and privatization. In comanagement the government delegates a limited role for users in management. In community-based management a community receives more or less complete control of the resources. In privatization government grants a nongovernmental organization, either nonprofit or for-profit, a mixture of control and management rights. The extent to which privatization of publicly owned resources will meet social and natural system sustainability is uncertain at this time.

U.S. fisheries are undergoing rapid change. Incorporating the needs of individuals for seafood and livelihoods while respecting the biological limits of coastal waters form the core of the ecosystem-based management challenge for the fisheries. Most seek sustainable social and natural systems, but the means for reaching them remain contentious and will be the subject of debate and experiment for years to come.

11

Conclusion

People are drawn to the sea. The number of individuals who live, work, and play along the coasts is larger than ever before and continuing to grow. Each day, this burgeoning population uses the coasts in a multitude of ways—for waste disposal, shipping, recreation, fishing, energy, housing, and many other aspects of life. Although these various activities may appear unrelated, they are connected through the flows of water, migration of organisms, dispersal of pollutants, human livelihoods, and community needs.

Governance, government complemented by nongovernmental means of shaping behavior, has and will continue to change for coastal lands and waters in response to changing values within society. Enhanced understanding of social and natural systems often creates new expectations for human activities. When new values shape a new common interest, new laws follow. The aggregate results of this process, as described in earlier chapters and summarized in figure 11.1, have been changes in approach to management. Sector-based management followed by spatial and more recently by ecosystem-based management exemplify the changes.

These management frameworks, although distinctive, are not exclusive. Rather, coastal lands and waters are subject to the simultaneous application of all three approaches. Before summarizing what the book has covered related to each management framework, it is useful to define the ends and means of coastal governance.

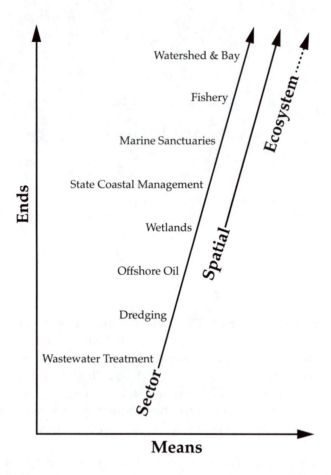

Figure 11.1. Coastal governance ends and means. Coastal governance has evolved as the society's ends have shifted. New means to implement change have been utilized, including those beyond direct governmental control. As a result, sector-based management has been augmented by spatial approaches and more recently by ecosystem-based management.

Ends and means

Evolution of coastal governance has resulted in the management frameworks described earlier in this book and schematically illustrated in figure 11.1. Each framework—sector, spatial, ecosystem—uses a mix of means to achieve a desired end. As pressures on resources increase and societal values shift, the end, or objective, changes. Consequently, new means—that is, policy instruments or tools—are needed. These simultaneous changes in ends and means are at the core of coastal governance and its change over time. The policy process establishes new programs in response to ends and creates means to reach them.

Until approximately the 1970s, it was acceptable to pave over marshes and dump wastes into estuaries. However, as it became clear that these activities were damaging fisheries, recreation, and natural processes, the national agenda shifted. A new public commitment to preserving natural systems and the services they deliver (the end) resulted in new policies (the means) to shape human behavior. This process has been repeated in the evolution to spatial management and more recently to ecosystem-based management. Spatial management ends focus on the suitability of specific activities in geographic regions, while ecosystem-based management maintains natural processes as a means to sustain social systems.

The most significant contemporary change in management reflects a new recognition that government, although important, need not be the exclusive means to guide human behavior. Increasingly, society uses tools beyond direct governmental intervention, such as public information campaigns, private markets, and family or community mores (table 2.1).

Sector-based management

Sector-based management focuses on a single activity or use of a particular resource and establishes a process to pursue it that is supervised by the government. This approach developed when the U.S. population was smaller, activities were less intense, and coastal resources seemed endless. Managers were not concerned with one use interfering with another. The means were straightforward. Top-down government action, usually through regulation, changed human behavior to meet objectives specified in the law. Sector-based management has successfully limited the discharge of wastes and improved coastal areas in many other ways. Most government activity in coastal areas is still sector-based, and it will continue to be an important aspect of most management schemes in the future.

However, as the number of coastal uses has grown and the intensity of virtually every one has rapidly increased, coordination of single-sector programs has proven to be difficult. Social and natural systems link human activities in multiple ways, while the horizontal and vertical dimensions of government break up management into ever smaller packets of responsibility and authority.

These cleavages in government are a source of innumerable difficulties for dredging and wetlands protection. Action for each requires navigating among congressional committees, multiple units of the executive branch, and the courts. This complexity cascades through federal, state, and local layers of government. U.S. laws and agencies not only encourage but also often mandate, that each sector of coastal activity be treated separately. Consequently, management decisions are frequently isolated and rarely take into account the cumulative effects of individual uses or the limits of the natural system. Nor does management adequately consider multiple stresses on social systems. These shortcomings are becoming painfully apparent as conflicting uses, such as fishing and waste disposal, butt up against one another.

In short, lack of coordination has led to a predicament in which both social and natural systems are degraded. Rather than solving conflicts among different users, a sector-based approach can amplify them. Their resolution, if it comes at all, takes time and money as users seek ever higher authority through the courts or the executive branch. Dredging matters have found their way to officials in the president's office because they could not be resolved elsewhere. Without overall goals for coasts and oceans, determination of a preferred use rests on complex and often indeterminate processes of bargaining. Instead of a coherent plan, sector-based management becomes a series of uncoordinated reactions. An alternative is to allocate space for certain purposes, an approach known as spatial management.

Spatial management

In early spatial management, the government designated specific locations for single uses, such as shipping channels or ocean dumping sites. Areas for oil and gas exploitation, coastal parks, marine protected areas, torpedo ranges, and a variety of other activities all found their way onto maps. Consequently, the geographic dimensions of single uses dominated early discussions of spatial management.

By the 1970s coastal management began to incorporate consideration of multiple uses. Many uses were vying for the same space, and a systematic way of sorting them out became necessary. Multiple use management has a long history related to the public lands onshore, and the Coastal Zone Management Act applied a similar set of considerations to state waters and a veneer of private lands along the coast. State coastal management initiatives rest on the assumption that context-specific plans and their implementation through zoning are well suited to equitably resolve issues. Zoning separates activities that might be injurious to one another and, as a result, protects people's health and safety. It can also be used to manage across multiple interests and environmental capacities. Public agreements about how lands and seas can be used, reflected in zoning plans, are converted into defined spaces with guidelines about preferred uses. This process rests on zoning all available space in some fashion. In short, the act signaled a change from regulation of isolated sectors to the potential for holistic examination of multiple uses on land and seascapes. Multiple use management requires trade-offs and produces maps showing plausible locations for uses.

The Coastal Zone Management Act clearly establishes a new spatial planning process led by the individual states, which have considerable discretion about whether to develop or protect a specific area. In fact both goals—development and conservation—are reflected in the law. Operationally, this means state programs include energy facility siting, expanded access to the shore, port and marina expansion, urban water-front renewal, and other development activities. At the same time, the law encourages protection of wetlands and dunes and can be used to limit ac-tivities on barrier beaches and islands. Thirty-five coastal and Great Lakes states practice various forms of spatial management along their shores through the act.

Spatial management ideally requires allocations to be established not through a battle of single interests, but rather through consideration of widely shared common interests. To the extent that shared values focus on sustainable environmental outcomes, spatial or multiple use manage-ment may advance environmental quality, but there is no assurance that this will always be the case. As a result, many believe that ecosystem-based management will more effectively provide long-term sustainability.

Ecosystem-based management

Ecosystem-based management is spatial management that recognizes the importance of natural systems as a means of improving human liveli-hoods and communities. Practitioners of ecosystem-based management recognize that ocean and coastal resources should be comprehensively managed to reflect relationships among all components of the system— including people (box 11.1). Meeting human necessities equitably and within the constraints imposed by natural systems is a persistent theme. Unlike space identified by political boundaries, ecosystems span geo-graphic regions such as watersheds and the coastal waters they influence. Ecosystem-based management also addresses fragmentation of govern-ment programs by focusing on uses within a geographic area and thereby providing a rationale and means for coordinating across agencies and

Box 11.1. Ecosystem-based Management in Practice

Elements of ecosystem-based management have been practiced in watershed and bay management as well as in fisheries. These cases in coastal governance share similar characteristics.

Stakeholders: Stakeholder participation contributes because program success depends on knowledge that stakeholders possess and on behavioral change they will implement. Resource users on the land in watersheds or in federal waters offshore both understand their respective systems and, with the creation of commonly shared public purpose, are equipped to advance programs. Furthermore, the federal fisheries management councils and regional river, watershed, or bay commissions exist to empower stakeholders to convert their deliberations into new policy initiatives.

Links among natural and social systems: Coastal governance objectives require a planning process that incorporates land and sea, as well as social and ecological systems. In both cases an ecosystem focus results in consideration of structural integrity and natural functioning as a basis for policy design. Restoring fish stocks means harvest must be reduced at least in the short run, which harms livelihoods and communities, hence the need to recognize social impacts of meeting biological objectives. In watersheds, farmers, water suppliers, fishers, and others depend on a single watershed–coastal waters system; the impacts of individual users flow downstream like the water itself and connect one user of the system to others. These connections among parts of the environment and across social and natural systems are more readily accommodated in ecosystem-based management programs and lead to proactive consideration of the cumulative impacts of various actions.

Organizations: Because ecosystem boundaries do not match political boundaries, ecosystem-based management requires new organizations that either directly manage regions or that connect to government entities in ways that produce meaningful action in the ecologically defined region. Watershed authorities or commissions and fishery management councils can resolve the matching of ecosystems with political units. The power to create programs and cause them to be implemented extends across organizations and as a result faces multiple checks and balances.

Behavioral change: Historically coastal governance has relied on top-down regulatory means. However, watersheds and fisheries use that approach and increasingly many other tools or instruments, including systems in which authorities are mixed between government and nongovernment approaches or in which voluntary approaches dominate. Comanagement, market incentives, and other means are frequently discussed and readily incorporated in watershed and fishery management.

Evaluation: Policy innovations incorporated in ecosystem-based management programs develop from evaluations of sector-based or spatial activities. In fact major opportunities may reside here as ecosystem-based management becomes seen as a solution to failures in existing approaches. Shortfalls with respect to sustainability, control of governmental fragmentation, or ability to advance common interests in sector-based or spatial initiatives lead stakeholders to consider ecosystem-based solutions.

levels of government. Finally, because it includes social systems and hence the needs of people, ecosystem thinking provides a basis for bridging social and natural systems.

Ecosystem-based management is in its formative stages and currently lacks comprehensive legal authority. However, increasingly actions taken by coastal managers are consistent with ecosystem-based management. In other words, incremental change within existing legal authorities allows applications of ecosystem-based management principles.

In spite of its challenges, ecosystem-based management has the potential to be just as significant, if not farther reaching, as the broad changes in environmental law enacted in the 1970s. This much needed transformation of coastal management necessitates double-loop learning on the part of government and society as a whole. In double-loop learning, as an organization seeks to improve performance, managers are willing to modify norms and objectives (Argyris and Schon, 1978). Adopting ecosystem-based management of the coasts will require diverse government organizations to work together to advance the broader public good and avoid being trapped as promoters of the much narrower interests of individual sectors.

Although ecosystem-based management is bold in concept, it is not exclusive in approach. For the foreseeable future coastal and ocean management will rely on a mix of the sector, spatial, and ecosystem-based approaches.

Change

The coasts and the individuals that inhabit them are continually changing, as are policy ends and the means to reach them. As a result, managers need to learn new things constantly. Changes in scientific understanding, values, and policy instruments restructure coastal management frameworks on a regular basis. Participants who learn the natural and social science, as well as the technology associated with key management challenges, can contribute most effectively to resolving societal problems. At the same time, professional coastal managers need to learn about the changing values of society. Values determine the desired ends for public policies. Management requires selecting among alternatives for encouraging changes in human behavior that are consistent with the values of the society. Over time, new instruments have been introduced. These new means for policy implementation include markets and comanagement, amongst other tools that are replacing command and control regulation.

Continuing change forces professionals to not only understand current situations but also to anticipate future challenges. As we have discussed, changes occur in both means and ends. When packaged together the combinations result in new frameworks. Hence, management has evolved from sector-based to spatial and ultimately ecosystem-based. Some important advances have been made in fishery and in watershed management. However, ecosystem-based management is likely to benefit from additional fundamental changes and may make present organizational structures obsolete. New policy designs that embrace change and value innovation will grow in importance.

Sector-based, spatial, and ecosystem-based management frameworks encompass our current repertoire of approaches, but they are unlikely to be all that the future holds. Future relationships between society and nature will inevitably spawn new frameworks for the coast. Whether those new frameworks create healthier coasts will depend on our ability to understand natural and social systems, apply that knowledge in the policy process, and ultimately manage human behavior. Each of these abilities is rooted in a clear comprehension of the policy process and familiarity with the successes as well as weaknesses of current management approaches. With the ability to understand and manage change, future leaders will be empowered to participate in effective coastal governance, narrowing the gap between the coasts we have and the coasts we want.

Questions for Discussion

Chapter 1

1. Describe the natural environment in either a coastal area or land near a river or stream in your community. You can use scientific or layman's terms. Has the environment changed over time? How? Explain.
2. Which of the drivers for change in coastal regions do you consider most important? Why? Did drivers affect the area you described above? Explain.
3. What are the impacts of global change in coastal regions? From what you have learned so far, how do you anticipate global change might affect coastal policy?

Chapter 2

1. Which coastal issues (table 2.2) have affected you recently, even if you live far from the coast? (Hints: Do rivers from your area drain to the sea? How do goods such as electronic devices get from where they are manufactured to you?)
2. Select a recent coastal or ocean article from the Web or your local newspaper. What stage or stages of the policy process (figure 2.1) apply to it? Why?
3. What policy instruments or tools (table 2.1) are being used or should be used to address the coastal problem you selected in the previous question? Explain the strengths and weaknesses of the policy instruments in terms of how effective you might expect them to be in resolving the issue.

Chapter 3

1. Explain the connection between wastewater and human health.
2. Identify and describe the contents of the primary law for controlling coastal water quality.
3. What are discharge permits? How are they used to protect coastal waters?

4. How does a sewage treatment plant work? What comes in? What goes out? What treatment technologies are used?

5. Characterize the primary changes in scientific understanding of the effects of wastewater, both untreated and treated, on coastal waters. From what you have seen in this chapter, how do scientific advances affect policies related to public health? Explain.

Chapter 4

1. How is oil formed? From what regions of the country does most U.S. offshore oil production come?

2. How much liquid petroleum has the United States produced in recent years? How many barrels of offshore oil have been produced in the United States in recent years? Is offshore oil an important part of U.S. energy supply? Explain.

3. What is a congressional moratorium? A presidential withdrawal? What areas of the United States have been subject to these measures? Why?

4. Describe primary environmental impacts from exploration, development, production, and refining of oil. How does offshore oil governance in the United States accommodate for the fact that oil production in federal waters has direct and indirect impacts on state lands and waters?

5. Name two issues that arose in the seaweed rebellion. In your opinion, have governmental arrangements evolved to equitably address each issue you have identified? Explain.

Chapter 5

1. Why do seaports in the United States seek ever deeper channels?

2. What environmental issues arise due to dredging? Due to dredged material disposal?

3. Which government agencies and laws are involved in dredging? How?

4. How is the disposal of contaminated sediments regulated?

5. Using your knowledge of interest group values and dredging laws, explain how gridlock might occur in this setting.

6. Define sector-based management.

7. Compare and contrast management for sewage and for dredging. In what circumstances does sector-based management work well? Poorly? Why? On the basis of these two issues, do you support or

oppose the use of single-purpose, sector-based management? Explain the position you take.

Chapter 6

1. What is the value of coastal wetlands? What human activities affect wetlands?
2. How has the government structured federal law to protect wetlands? Name the section of the law and the actions taken under it.
3. Define each of the following with respect to wetlands: restoration, mitigation, compensation, and no net loss.
4. What is a wetland bank and how does it work? Is wetland banking a legitimate environmental technique? Explain pro or con.
5. Review the chapter and identify causes for intertidal wetland loss. Select an important cause and explain what action should be taken to limit it.

Chapter 7

1. Define exclusive, compatible or multiple, and displaceable uses of coastal areas.
2. If two or more uses vie for a location where they will directly or indirectly conflict, how is the matter resolved under sector-based management? Under spatial management?
3. What are the goals of the U.S. Coastal Zone Management Act? How are state programs created to meet the national goals? At the state level what actions do government officials take? How?
4. What is consistency?
5. Name and explain three important tools or techniques that are used in zoning. Select one that can reduce human risk from coastal hazards. How does the risk reduction technique work?
6. Define sprawl. What drives it? Has coastal management in the United States reduced sprawl? Why or why not?

Chapter 8

1. What causes low oxygen conditions in the Gulf of Mexico? Explain natural processes and human activities related to the problem.
2. What change(s) in public policy could be used to reduce the size of the dead zone in the Gulf of Mexico? What tool or tools would be used to implement the policy?
3. From what you have learned so far, define and give examples of

196 QUESTIONS FOR DISCUSSION

targets and agents in an ecosystem-based management program for coastal waters.

4. Use examples to illustrate the similarities and differences between incremental and fundamental change to advance ecosystem-based management. Which approach is likely to be most successful? Why?

5. What are ecosystem services? Select one. What type of service is it? How does it relate to social systems? To natural systems?

6. Define an ecosystem service district. If you were to create an ecosystem service district to control nitrogen, what three factors would be most useful to include in your design? Explain each and how it would contribute.

Chapter 9

1. How are watersheds defined? Some are concerned that most watershed boundaries do not coincide with political boundaries. Define a political boundary. Why should one care if these boundaries are different?

2. The concept of managing watersheds as single units has fallen in and out of fashion. What is responsible for these changes? Where does this issue stand today?

3. Name two federal agencies that are involved in river or watershed management. For each agency explain the nature of its responsibilities and how they are implemented.

4. What are the primary water quality goals for Chesapeake Bay? Who participated in establishing the policy goals for the bay? Through which organizations? Over what time period?

5. What is the status of the Chesapeake Bay today? What might be done to improve it? Explain how two sections of federal law have been used in this context.

6. Select an ecosystem-based management principle and explain how it could be used in watershed and coastal management.

Chapter 10

1. What factors enabled an expansion of U.S. fishery harvest over time? What factors have limited fishery harvest since the mid-1990s?

2. What is the role of fisheries management councils in the U.S. fisheries? Who chartered them and how? Who participates in making decisions at the councils? What is in a fisheries management plan?

3. Contrast traditional fisheries management with ecosystem-based

fishery management. What are the new elements that the latter concept introduces?

4. Explain processes for and examples of incremental change in fisheries management. Do the same for fundamental change in fisheries management.

5. Should U.S. fisheries be privatized? Would that make them more sustainable? Explain.

Chapter 11

1. Briefly define sector-based, spatial, and ecosystem-based management. Which is the most difficult to implement? Why?

2. Assume you are a strong proponent of sector-based management. How would you revise the processes used in reaching decisions for sprawl or for coastal water quality related to land use?

3. To what extent are multiple use management and spatial management one and the same? Different? Explain.

4. Compare and contrast spatial management and ecosystem-based management.

5. At what stage of the policy process would you expect to see the greatest change if ecosystem-based management were adopted for fisheries? For watersheds and coasts?

References

Adler, R. 1995. Addressing barriers to watershed protection. *Environmental Law* 25:973–1106.

Adler, R. W., J. C. Landman, and D. M. Cameron. 1993. *The Clean Water Act 20 Years Later.* Washington, D.C.: Island Press.

Anderson, J. 1979. *Public Policy Making.* New York: Holt, Rinehart and Winston.

Anderson, S. 1999. Watershed management and nonpoint source pollution: The Massachusetts approach. *Boston College Environmental Affairs Law Review* 26:339–386.

Argyris, C., and D. Schön. 1978. *Organizational Learning: A Theory of Action Perspective.* Reading, MA: Addison-Wesley Publishing Company.

Arkema, K. K., S. C. Abramson, and B. M. Dewsbury. 2006. Marine ecosystem-based management: From characterization to implementation. *Frontiers in Ecology and the Environment* 4(10):525–532.

Arnstein, S. 1969. A ladder of citizen participation. *Journal of the American Planning Association* 35:216–224.

Babcock, E. A., and E. K. Pikitch. 2004. Can we reach agreement on a standardized approach to ecosystem-based fishery management? *Bulletin of Marine Science* 74:685–692.

Bagley, P. R. 2003. Don't forget about the fishermen: In the battle over fisheries conservation and management, a conservation ethic has trumped economic concerns of the community—or has it? *Suffolk University Law Review* 36:765–786.

Bagstad, K. J., K. Stapleton, and J. R. D'Agostino. 2007. Taxes, subsidies, and insurance as drivers of United States coastal development. *Ecological Economics* 63:285–298.

Baldwin, M. 1970. The Santa Barbara oil spill. In M. Baldwin and J. Page, eds., *Law and the Environment.* New York: Walker and Company.

Baldwin, P., and M. Baldwin. 1975. *Onshore Planning for Offshore Oil: Lessons from Scotland.* Washington, D.C.: The Conservation Foundation.

Bardach, E. 1977. *The Implementation Game: What Happens After a Bill Becomes a Law.* Cambridge, MA: The MIT Press.

Bardach, E. 2009. *A Practical Guide for Policy Analysis: The Eightfold Path to More Effective Problem Solving.* Washington, D.C.: CQ Press.

Barras, J., S. Beville, D. Britsch, S. Hartley, S. Hawes, J. Johnston, P. Kemp, Q. Kinler, A. Martucci, J. Porthouse, D. Reed, K. Roy, S. Sapkota, and J. Suhayda. 2004. Historical and projected coastal Louisiana land changes: 1978–2050. Washington, D.C.: United States Geological Survey, USGS Open File Report 03-334.

Barrow, C. 1998. River basin development planning and management: A critical review. *World Development* 26(1):171–186.

Beatley, T., D. J. Brower, and A. K. Schwab. 2002. *An Introduction to Coastal Zone Management,* 2nd ed. Washington, D.C.: Island Press.

Beebe, B. 1961. Drilling the exploratory well. In G. Moody, ed., *Petroleum Exploration Handbook*. New York: McGraw-Hill Book Company.

Berkes, F. 1994. Co-management: Bridging the two solitudes. *Northern Perspectives* 22(2–3):18–20.

Birkland, T. 1997. *After Disaster: Agenda Setting, Public Policy and Focusing Events*. Washington, D.C.: Georgetown University Press.

Birkland, T. 2005. *An Introduction to the Policy Process: Theories, Concepts, and Models of Public Policy Making*. Armonk, NY: M. E. Sharpe.

Bloomberg, M. R., and E. Lloyd. 2007. *New York City's Wastewater Treatment System*. New York: New York City Department of Environmental Protection.

Blume, A. 2002. A proposal for funding port dredging to improve the efficiency of the nation's marine transportation system. *Journal of Maritime Law and Commerce* 33:37–89.

Boesch, D., and E. Goldman. 2009. Chesapeake Bay, USA. In K. McLeod and H. Leslie, eds., *Ecosystem-Based Management for the Oceans*. Washington, D.C.: Island Press, 268–293.

Born, S., and A. Miller. 1988. Assessing networked coastal zone management programs. *Coastal Management* 16:229–243.

Brauman, K., G. Daily, T. Duarte, and H. Mooney. 2007. The nature and value of ecosystem services: An overview highlighting hydrologic services. *Annual Review of Environment and Resources* 32:67–98.

Brax, J. 2002. Zoning the oceans: Using the National Marine Sanctuaries Act and the Antiquities Act to establish marine protection areas and marine reserves in America. *Ecology Law Quarterly* 29:71–129.

Brewer, G., and P. deLeon. 1983. *The Foundations of Policy Analysis*. Homewood, IL: The Dorsey Press.

Brookfield, K., T. Gray, and J. Hatchard. 2005. The concept of fisheries-dependent communities. A comparative analysis of four UK case studies: Shetland, Peterhead, North Shields and Lowestoft. *Fisheries Research* 72:55–69.

Brown, K., E. Tompkins, and W. Adger. 2002. *Making Waves: Integrating Coastal Conservation and Development*. London: Earthscan.

Brunner, R., and T. Clark. 1997. A practice-based approach to ecosystem management. *Conservation Biology* 11(1):48–58.

Burroughs, R. 1981. OCS oil and gas: Relationships between resource management and environmental research. *Coastal Zone Management Journal* 9:77–88.

Burroughs, R. 1986. Seafloor area within reach of petroleum technology. *Ocean Management* 10:125–135.

Burroughs, R. 1988. Ocean dumping: Information and policy development in the USA. *Marine Policy* 12:96–104.

Burroughs, R. 1999. When stakeholders choose: Process, knowledge, and motivation in water quality decisions. *Society and Natural Resources* 12(8):797–809.

Burroughs, R. 2003. Goal and trend assessment to define coastal ecosystem management initiatives. *Local Environment* 8:277–329.

Burroughs, R. 2005. Institutional change in the Port of New York. *Maritime Policy and Management* 32(3):315–328.

Burroughs, R., and T. Clark. 1995. Ecosystem management: A comparison of Greater Yellowstone and Georges Bank. *Environmental Management* 19:649–663.

Busch, C. B., D. L. Kirp, and D. F. Schoenholz. 1998. Taming adversarial legalism: The Port of Oakland's dredging saga revisited. *New York University School of Law Journal of Legislation and Public Policy* 2:179–216.

Capper, J., G. Power, and F. Shivers. 1983. *Chesapeake Waters: Pollution, Public Health, and Public Opinion, 1607–1972*. Centreville, MD: Tidewater Publishers.

Carter, R. W. G. 1988. *Coastal Environments: An Introduction to the Physical, Ecological, and Cultural Systems of Coastlines*. New York: Academic Press.

Chandler, W., and H. Gillelan. 2004. The history and evolution of the National Marine Sanctuaries Act. *Environmental Law Reporter* 34:10505–10565.

Chertow, M. 2001. The IPAT equation and its variants. *Journal of Industrial Ecology* 4:13–29.

Chesapeake Bay Agreement. 1987. www.cheaspeakebay.net.

Christie, P., R. Pollnac, D. Fluharty, M. Hixon, G. K. Lowry, R. Mahon, D. Pietri, B. Tissot, A. White, N. Armada, and R.-L. Eisma-Osorio. 2009. Tropical marine EBM feasibility: A synthesis of case studies and comparative analyses. *Coastal Management* 37:374–385.

Cicin-Sain, B., and R. Knecht. *The Future of U.S. Ocean Policy*. Washington, D.C.: Island Press.

Clark, R. 2001. *Marine Pollution*. Oxford, UK: Oxford University Press.

Clark, T. 2002. *The Policy Process: A Practical Guide for Natural Resource Professionals*. New Haven, CT: Yale University Press.

Cohen, M., J. Marsh, and J. Olsen. 1972. A garbage can model of organizational choice. *Administrative Science Quarterly* 17:1–25.

Cook, E. 1976. *Man, Energy, Society*. San Francisco: W.H. Freeman and Company.

Cortner, H., and M. Moote. 1999. A paradigm shift? In *The Politics of Ecosystem Management*. Washington, D.C.: Island Press, 37–55.

Costanza, R., and J. Greer. 1995. The Chesapeake Bay and its watershed: A model for sustainable ecosystem management? In L. Gunderson, C. Holling, and S. Light, eds., *Barriers and Bridges to the Renewal of Ecosystems and Institutions*. New York: Columbia University Press, 169–213.

Costanza, R., F. Andrade, P. Antunes, M. Belt, D. Boersma, D. Boesch, F. Catarino, S. Hanna, K. Limburg, B. Low, M. Molitor, J. Pereira, S. Rayner, R. Santos, J. Wilson, and M. Young. 1998. Principles for sustainable governance of the oceans. *Science* 281(5374):198–199.

Costanza, R., O. Perez-Maqueo, M. Martinez, P. Sutton, S. Anderson, and K. Mulder. 2008. The value of coastal wetlands for hurricane protection. *Ambio* 37(4):241–248.

Cotgreave, P., and I. Forseth. 2002. *Introductory Ecology*. Oxford, UK: Blackwell Science Ltd.

Council on Environmental Quality. 1970. *Ocean Dumping: A National Policy*. Washington, D.C.: U.S. Government Printing Office.

Council on Environmental Quality. 1974. OCS Oil and Gas: An Environmental Assessment. Washington, D.C.: U.S. Government Printing Office.

Cowen, R. 1960. *Frontiers of the Sea: The Story of Oceanographic Exploration*. New York: Bantam Books.

Crawford, T. 2007. Where does the coast sprawl the most? Trajectories of residential development and sprawl in coastal North Carolina, 1971–2000. *Landscape and Urban Planning* 83:294–307.

Crossett, K., T. Culliton, P. Wiley, and T. Goodspeed. 2004. *Population Trends along the Coastal United States, 1980–2008*. Washington, D.C.: National Oceanic and Atmospheric Administration.

Crossland, C., H. Kremer, H. Lindeboom, J. Crossland, and M. Le Tissier, eds. 2005. *Coastal Fluxes in the Anthropocene*. Berlin: Springer-Verlag.

Crowder, L., G. Osherenko, O. Young, S. Airame, E. Norse, N. Baron, J. Day, F. Douvere, C. Ehler, B. Halpern, S. Langdon, K. McLeod, J. Ogden, R. Peach, A. Rosenberg, and J. Wilson. 2006. Resolving mismatches in U.S. ocean governance. *Science* 313:617–618.

Culliton, T. J., J. McDonough, D. Remer, and D. Lott. 1992. *Building America's Coasts: 20 Years of Building Permits, 1970–1989*. Rockville, MD: National Oceanic and Atmospheric Administration.

Dahl, T. 2006. *Status and Trends of Wetlands in the Conterminous United States 1998 to 2004*. Washington, D.C.: U.S. Fish and Wildlife Service.

Daily, G. 1997. Introduction: What are ecosystem services? In G. C. Daily, ed., *Nature's Services: Societal Dependence on Natural Ecosystems*. Washington, D.C.: Island Press, 1–10.

Daily, G., and P. Matson. 2008. Ecosystem services: From theory to implementation. *Proceedings of the National Academy of Sciences* 105(28):9455–9456.

Dalton, T., R. Thompson, and D. Jin. 2010. Mapping human dimensions in marine spatial planning and management: An example from Narragansett Bay, Rhode Island. *Marine Policy* 34:309–319.

Davies, J., and J. Mazurek. 1998. *Pollution Control in the United States: Evaluating the System*. Washington, D.C.: Resources for the Future.

Davis, B. 2001. Judicial interpretations of federal consistency under the Coastal Zone Management Act. *Coastal Management* 29:341–352.

Davis, B. 2004. Regional planning in the U.S. coastal zone: A comparative analysis of 15 special area plans. *Ocean and Coastal Management* 47:79–94.

Day, Jr., J. W., C. A. S. Hall, W. M. Kemp, and A. Yanez-Arancibia. 1989. *Estuarine Ecology*. New York: John Wiley & Sons.

Day, Jr., J., D. Boesch, E. Clairain, G. Kemp, S. Laska, W. Mitsch, K. Orth, H. Mashriqui, D. Reed, L. Shabman, C. Simenstad, B. Streever, R. Twilley, C. Watson, J. Wells, and D. Whigham. 2007. Restoration of the Mississippi Delta: Lessons from hurricanes Katrina and Rita. *Science* 315:1679–1684.

Dayton, P., M. Tegner, P. Edwards, and K. Riser. 1998. Sliding baselines, ghosts, and reduced expectations in kelp forest communities. *Ecological Applications* 8:309–322.

Deffeyes, K. 2005. *Beyond Oil: A View from Hubbert's Peak*. New York: Hill and Wang.

Department of Defense and U.S. Environmental Protection Agency. 2008. Compensatory mitigation for losses of aquatic resources. *Federal Register* 73(70):19594–19705.

Done, T. J., and R. E. Reichelt. 1998. Integrated coastal zone and fisheries ecosystem management: Generic goals and performance indices. *Ecological Applications* S110-S118.

Douvere, F. 2008. The importance of marine spatial planning in advancing ecosystem-based sea use management. *Marine Policy* 32:762–771.

Douvere, F., and C. Ehler. 2009. New perspectives on sea use management: Initial findings from European experience with marine spatial planning. *Journal of Environmental Management* 90:77–88.

Eagle, J., and B. Thompson. 2003. Answering Lord Perry's question: Dissecting regulatory overfishing. *Ocean and Coastal Management* 46:649–679.

Eagle, J., S. Newkirk, and B. Thompson. 2003. Taking Stock of the Regional Fisheries Management Councils. Washington, D.C.: Island Press.

Ecosystem Principles Advisory Panel. 1999. Ecosystem-based fishery management: A report to the Congress by the Ecosystem Principles Advisory Panel. Silver Spring, MD: National Marine Fisheries Service.

Ehler, C. 2008. Conclusions: Benefits, lessons learned, and future challenges of marine spatial planning. *Marine Policy* 32:840–843.

Ehrlich, P., and A. Ehrlich. 1990. *The Population Explosion*. New York: Simon and Schuster.

Energy Information Administration. 2009. Annual Energy Review 2008. Washington, D.C.: Energy Information Administration.

Environmental Law Institute. 2006. The Status and Character of In-lieu Fee Mitigation in the United States. Washington, D.C.: Environmental Law Institute, 1–11.

Environmental Protection Agency. 1991. Evaluation of Dredged Material Proposed for Ocean Disposal—Testing Manual. Washington, D.C.: EPA, EPA-503/B-91/001.

Environmental Protection Agency. 1998. EPA's Contaminated Sediment Management Strategy. Washington, D.C.: EPA, EPA-823-R-98-001.

Environmental Protection Agency. 1999a. Chlorine Disinfection. Washington, D.C.: EPA, EPA 832-F-99-062.

Environmental Protection Agency. 1999b. Ozone Disinfection. Washington, D.C.: EPA, EPA 832-F-99-063.

Environmental Protection Agency. 1999c. Ultraviolet Disinfection. Washington, D.C.:EPA, EPA 832-F-99-064.

Environmental Protection Agency. 1999d. Biosolids Generation, Use, and Disposal in the United States. Washington, D.C.: EPA, EPA 530-R-99-09.

Environmental Protection Agency. 2004. Primer for Municipal Wastewater Treatment Systems. Washington, D.C.: EPA, EPA 832-R-04-001.

Environmental Protection Agency. 2006. Saving the Chesapeake Bay Watershed Requires Better Coordination of Environmental and Agricultural Resources. Washington, D.C.: EPA, EPA OIG Report No. 2007-P-00004.

Environmental Protection Agency. 2007. Development growth outpacing progress in watershed efforts to restore Chesapeake Bay. Washington, D.C.: EPA, EPA OIG Report No. 2007-P-00031.

Environmental Protection Agency. 2008a. National Coastal Condition Report III. Washington, D.C.: EPA, EPA 842-R-08-002.

Environmental Protection Agency. 2008b. EPA's BEACH Report: 2007 Swimming Season. Washington, D.C.: EPA, EPA 823-F-08-006.

Environmental Protection Agency and the Army Corps of Engineers. 1998. Evaluation of Dredged Material Proposed for Discharge in Waters of the U.S.—Testing Manual (Inland Testing Manual). Washington, D.C.: EPA and Corps of Engineers, EPA-823-B-98-004.

Ernst, H. 2003. *Chesapeake Bay Blues: Science, Politics, and the Struggle to Save the Bay*. Lanham, MD: Rowman & Littlefield Publishers, Inc.

Ewel, K. C. 1997. Water quality improvements by wetlands. In G. C. Daily, ed., *Nature's*

Services: Societal Dependence on Natural Ecosystems. Washington, D.C.: Island Press, 329–344.

Farber, S., R. Costanza, D. Childers, J. Erickson, K. Gross, M. Grove, C. Hopkinson, J. Kahan, S. Pincetl, A. Troy, P. Warren, and M. Wilson. 2006. Linking ecology and economics for ecosystem management. *BioScience* 56(2):121–133.

Federal Energy Administration. 1974. Project Independence Report. Washington, D.C.: US Government Printing Office.

Federal Water Pollution Control Act Amendments of 1972. 33 United States Code 1251 et seq.

Ferejohn, J. A. 1974. *Pork Barrel Politics: Rivers and Harbors Legislation, 1947–1968.* Stanford, CA: Stanford University Press.

Field, J. C., and R. C. Francis. 2006. Considering ecosystem-based fisheries management in the California current. *Marine Policy* 30:552–569.

Fishery Conservation and Management Act. 16 United States Code 1801 et seq.

Fitzgerald, E. 2001. *The Seaweed Rebellion: Federal-State Conflicts over Offshore Energy Development.* Lanham, MD: Lexington Books.

Flow Rate Technical Group, National Incident Command. 2010. U.S. Scientific Teams Refine Estimates of Oil Flow from BP's Well Prior to Capping. Deepwater Horizon Incident Joint Information Center. August 2. http://www.deepwater horizonresponse.com/go/doc/2931/840475/. Accessed Aug. 3, 2010.

Fluharty, D. 2005. Evolving ecosystem approaches to management of fisheries in the USA. *Marine Ecology Progress Series* 300:241–296.

Food and Agriculture Organization. 2003. The ecosystem approach to fisheries. FAO Technical Guidelines for Responsible Fisheries No. 4, Supplement 2. Rome: FAO.

Food and Agriculture Organization of the United Nations. 2005. Review of the State of World Marine Fishery Resources. FAO Fisheries Technical Paper 457. Rome: FAO.

Francis, R., M. Hixon, M. Clarke, S. Murawski, and S. Ralston. 2007. Ten commandments for ecosystem-based fisheries scientists. *Fisheries* 32(5):217–228.

Freeman, A. 1990. Water pollution policy. In P. R. Portney, ed., *Public Policies for Environmental Protection.* Washington, D.C.: Resources for the Future, 97–149.

Freudenburg, W., and R. Gramling. 1994. *Oil in Troubled Waters: Perceptions, Politics, and the Battle over Offshore Drilling.* Albany: State University of New York Press.

Garcia, S. M., and K. L. Cochrane. 2005. Ecosystem approach to fisheries: A review of implementation guidelines. *ICES Journal of Marine Science* 62:311–318.

Gedan, K., B. Silliman, and M. Bertness. 2009. Centuries of human-driven change in salt marsh ecosystems. *Annual Review of Marine Science* 1:117–141.

Ginter, J. 1995. The Alaska community development quota fisheries management program. *Ocean and Coastal Management* 28:147–163.

Goins, W., and R. Sheffield. 1983. *Blowout Prevention.* Houston, TX: Gulf Publishing Company.

Goldfarb, W. 1994. Watershed management: Slogan or solution? *Boston College Environmental Affairs Law Review* 21(3):483–510.

Goldman, J. 1997. *Building New York's Sewers: Developing Mechanisms of Urban Management.* West Lafayette, IN: Purdue University Press.

Goldsmith, R. 2005. Deepwater wells: High production, high risk. *Offshore* 65(3) March 1, 2005.

Good, J., J. Weber, and J. Charland. 1999. Protecting estuaries and coastal wetlands through state coastal zone management programs. *Coastal Management* 27:139–186.

Government Accountability Office. 2008a. Coastal Zone Management: Measuring Program's Effectiveness Continues to be a Challenge. Washington, D.C.: GAO, GAO-08-1045.

Government Accountability Office. 2008b. Chesapeake Bay program: Recent actions are positive steps toward more effectively guiding the restoration effort. Washington, D.C.: GAO-08-1033T.

Graff, W. 1981. *Introduction to Offshore Structures*. Houston, TX: Gulf Publishing.

Gramling, R., and W. Freudenburg. 2006. Attitudes toward offshore oil development: A summary of current evidence. *Ocean & Coastal Management* 49:442–461.

Gregersen, H., P. Ffolliot, and K. Brooks. 2007. *Integrated Watershed Management: Connecting People to Their Land and Water*. Oxfordshire, UK: CAB International.

Grigalunas, T., J. Opaluch, J. Diamantides, and M. Mazzotta. 1998. Liability for oil spill damages: Issues, methods, and examples. *Coastal Management* 26:61–77.

Hassett, B., M. Palmer, E. Bernhardt, S. Smith, J. Carr, and D. Hart. 2005. Restoring watersheds project by project: Trends in Chesapeake Bay tributary restoration. *Frontiers in Ecology and the Environment* 3(5):259–267.

Hatry, H., R. Winnie, and D. Fisk. 1981. *Practical Program Evaluation for State and Local Governments*. Washington, D.C.: The Urban Institute Press.

Heal, G., G. Daily, P. Ehrlich, J. Salzman, C. Boggs, J. Hellmann, J. Hughes, C. Kremen, and T. Ricketts. 2001. Protecting natural capital through ecosystem service districts. *Stanford Environmental Law Journal* 20:333–364.

Healy, M. 1997. Still dirty after twenty-five years: Water quality standard enforcement and the availability of citizen suits. *Ecology Law Quarterly* 24:271–273.

Hennessey, T. 1994. Governance and adaptive management for estuarine ecosystems: The case of Chesapeake Bay. *Coastal Management* 22:119–145.

Hershman, M., J. Good, T. Bernd-Cohen, R. Goodwin, V. Lee, and P. Pogue. 1999. The effectiveness of coastal zone management in the United States. *Coastal Management* 27:113–138.

Hilborn, R. 2007. Moving to sustainability by learning from successful fisheries. *Ambio* 36:296–303.

Holdway, D. 2002. The acute and chronic effects of wastes associated with offshore oil and gas production on temperate and tropical marine ecological processes. *Marine Pollution Bulletin* 44:185–203.

Holling, C. S., ed. 1978. *Adaptive Environmental Assessment and Management*. New York: John Wiley.

Houck, O. 2002. *The Clean Water Act TMDL Program: Law, Policy, and Implementation*. Washington, D.C.: Environmental Law Institute.

Howlett, M., and M. Ramesh. 1995. *Studying Public Policy: Policy Cycles and Policy Subsystems*. Oxford: Oxford University Press.

Hubbert, Marion K. "Nuclear Energy and the Fossil Fuels," in *Drilling and Production Practice*, American Petroleum Institute Proceedings of Spring Meeting, San Antonio (1956).

Hughey, K., R. Cullen, and G. Kerr. 2000. Stakeholder groups in fisheries management. *Marine Policy* 24:119–127.

Intergovernmental Panel on Climate Change (IPCC). 2007a. Summary for Policymakers. In *Climate Change 2007: The Physical Science Basis. Contribution of Working Group I to the Fourth Assessment Report of the Intergovernmental Panel on Climate Change*. S. Solomon, D. Qin, M. Manning, Z. Chen, M. Marquis, K. Averyt, M. Tignor, and H. Miller, eds. Cambridge, UK: Cambridge University Press.

IPCC. 2007b. *Climate Change 2007: The Physical Science Basis. Contribution of Working Group I to the Fourth Assessment Report of the Intergovernmental Panel on Climate Change*. S. Solomon, D. Qin, M. Manning, Z. Chen, M. Marquis, K. Averyt, M. Tignor, and H. Miller, eds. Cambridge, UK: Cambridge University Press.

IPCC. 2007c. Summary for Policymakers. In *Climate Change 2007: Impacts, Adaptation, and Vulnerability. Working Group II Contribution to the Intergovernmental Panel on Climate Change Fourth Assessment Report*. M. Parry, O. Canziani, J. Palutikof, P. van der Linden, and C. Hansen, eds. Cambridge, UK: Cambridge University Press.

Jackson, J., M. Kirby, W. Berger, K. Bjorndal, L. Botsford, B. Bourque, R. Bradbury, R. Cooke, J. Erlandson, J. Estes, T. Hughes, S. Kidwell, C. Lange, H. Lenihan, J. Pandolfi, C. Peterson, R. Steneck, M. Tegner, and R. Warner. 2001. Historical overfishing and the recent collapse of coastal ecosystems. *Science* 293:629–638.

Jentoft, S. 2004. Institutions in fisheries: What they are, what they do, and how they change. *Marine Policy* 28:137–149.

Jentoft, S. 2007. Limits of governability: Institutional implications for fisheries and coastal governance. *Marine Policy* 31:360–370.

Jentoft, S., and B. McCay. 1995. User participation in fisheries management: Lessons drawn from international experiences. *Marine Policy* 19:227–246.

Johnson, K. 1999. The mythical giant: Clean Water Act Section 401 and nonpoint source pollution. *Environmental Law* 29:417–461.

Jones, C. O. 1984. *An Introduction to the Study of Public Policy*. Monterey, CA: Brooks/Cole.

Juda, L. 1993. Ocean policy, multi-use management, and the cumulative impact of piecemeal change: The case of the United States outer continental shelf. *Ocean Development and International Law* 24:355–376.

Juda, L. 1999. Considerations in developing a functional approach to the governance of large marine ecosystems. *Ocean Development and International Law* 30:89–125.

Juda, L., and R. Burroughs. 2004. Dredging navigational channels in a changing scientific and regulatory environment. *Journal of Maritime Law and Commerce* 35(2):171–218.

Juda, L., and T. Hennessey. 2001. Governance profiles and the management of the uses of large marine ecosystems. *Ocean Development and International Law* 32:43–69.

Kagan, R. A. 1991. The dredging dilemma: Economic development and environmental protection in Oakland Harbor. *Coastal Management* 19:313–341.

Kagan, R. A. 2001. *Adversarial Legalism: The American Way of Law*. Cambridge, MA: Harvard University Press.

Kash, D., I. White, K. Bergey, M. Chartock, M. Devine, R. Leonard, S. Salomon, and H. Young. 1973. *Energy Under the Oceans: A Technology Assessment of Outer Continental Shelf Oil and Gas Operations*. Norman, OK: University of Oklahoma Press.

Kay, R., and J. Alder. 2005. *Coastal Planning and Management*. London: Taylor & Francis Group.

Kennish, M. 1991. *Ecology of Estuaries: Anthropogenic Effects*. Boca Raton, FL: CRC Press, 357–397.

Kennish, M. 1997. Dredging and dredged-spoil disposal. In M. Kennish, ed., *Practical Handbook of Estuarine and Marine Pollution*. Boca Raton, FL: CRC Press, 447–477.

Ketchum, B., ed. 1972. *The Water's Edge: Critical Problems of the Coastal Zone*. Cambridge, MA: The MIT Press.

Knecht, R., B. Cicin-Sain, and G. W. Fisk. 1996. Perceptions on the performance of state coastal zone management programs in the United States. *Coastal Management* 24:141–164.

Ko, J., and J. Day. 2004. A review of ecological impacts of oil and gas development on coastal ecosystems in the Mississippi Delta. *Ocean & Coastal Management* 47:597–623.

Kurlansky, M. 2006. *The Big Oyster: History on the Half Shell*. New York: Random House, Inc.

Kusler, J., and M. Kentula, eds. 1990. *Wetland Creation and Restoration: The Status of the Science*. Washington, D.C.: Island Press.

Labaree, B. W., W. M. Fowler, E. W. Sloan, J. B. Hattendorf, J. J. Safford, and A. W. German. 1998. *America and the Sea: A Maritime History*. Mystic, CT: Mystic Seaport Museum, Inc.

LaBelle, R. 2001. Overview of U.S. Minerals Management Service activities in deepwater research. *Marine Pollution Bulletin* 43:256–261.

Lant, C., J. Ruhl, and S. Kraft. 2008. The tragedy of ecosystem services. *Bioscience* 58(10):969–974.

Lasswell, H. 1971. *A Pre-View of Policy Sciences*. New York: American Elsevier.

Laws, E. A. 2000. *Aquatic Pollution: An Introductory Text*, 3rd ed. New York: John Wiley & Sons, Inc.

Layzer, J. 2008. *Natural Experiments: Ecosystem-based Management and the Environment*. Cambridge, MA: The MIT Press.

Lee, K. 1999. Appraising adaptive management. *Ecology and Society* 3(2): article 3 www.consecol.org/vol3/iss2/art3/.

Lemos, M., and A. Agrawal. 2006. Environmental governance. *Annual Review of Environment and Resources* 31:297–325.

Leschine, T., B. Ferriss, K. Bell, K. Bartz, S. MacWilliams, M. Pico, and A. Bennett. 2003. Challenges and strategies for better use of scientific information in the management of coastal estuaries. *Estuaries* 26(4B):1189–1204.

Levin, S., and J. Lubchenco. 2008. Resilience, robustness, and marine ecosystem-based management. *Bioscience* 58(1):27–32.

Lewis, Jr., W. 2001. *Wetlands Explained: Wetland Science, Policy, and Politics in America*. New York: Oxford University Press.

Lindblom, C. 1959. The science of "muddling through." *Public Administration Review* 19(2):79–88.

Link, J. S. 2002a. Ecological considerations in fisheries management: When does it matter? *Fisheries* 27(4):10–17.

Link, J. S. 2002b. What does ecosystem-based fisheries management mean? *Fisheries* 27(4):18–21.

Long, E. 2000. Degraded sediment quality in U.S. estuaries: A review of magnitude and ecological implications. *Ecological Applications* 10:338–349.

Long, E., and P. Chapman. 1985. A sediment quality triad: Measures of sediment contamination, toxicity, and infaunal community composition in Puget Sound. *Marine Pollution Bulletin* 16:405–415.

Lubchenco, J., S. Palumbi, S. Gaines, and S. Andelman. 2003. Plugging a hole in the ocean: The emerging science of marine reserves. *Ecological Applications* 13(1) Supplement:S3-S7.

Lubell, M. 2005. Do watershed partnerships enhance beliefs conducive to collective action? In P. Sabatier, W. Focht, M. Lubell, Z. Trachtenberg, A. Vedlitz, and M. Matlock, eds., *Swimming Upstream: Collaborative Approaches to Watershed Management.* Cambridge, MA: The MIT Press, 201–232.

Mace, P. M. 2001. A new role for MSY. *Fish and Fisheries* 2:2–32.

Macinko, S., and D. Bromley. 2002. *Who Owns America's Fisheries?* Philadelphia: The Pew Charitable Trusts.

Mangel, M., and P. S. Levin. 2005. Regime, phase and paradigm shifts: Making community ecology the basic science for fisheries. *Philosophical Transactions of the Royal Society* 360:95–105.

Marasco, R. J., D. Goodman, C. B. Grimes, P. W. Lawson, A. E. Punt, and T. J. Quinn II. 2007. Ecosystem-based fisheries management: Some practical suggestions. *Canadian Journal of Fisheries and Aquatic Sciences* 64:928–939.

March, J., and H. Simon. 1958. *Organizations.* New York: John Wiley & Sons.

Marine Protection Research and Sanctuaries Act of 1972. 33 USC 1401 et seq.

Mayo, R., and L. O'Brien. 2006. Status of Fishery Resources off the Northeastern US—Atlantic Cod. Woods Hole, MA: Northeast Fisheries Science Center (NEFSC), NEFSC Reference Document 06-02.

Mazmanian, D., and P. Sabatier. 1989. *Implementation and Public Policy with a New Postscript.* Lanham, MD: University Press of America.

McCauley, D. 2006. Selling out on nature. *Nature* 443(7):27–28.

McLeod, K., and H. Leslie, eds. 2009. *Ecosystem-based Management for the Oceans.* Washington, D.C.: Island Press.

McLeod, K., and H. Leslie. 2009. State of the practice. In K. McLeod and H. Leslie, eds., *Ecosystem-based Management for the Oceans.* Washington, D.C.: Island Press, 314–321.

McLeod, K., J. Lubchenco, S. Palumbi, and A. Rosenberg. 2005. Scientific consensus statement on marine ecosystem-based management. Communication Partnership on Science and the Sea. compassonline.org/?q=EBM

McLusky, D., and M. Elliott. 2004. *The Estuarine Ecosystem: Ecology, Threats, and Management,* 3rd ed. Oxford, UK: Oxford University Press.

Mitsch, W. J., and J. G. Gosselink. 2000. *Wetlands,* 3rd ed. New York: John Wiley & Sons, Inc.

Mitsch, W. J., and J. G. Gosselink. 2007. *Wetlands,* 4th ed. Hoboken, NJ: John Wiley & Sons, Inc.

Moore, K., and R. Russell. 2009. Toward a new ethic for the oceans. In K. McLeod and H. Leslie, eds., *Ecosystem-based Management for the Oceans.* Washington, D.C.: Island Press, 325–340.

Mead, W., A. Moseidjord, D. Muraoka, and P. Sorensen. 1985. *Offshore Lands: Oil and*

Gas Leasing and Conservation on the Outer Continental Shelf. San Francisco, CA: Pacific Institute for Public Policy Research.

Mueller, J., and A. Anderson. 1983. Municipal sewage systems. In E. Myers and E. Harding, eds., *Ocean Disposal of Municipal Wastewater: Impacts on the Coastal Environment.* Washington, D.C.: National Oceanic and Atmospheric Administration, volume 1:37–92.

National Center for Ecological Analysis and Synthesis. 2001. Scientific consensus statement on marine reserves and marine protected areas. Santa Barbara, CA: National Center for Ecological Analysis and Synthesis. www.nceas.ucsb.edu/Consensus

National Marine Fisheries Service. 2008. 2007 Report to Congress: The Status of U.S. Fisheries. Silver Spring, MD: National Marine Fisheries Service.

National Oceanic and Atmospheric Administration. 2009. CZMA federal consistency overview. Silver Spring, MD: NOAA.

National Oceanic and Atmospheric Administration (NOAA) Fish Stock Sustainability Index (FSSI). 2009. http://www.nmfs.noaa.gov/sfa/statusoffisheries/SOSmain.htm

National Research Council. 1978a. *Multimedium Management of Municipal Sludge.* Washington, D.C.: National Academy of Sciences.

National Research Council. 1978b. *OCS Oil & Gas: An Assessment of the Department of the Interior Environmental Studies Program.* Washington, D.C.: National Academy of Sciences.

National Research Council. 1981. *Safety and Offshore Oil.* Washington, D.C.: National Academies Press.

National Research Council. 1985a. *Oil in the Sea: Inputs, Fates, and Effects.* Washington, D.C.: National Academies Press.

National Research Council. 1985b. *Dredging Coastal Ports: An Assessment of the Issues.* Washington, D.C.: National Academies Press.

National Research Council. 1993. *Managing Wastewater in Coastal Urban Areas.* Committee on Wastewater Management for Coastal Urban Areas. Washington, D.C.: National Academies Press.

National Research Council. 1999. *New Strategies for America's Watersheds.* Washington, D.C.: National Academies Press.

National Research Council. 2003. *Oil in the Sea III: Inputs, Fates, and Effects.* Washington, D.C.: The National Academies Press.

National Research Council—Transportation Research Board (TRB). 2008. *Potential Impacts of Climate Change on U.S. Transportation.* Washington, D.C.: National Academy of Sciences, TRB Special Report 290.

National Wetlands Policy Forum. 1988. *Protecting America's Wetlands: An Action Agenda.* Washington, D.C.: Conservation Foundation.

Nelson, G., E. Bennett, A. Berhe, K. Cassman, R. DeFries, T. Dietz, A. Dobermann, A. Dobson, A. Janetos, M. Levy, D. Marco, N. Nakicenovic, B. O'Neill, R. Norgaard, G. Petschel-Held, D. Ojima, P. Pingali, R. Watson, and M. Zurek. 2006. Anthropogenic drivers of ecosystem change: An overview. *Ecology and Society* 11(2): article 29. www.ecologyandsociety.org/vol11/iss2/art29/

Newell, R., L. Seiderer, and D. Hitchcock. 1998. The impact of dredging works on coastal waters: A review of the sensitivity to disturbance and subsequent recovery of biological resources on the sea bed. *Oceanography and Marine Biology Annual Review* 36:127–178.

Noble, B. F. 2000. Institutional criteria for co-management. *Marine Policy* 24:69–77.

Norton, R. 2005. More and better local planning: State-mandated local planning in coastal North Carolina. *Journal of the American Planning Association* 71(1):55–71.

Ocean Policy Task Force. 2009. Interim Framework of Effective Coastal and Marine Spatial Planning. Washington, D.C.: The White House Council on Environmental Quality.

Office of Federal Register. 2008. *United States Government Manual 2008–2009.* Washington, D.C.: U.S. Government Printing Office.

Office of Technology Assessment (OTA). 1990. Coping with an Oiled Sea: Background Paper. Washington, D.C.: Congress of the United States, OTA.

Okey, T. A. 2003. Membership of the eight regional fishery management councils in the United States: Are special interests over-represented? *Marine Policy* 27:193–206.

Orlando, S., F. Shirzad, J. Schuerholz, D. Mathieux, and S. Strassner. 1988. *National Estuarine Inventory: Shoreline Modification, Dredged Channels and Dredged Material Disposal Areas in the Nation's Estuaries.* Rockville, MD: National Oceanic and Atmospheric Administration.

Owens, D. 1992. National goals, state flexibility, and accountability in coastal zone management. *Coastal Management* 20:143–165.

Paganie, D. 2010. Reloading the Gulf. *Offshore* 70 (issue 50).

Parsons, S. 2005. Ecosystem considerations in fisheries management: Theory and practice. *The International Journal of Marine and Coastal Law* 20(3–4):381–422.

Pauly, D. 1995. Anecdotes and the shifting baseline syndrome of fisheries. *Trends in Ecology and Evolution* 10:430.

Pauly, D., and R. Watson. 2003. Counting the last fish. *Scientific American* (July):42–47.

Pew Oceans Commission. 2003. *America's Living Oceans: Charting a Course for Sea Change.* Arlington, VA: Pew Oceans Commission. www.pewoceans.org.

Pezeshki, S., M. Hester, Q. Lin, and J. Nyman. 2000. The effects of oil spill clean-up on dominant U.S. Gulf Coast marsh macrophytes: A review. *Environmental Pollution* 108:129–139.

Pikitch, E., S. Santora, E. Babcock, A. Bakun, R. Bonfil, D. Conover, P. Dayton, P. Doukakis, D. Fluharty, B. Heneman, E. Houde, J. Link, P. Livingston, M. Magnel, M. McAllister, J. Pope, and K. Sainsbury 2004. Ecosystem-based fishery management. *Science* 305:346–347.

Platt, R. H. 1996. *Land Use and Society: Geography, Law, and Public Policy.* Washington, D.C.: Island Press.

Plummer, R., and J. FitzGibbon. 2004. Some observations on the terminology in co-operative environmental management. *Journal of Environmental Management* 70:63–72.

Pollnac, R., S. Abbott-Jamieson, C. Smith, M. Miller, P. Clay, and B. Oles. 2006. Toward a model for fisheries social impact assessment. *Marine Fisheries Review* 68(1–4):1–18.

Pomeroy, R., and F. Berkes. 1997. Two to tango: The role of government in fisheries co-management. *Marine Policy* 21:465–480.

Pressman, J., and A. Wildavsky. 1973. *Implementation: How Great Expectations in*

Washington Are Dashed in Oakland. Berkeley, CA: University of California Press.

Rabalais, N., and D. Gilbert. 2009. Distribution and consequences of hypoxia. In E. R. Urban, B. Sundby, P. Malanotte-Rizzoli, and J. Milello, eds., *Watersheds, Bays, and Bounded Seas: The Science and Management of Semi-Enclosed Marine Systems.* Washington, D.C.: Island Press, 209–225.

Randall, R. E. 2004. Dredging. In G. Tsinker, ed., *Port Engineering: Planning, Construction, Maintenance, and Security.* Hoboken, NJ: John Wiley & Sons, Inc., 731–825.

Raymond, M., and W. Leffler. 2006. *Oil and Gas Production in Nontechnical Language.* Tulsa, OK: PennWell Corporation.

Reed, D. J. 2002. Sea-level rise and coastal marsh sustainability: Geological and ecological factors in the Mississippi delta plain. *Geomorphology* 48:233–243.

Roberts, C. 2007. *The Unnatural History of the Sea.* Washington, D.C.: Island Press.

Roheim, C. 2008. The economics of ecolabeling. In T. Ward and B. Phillips, eds., *Seafood Ecolabeling: Principles and Practices.* Oxford, UK: Blackwell Publishing, 38–57.

Rosenberg, A., and P. Sandifer. 2009. What do managers need? In K. McLeod and H. Leslie, eds., *Ecosystem-based Management for the Oceans.* Washington, D.C.: Island Press, 13–30.

Rozan, T., and G. Benoit. 2001. Mass balance of heavy metals in New Haven harbor, Connecticut: Predominance of nonpoint sources. *Limnology and Oceanography* 46:2032–2049.

Ruhl, J. 2000. Farms, their environmental harms, and environmental law. *Ecology Law Quarterly* 27:263–349.

Ruhl, J., S. Kraft, and C. Lant. 2007. *The Law and Policy of Ecosystem Services.* Washington, D.C.: Island Press.

Ryther, J. 1969. Photosynthesis and fish production in the sea. *Science* 166(3901):72–76.

Sabatier, P., W. Focht, M. Lubell, Z. Trachtenberg, A. Vedlitz, and M. Matlock, eds. 2005a. *Swimming Upstream: Collaborative Approaches to Watershed Management.* Cambridge, MA: The MIT Press.

Sabatier, P., C. Weible, and J. Ficker. 2005b. Eras of water management in the United States: Implications for collaborative watershed approaches. In P. Sabatier, W. Focht, M. Lubell, Z. Trachtenberg, A. Vedlitz, and M. Matlock, eds., *Swimming Upstream: Collaborative Approaches to Watershed Management.* Cambridge, MA: The MIT Press, 23–52.

Salazar, K. 2010a. Establishment of the Bureau of Ocean Energy Management, the Bureau of Safety and Environmental Enforcement, and the Office of Natural Resources Revenue. Secretary of the Interior Order No. 3299.

Salazar, K. 2010b. Change of the name of the Minerals Management Service to the Bureau of Ocean Energy Management, Regulation, and Enforcement. Secretary of the Interior Order No. 3302.

Salcido, R. 2008. Offshore federalism and ocean industrialization. *Tulane Law Review* 82:1355–1445.

Salvesen, D. 2005. The Coastal Barrier Resources Act: Has it discouraged development? *Coastal Management* 33:181–195.

Schmitz, O. 2007. *Ecology and Ecosystem Conservation.* Washington, D.C.: Island Press.

Schneider, A., and H. Ingram. 1997. *Policy Design for Democracy.* Lawrence: University Press of Kansas.

Schneider, A., and M. Sidney. 2009. What's next for policy design and social construction theory? *Policy Studies Journal* 37:103–119.

Searles Jones, J., and S. Ganey. 2009. Building the legal and institutional framework. In K. McLeod and H. Leslie, eds., *Ecosystem-based Management for the Oceans*. Washington, D.C.: Island Press, 162–179.

Siry, J. 1984. *Marshes of the Ocean Shore: Development of an Ecological Ethic*. College Station: Texas A&M University Press.

Skinner, B., and K. Turekian. 1973. *Man and the Ocean*. Englewood Cliffs, NJ: Prentice-Hall, Inc.

Slocombe, S. 1998. Defining goals and criteria for ecosystem-based management. *Environmental Management* 22(4):483–493.

Smith, M. 2006. Cumulative impact assessment under the National Environmental Policy Act: An analysis of recent case law. *Environmental Practice* 8(4):228.

Sorensen, J. 1997. National and international efforts at integrated coastal management: Definition, achievements, and lessons. *Coastal Management* 25:3–41.

Tacconi, L. 2007. Decentralization, forests, and livelihoods: Theory and narrative. *Global Environmental Change* 17:338–348.

Tang, Z. 2008. Evaluating local coastal zone land use planning capacities in California. *Ocean & Coastal Management* 51:544–555.

Tchobanoglous, G., and E. Schroeder. 1987. *Water Quality: Characteristics, Modeling, Modification*. Reading, MA: Addison-Wesley Publishing Company.

Titus, J., K. Anderson, D. Cahoon, D. Gesch, S. Gill, B. Gutierrez, E. Thieler, and J. Williams. 2009. Coastal Elevations and Sensitivity to Sea-Level Rise: A Focus on the Mid-Atlantic Region. Washington, D.C.: EPA, U.S. Climate Change Science Program Synthesis and Assessment Product 4.1.

Tudela, S., and K. Short. 2005. Paradigm shifts, gaps, inertia, and political agendas in ecosystem-based fisheries management. *Marine Ecology Progress Series* 300:282–286.

Turner, R. E., J. Baustian, E. Swenson, and J. Spicer. 2006. Wetland sedimentation from hurricanes Katrina and Rita. *Science* 313:1713–1715.

United Nations Environment Program. 2006. Marine and coastal ecosystems and human well-being: A synthesis report based on the findings of the Millennium Ecosystem Assessment. Nairobi, Kenya: UNEP.

U.S. Census Bureau. 2007. Hurricane Data and Emergency Preparedness: Additional Information on Coastal Counties. Accessed 6/6/07. www.census.gov/Press -Release/www/emergencies/coast_areas.html.

U.S. Commission on Marine Science, Engineering, and Resources (Stratton Commission). 1969. *Our Nation and the Sea*—Panel Reports on Marine Science, Engineering, and Resources. Washington, D.C.: U.S. Government Printing Office.

U.S. Commission on Ocean Policy (USCOP). 2004. *An Ocean Blueprint for the 21st Century: Final Report*. Washington, D.C. www.oceancommission.gov.

Vestal, B., and A. Rieser. 1995. Methodologies and mechanisms for management of cumulative coastal environmental impacts—Synthesis. NOAA Coastal Ocean Program Decision Analysis Series No. 6. Silver Spring, MD: NOAA.

von Weizsacker, E., O. Young, and M. Finger, eds. 2005. *Limits to Privatization: How to Avoid Too Much of Good Thing*. London: Earthscan.

Walker, B., and D. Salt. 2006. *Resilience Thinking: Sustaining Ecosystems and People in a Changing World.* Washington, D.C.: Island Press.

Weimer, D., and A. Vining. 1992. *Policy Analysis: Concepts and Practice.* Englewood Cliffs, NJ: Prentice-Hall.

Wengert, N. 1985. The river basin concept as seen from a management perspective in the USA. In J. Lundqvist, U. Lohm, and M. Falkenmark, eds., *Strategies for River Basin Management.* Dordrecht: D. Reidel Publishing Company, 299–305.

White, G. 1969. *Strategies of American Water Management.* Ann Arbor: The University of Michigan Press.

Worm, B., R. Hilborn, J. Baum, T. Branch, J. Collie, C. Costello, M. Fogarty, E. Fulton, J. Hutchings, S. Jennings, O. Jensen, H. Lotze, P. Mace, T. McClanahan, C. Minto, S. Palumbi, A. Parma, D. Ricard, A. Rosenberg, R. Watson, and D. Zeller. 2009. Rebuilding global fisheries. *Science* 235:578–585.

Yaffee, S. 1999. Three faces of ecosystem management. *Conservation Biology* 13(4): 713–725.

Young, O. 1982. The political economy of fish: The Fishery Conservation and Management Act of 1976. *Ocean Development & International Law* 10:199–273.

Young, O., G. Osherenko, J. Ekstrom, L. Crowder, J. Ogden, J. Wilson, J. Day, F. Douvere, C. Ehler, K. McLeod, B. Halpern, and R. Peach. 2007. Solving the crisis in ocean governance: Place-based management of marine ecosystems. *Environment* 49(4):21–32.

Zile, Z. 1974. A legislative-political history of the Coastal Zone Management Act of 1972. *Coastal Zone Management Journal* 1:235–274.

Further Reading

CHAPTER 1

Ehrlich, P., and A. Ehrlich. 1990. *The Population Explosion*. New York: Simon and Schuster.

Houghton, J. 2009. *Global Warming: The Complete Briefing*. Cambridge, UK: Cambridge University Press.

Kaufman, W., and O. Pilkey. 1983. *The Beaches Are Moving: The Drowning of America's Shoreline*. Durham, NC: Duke University Press.

U.S. Commission on Ocean Policy (USCOP). 2004. *An Ocean Blueprint for the 21st Century: Final Report*. Washington, D.C.

CHAPTER 2

Baumgartner, F., and B. Jones. 2002. *Policy Dynamics*. Chicago: The University of Chicago Press.

Clark, T. 2002. *The Policy Process: A Practical Guide for Natural Resource Professionals*. New Haven, CT: Yale University Press.

Kingdon, J. 1995. *Agendas, Alternatives, and Public Policies*. New York: Longman.

Lasswell, H. 1971. *A Pre-View of Policy Sciences*. New York: American Elsevier.

Majone, J. 1989. *Evidence, Argument and Persuasion in the Policy Process*. New Haven, CT: Yale University Press.

Sabatier, P., and H. Jenkins-Smith. 1993. *Policy Change and Learning: An Advocacy Coalition Approach*. Boulder, CO: Westview Press.

CHAPTER 3

National Research Council. 1993. *Managing Wastewater in Coastal Urban Areas*. Washington, D.C.: National Academies Press.

Davies, J. C., and J. Mazurek. 1998. *Pollution Control in the United States: Evaluating the System*. Washington, D.C.: Resources for the Future.

Kurlansky, M. 2006. *The Big Oyster: History on the Half Shell*. New York: Random House, Inc.

Laws, E. A. 2000. *Aquatic Pollution: An Introductory Text*, 3rd ed. New York: John Wiley & Sons, Inc.

Tchobanoglous, G., and E. Schroeder. 1987. *Water Quality: Characteristics, Modeling, Modification*. Reading, MA: Addison-Wesley Publishing Company.

CHAPTER 4

Burger, J. 1997. *Oil Spills*. New Brunswick, NJ: Rutgers University Press.

Deffeyes, K. 2005. *Beyond Oil: A View from Hubbert's Peak*. New York: Hill and Wang.

Fitzgerald, E. 2001. *The Seaweed Rebellion: Federal-State Conflicts over Offshore Energy Development*. Lanham, MD: Lexington Books.

Freudenburg, W., and R. Gramling. 1994. *Oil in Troubled Waters: Perceptions, Politics, and the Battle over Offshore Drilling.* Albany: State University of New York Press.

National Research Council. 2003. *Oil in the Sea III: Inputs, Fates, and Effects.* Washington, D.C.: The National Academies Press.

Raymond, M., and W. Leffler. 2006. *Oil and Gas Production in Nontechnical Language.* Tulsa, OK: PennWell Corporation.

CHAPTER 5

Brown, P. 2009. *America's Waterfront Revival: Port Authorities and Urban Redevelopment.* Philadelphia: University of Pennsylvania Press.

Hershman, M. 1988. *Urban Ports and Harbor Management: Responding to Change along US Waterfronts.* New York: Taylor and Francis.

Kennish, M. J. 1997. *Practical Handbook of Estuarine and Marine Pollution.* Boca Raton, FL: CRC Press.

Lechich, A. 2006. *A Storm in the Port: Keeping the Port of New York and New Jersey Open.* Hanover, NH: Dartmouth College Press/University of New England Press.

Newell, R., L. Seiderer, and D. Hitchcock. 1998. The impact of dredging works on coastal waters: A review of the sensitivity to disturbance and subsequent recovery of biological resources on the sea bed. *Oceanography and Marine Biology Annual Review* 36:127–178.

Tsinker, G. ed., 2004. *Port Engineering: Planning, Construction, Maintenance, and Security.* Hoboken, NJ: John Wiley & Sons, Inc.

CHAPTER 6

Freudenburg, W., R. Gramling, S. Laska, and K. Erikson. 2009. *Catastrophe in the Making: The Engineering of Katrina and the Disasters of Tomorrow.* Washington, D.C.: Island Press.

Lewis Jr., W. 2001. *Wetlands Explained: Wetland Science, Policy, and Politics in America.* New York: Oxford University Press.

Mitsch, W. J., and J. G. Gosselink. 2007. *Wetlands,* 4th ed. Hoboken, NJ: John Wiley & Sons, Inc.

Teal, J., and M. Teal. 1969. *Life and Death of the Salt Marsh.* New York: Ballantine Books, Inc.

Pittman, C., and M. Waite. 2009. *Paving Paradise: Florida's Vanishing Wetlands and the Failure of No Net Loss.* Gainesville: University Press of Florida.

CHAPTER 7

Beatley, T., D. J. Brower, and A. K. Schwab. 2002. *An Introduction to Coastal Zone Management,* 2nd ed. Washington, D.C.: Island Press.

Brown, K., E. Tompkins, and W. Adger. 2002. *Making Waves: Integrating Coastal Conservation and Development.* London: Earthscan.

Gibbons, B. 1977. *Wye Island.* Baltimore, MD: Johns Hopkins University Press.

Gubbay, S., ed. 1995. *Marine Protected Areas: Principles and Techniques for Management.* London, UK: Chapman and Hall.

Kay, R., and J. Alder. 2005. *Coastal Planning and Management.* London: Taylor & Francis Group.

Platt, R. H. 1996. *Land Use and Society: Geography, Law, and Public Policy.* Washington, D.C.: Island Press.

Wholey, J., H. Hatry, and K. Newcomer, eds. 2004. *Handbook of Practical Program Evaluation,* 2nd ed. San Francisco: Jossey-Bass/John Wiley & Sons, Inc.

CHAPTER 8

Cortner, H., and M. Moote. 1999. A paradigm shift? In *The Politics of Ecosystem Management.* Washington, D.C.: Island Press.

Daily, G. C., ed. 1997. *Nature's Services: Societal Dependence on Natural Ecosystems.* Washington, D.C.: Island Press.

Layzer, J. 2008. *Natural Experiments: Ecosystem-based Management and the Environment.* Cambridge, MA: The MIT Press.

McLusky, D., and M. Elliott. 2004. *The Estuarine Ecosystem: Ecology, Threats, and Management,* 3rd ed. Oxford, UK: Oxford University Press.

McLeod, K., and H. Leslie, eds. 2009. *Ecosystem-based Management for the Oceans.* Washington, D.C.: Island Press.

Walker, B., and D. Salt. 2006. *Resilience Thinking: Sustaining Ecosystems and People in a Changing World.* Washington, D.C.: Island Press.

CHAPTER 9

Brauman, K., G. Daily, T. Duarte, and H. Mooney. 2007. The nature and value of ecosystem services: An overview highlighting hydrologic services. *Annual Review of Environment and Resources* 32:67–98.

Ernst, H. 2003. *Chesapeake Bay Blues: Science, Politics, and the Struggle to Save the Bay.* Lanham, MD: Rowman & Littlefield Publishers, Inc.

Gregersen, H., P. Ffolliot, and K. Brooks. 2007. *Integrated Watershed Management: Connecting People to Their Land and Water.* Oxfordshire, UK: CAB International.

Houck, O. 2002. *The Clean Water Act TMDL Program: Law, Policy, and Implementation.* Washington, D.C.: Environmental Law Institute.

Lee, K. 1993. *Compass and Gyroscope: Integrating Science and Politics for the Environment.* Washington, D.C.: Island Press.

Sabatier, P., W. Focht, M. Lubell, Z. Trachtenberg, A. Vedlitz, and M. Matlock, eds. 2005. *Swimming Upstream: Collaborative Approaches to Watershed Management.* Cambridge, MA: The MIT Press.

Urban, E., B. Sundby, P. Malanotte-Rizzoli, and J. Melillo. 2009. *Watersheds, Bays, and Bounded Seas: The Science and Management of Semi-enclosed Marine Systems.* SCOPE 70. Washington, D.C.: Island Press.

White, G. 1969. *Strategies of American Water Management.* Ann Arbor: The University of Michigan Press.

CHAPTER 10

Helfman, G. 2007. *Fish Conservation: A Guide to Understanding and Restoring Global Aquatic Biodiversity and Fishery Resources.* Washington, D.C.: Island Press.

Ostrom, E. 1990. *Governing the Commons: Evolution of Institutions for Collective Action.* Cambridge, UK: Cambridge University Press.

Warner, W. 1977. *Distant Water: The Fate of the North Atlantic Fisherman.* Boston, MA: Little, Brown and Company.

Weber, M. 2002. *From Abundance to Scarcity: A History of U.S. Marine Fisheries Policy.* Washington, D.C.: Island Press.

Worm, B., R. Hilborn, J. Baum, T. Branch, J. Collie, C. Costello, M. Fogarty, E.

Fulton, J. Hutchings, S. Jennings, et al. 2009. Rebuilding global fisheries. *Science* 235:578–585.

CHAPTER 11

Argyris, C., and D. Schon. 1978. *Organizational Learning: A Theory of Action Perspective.* Reading, MA: Addison-Wesley Publishing Company.

Glossary

Acute toxicity: Lethal amount of a toxin administered as a single dose or exposure.

Adaptive management: A decision process that acknowledges that action often occurs before a perfect understanding is available. Therefore, as new information becomes apparent the original management approach must change in response to the new information, much in the way one can learn from an experiment.

Adversarial legalism: Policy making, policy implementation, and dispute resolution by means of lawyer-dominated procedures that provides a means to help disputants when they believe that they have been wronged.

Agent: Individual operating under statutes and possessing the means (tools, rules, or rationales) to deliver policy to target populations.

Anadromous: Species that spawn in freshwater and spend most of their lives in saltwater.

Anoxia (anoxic): The absence of free oxygen (O_2).

Aquaculture: The breeding, rearing, and harvesting of plants and animals in all types of water environments, including aquaria, ponds, rivers, lakes, and the ocean.

Barrel: A unit of volume for liquid petroleum production equivalent to 42 U.S. gallons (159 liters).

Baseline: (1) Boundary dividing land from ocean, normally indicated by the low (or lower low) water line and extending across rivers and bays and along outer points of complex coastlines. (2) The status of a natural system at some point in time that may be established prior to major anthropogenic change.

Beneficial use (of dredge spoil): Using dredged material for another purpose such as building a beach or a marsh, rather than just disposing of it.

Benthic/benthos: Organisms that live on or in the seafloor.

Best management practices: Technology or management determined to be the most effective way of controlling point and/or nonpoint source pollution from a technical, economic, and institutional point of view.

Bill: Formally introduced legislation or a proposed law requiring the approval of both the House of Representatives and the Senate and the signature of the president to become a law.

Bioaccumulation: The buildup of chemical substances in the cell or tissue of an organism.

Biochemical oxygen demand (BOD): A measure of the amount of oxygen consumed in the biological processes that break down organic matter in water. Elevated levels of this measure signify greater pollution.

Biodiversity: Biological variety at all levels of organization that can range from genetic variety within a species to the number of species within an ecological community.

Biogeochemical cycling: The cycling of chemical compounds among biotic and abiotic ecosystem components due to biological, chemical, physical, or geological processes.

Biological nitrogen removal: A temperature-dependent process in which the ammonia-nitrogen present in raw wastewater is converted by bacteria to nitrate-nitrogen and ultimately to nitrogen gas.

Biological opinion: The assessment provided by the U.S. Fish and Wildlife Service or the National Marine Fisheries Service when another federal agency is considering a decision that could affect an endangered species.

Biomass: The quantity of living matter expressed as grams per unit area or unit volume.

Biosolid: The nutrient-rich organic materials resulting from composting or other treatment of domestic sewage sludge.

Blowout: Occurs when high-pressure fluids from deep in the earth enter the well bore and escape in an uncontrolled fashion at the surface. Can involve explosion, fire, and/or loss of life and equipment.

Blow-out preventer: Hydraulically operated ram to prevent uncontrolled flow of fluids to the surface. It may close around the drill pipe, close against the drill pipe and pinch it together, or close off the well when there is no pipe in the hole.

Bonus bid: Nonrefundable lump sum cash payment made by the entity seeking access to potential oil and gas deposits at the time the owner of the resource grants the lease.

Boom: An air- or foam-filled flotation tube with a weighted skirt beneath it used to control the spread of oil on the surface of the sea or to concentrate that oil into thicker surface layers so it may be recovered.

Bounded rationality: Acting as rationally as possible given limits in human ability, time, and information to be consistent with appropriate goals but only after greatly simplifying the choices available.

Bycatch: The incidental harvest of nontargeted species.

Cap and trade: A system in which an entity, usually the government, establishes a limited amount of pollution that can be emitted. Emissions permits or credits can be sold or transferred to other firms, with the goal that government action and market mechanisms can reduce emissions.

Cap rock: Layer of impervious rock that prevents migration of hydrocarbons or water.

Capping (of dredged material): Use of clean dredged materials to cover contaminated dredged sediments, which are usually deposited in a depression in the seafloor.

Carrying capacity: The number of individuals a habitat or area can support given the supply of resources necessary for survival and replacement reproduction.

Casing: Steel pipe that lines a well as drilling progresses to prevent the hole from caving in and to control of the flow of fluids in the well.

Catch per unit effort (CPUE): A measure indicating the efficiency of a fishery, computed by dividing the catch data for a given place and time period by the corresponding fishing effort data.

Chlorination: Addition of chlorine to effluent waters of a sewage treatment plant to disinfect the waste stream.

Cholera: A diarrheal illness that ranges from mild to severe and is caused by infection of the intestine with the bacterium *Vibrio cholerae*.

Clean Water Act: Current name for the Federal Water Pollution Control Act Amendments of 1972, which were established to restore and maintain the chemical, physical, and biological integrity of the nation's waters by eliminating discharge of pollutants and ensuring water quality at a level adequate to protect fish, shellfish, wildlife, and human recreational activities.

Coastal ecosystem governance: Recognizes the interrelationships among natural (biological, chemical, geological, physical) systems and associated social systems that straddle land and sea and seeks to shape human behavior so that the systems are sustained using both governmental (law, regulation) and non-governmental (markets, voluntary organizations, social mores, information) means.

Comanagement: System of management that includes some form of community participation in the development of implementation of resource policy.

Combined sewer overflows: Wet weather discharges of untreated human sewage and stormwater from streets to rivers and estuaries. Occurs when the capacity of the treatment facility is exceeded due to stormwater runoff.

Community-based management: An approach to fisheries management in which individual communities take a lead role in making decisions concerning how a fishery should be managed to protect the community as well as the resource.

Compatible uses: Those uses in the same coastal area that can coexist without conflict.

Conditions: Environmental situations that may be unpleasant but about which nothing can be done, usually due to the lack of feasible technical or political solutions.

Confined disposal facility: A structure to receive sediments dredged from a navigation channel, which is designed to contain the contaminants and prevent their reentry into the waterway.

Congressional moratoria: Temporary exclusion of specific offshore areas from leasing. Created by restrictions in how the Department of the Interior budget may be spent.

Consistency (of federal actions): A Coastal Zone Management Act requirement wherein federal activities such as a permit approval that will have an effect on land, water, or natural resource use of the coastal zone must be consistent with the policies of a coastal state's federally approved coastal management program.

Constitutive decision process: Deciding how to decide about the creation of new policies that support common interests and are enforceable.

Container (for cargo on a ship): A box packed by the sender that is usually 40 feet x 8 feet 6 inches x 8 feet 6 inches (12.2 meters x 2.6 meters x 2.6 meters). Minimizes the turnaround time of the ship because the container can be moved quickly.

Contaminated sediments: Deposits that include elevated concentrations of materials that have been released to the environment and accumulate in the silt and mud on the bottoms of rivers, lakes, estuaries, and oceans.

Continental margin: Submerged edge of continent that includes the continental shelf, continental slope, and continental rise.

Continental rise: Accumulations of sediment at the base of the slope; often extend several hundred kilometers in width.

Continental slope: Extends downward at an average of four degrees from the shelf to the top of the rise with a total relief of 0.6 to 6 miles (one to ten kilometers).

Crude oil (petroleum): Naturally occurring liquid hydrocarbons formed by decay of organic matter.

Cumulative impact: Environmental impacts that are independently insignificant but when summed become harmful.

Dead zone: Hypoxic (low dissolved oxygen) or anoxic (no dissolved oxygen) area in marine waters.

Development right: The legal entitlement to improve a piece of land.

Development stage: Period after discovery of commercial quantities of oil and gas during which the extent of the reserves and production rates are estimated and construction of facilities to produce and transport the product are completed.

Disinfection: The use of a chemical or physical process to kill pathogenic organisms.

Dispersants: When sprayed on oil these chemicals will break down the slick into small droplets.

Displaceable use: An activity that can be moved elsewhere if the economic, social, and political pressures are sufficiently great.

Dissolved oxygen (DO): The concentration of free molecular oxygen dissolved in seawater, which may vary in response to physical, chemical, and biological factors.

Double-loop learning: A process whereby an organization detects an error and corrects the situation by changing the organization's underlying norms and objectives.

Draft: The depth of a vessel below its waterline.

Dredge and fill: The removal of sediments and disposal of those materials in another area. Requires a permit from the U.S. Army Corps of Engineers, and has been most controversial in the cases where the U.S. Environmental Protection Agency has vetoed an approval by the Corps.

Drill bit: The cutting or boring element used in drilling.

Drill string: Thirty-foot-long (nine-meter) drill pipes coupled together with joints and used to transmit fluid and rotational power to the drill bit.

Drilling mud or fluid: A liquid usually composed of clay, water, and various additives, which, when circulated, carries the cuttings of rock to the surface and with appropriate density and pressure is also used to counter formation pressure on the well during drilling.

Ecolabel: A label provided by an independent certification body on a product or service that certifies voluntary adherence to the goals of minimizing environmental impacts, promoting sustainable harvest, and producing in conformance with specific environmental expectations.

Ecosystem-based management: Structuring societal behavior in ocean and coastal systems so that humans promote ecosystem health and resilience while allowing sustainable uses of goods and services.

Ecosystem-based fisheries management: Promotion of ecosystem health and resilience rather than single-species management when considering harvest, habitat, predators, and prey of the target species in addition to other interactions.

Ecosystem engineer: Any organism that creates or modifies habitat.

Ecosystem governance: Recognizes the interrelationships among natural (biological, chemical, geological, physical) systems and related social systems and seeks to shape human behavior so that both are sustained using both governmental (law, regulation) and nongovernmental (markets, voluntary organizations, social mores, information) means.

Ecosystem indices: Quantitative measures that provide a condensed description of multidimensional environmental states by aggregating several variables (or indicators) into a single quantity.

Ecosystem services: Benefits that flow to humans from naturally functioning systems, including aspects such as provisioning of food, regulating climate, cultural enrichment through recreation, and supporting activities such as maintenance of nutrient cycles.

Effectiveness: The extent to which targets that focus on cause-effect relationships are being met and the extent to which a particular policy produces the desired outcome.

Efficiency: Getting the most out of the resources used to produce goods and services. Efficiency is likely to be greatest when information is comprehensive.

Environmental Impact Statement: A legally mandated and publicly available document that requires several alternatives to be considered along with their environmental impacts before a federal agency selects a preferred course of action.

Equity: The concept of fairness in the distribution of the gains from economic activity throughout the society.

Essential fish habitat: The water column and the underlying seafloor of a particular area essential to the long-term survival and health of commercially important marine species during each life stage of the organism.

Estuary: Semienclosed coastal body of water connected to the ocean and usually receiving freshwater.

Eustatic sea level rise: The alteration of global sea level, such as a change in the volume of water in the world oceans or a change in the volume of an ocean basin.

Eutrophication: Addition of dissolved nutrients to a water body resulting in large increases in phytoplankton production and microbial activity often accompanied by low dissolved oxygen levels.

Evaluation: The process of investigating whether and to what extent a program has accomplished its desired effect.

Exclusive economic zone: The area specified in the United Nations Convention on the Law of the Sea that extends 200 nautical miles (370 kilometers) seaward from baselines for the territorial sea and that includes the legal rights to explore, exploit, conserve, and manage natural resources located below, on, or above the seabed.

Exclusive use: A use that is, by nature, totally incompatible with any other use.

Exploration stage: Includes a sequence of regional geophysical surveys to identify promising geological formations, detailed surveys to evaluate the potential of specific structures, and exploratory drilling to determine whether oil and gas are present.

Federal consistency: A legal requirement that federal agency activities with reasonably foreseeable effects on coastal uses or resources be consistent to the maximum extent practicable with enforceable policies of a state's federally approved coastal management program.

Federal Water Pollution Control Act Amendments (FWPCA) of 1972: See Clean Water Act.

Fee-simple property acquisition: Obtaining the full bundle of rights associated with a parcel of land.

Fisheries Conservation and Management Act (FCMA): An act that extended the fishery conservation zone to 200 nautical miles (370 kilometers) and created eight regional fishery management councils to develop management plans for each commercially and recreationally important species.

Fisheries management council: Decision-making body composed of stakeholders including fishers that develops management measures for fisheries subject to approval and implementation by the National Marine Fisheries Service and the Secretary of Commerce.

Fisheries management plan: Plan developed by a fisheries management council. Sets standards and guidelines for each fishery using biological details of the fishery, as well as social, economic, and human considerations that will allow for sustainable management.

Focusing event: A sudden event that generates public attention related to harmful situations. Can also be a powerful symbol that many adopt, or personal experience that affects a policy maker.

Formation pressure: The force exerted by fluids in a formation recorded in the hole at the level of the formation.

Fragmentation (in government): The separation of power among branches of government (executive, legislative, and judicial), between states and the federal government, and among the departments/agencies or congressional committees at the state or federal level.

Garbage can policy process: Decision-making process that uses a theoretical "garbage can" of options. The can contains solutions looking for problems as much as the reverse. The participants, often with their own favorite problems and/or solutions in mind, seek to unite the two.

Gastroenteritis: A condition that causes irritation and inflammation of the stomach and intestines and is caused by bacterial pathogens *Salmonella* and *Shigella*. These pathogens are excreted in the feces of an infected person.

Geoengineering: The deliberate modification of earth's environment on a large scale to suit human needs and promote habitability. Often taken to mean proposals to deliberately manipulate the earth's climate to counteract the effects of global warming from greenhouse gas emissions.

Governance: Political authority to manage society's affairs. Shifting from traditional bureaucratic heirarchies toward greater use of markets, networks, and other means to control activity and deliver public services.

Gridlock (in a political system): A complete lack of movement or progress resulting in a backup or stagnation.

Harmful algal bloom: Rapid increase of, typically, one or a few plankton species, resulting in discoloration of the water and presence of naturally occurring biotoxins, some of which affect neurological functions in wildlife and humans.

Hepatitis: Inflammation of the liver caused by the hepatitis virus, which is a pathogen excreted in the feces of an infected person.

Hydric soil: A soil supporting primarily vegetation that requires a habitat of water or wet conditions. Formed under conditions of saturation or flooding long enough to develop anaerobic conditions in the upper part of the soil during the growing season.

Hydrologic cycle: Terrestrial, oceanic, and atmospheric exchange of water by processes including evaporation, precipitation, groundwater flow, and surface runoff.

Hydrophytic vegetation: Vegetation requiring a habitat of water or wet conditions, capable of growing in soils deficient in oxygen as a result of inundation with water.

Hypoxia (hypoxic): Very low levels of oxygen in water, usually defined as less than two parts per million.

Implementation: The process by which policies enacted by government are put into effect by the relevant agencies or other entities.

Incremental decision making: A model of decision making in which policy change is accomplished through small steps that allow decision makers to adjust policies as they learn from their successes and failures.

In lieu fee mitigation: An agreement between a regulatory agency and a sponsor, which is usually a public agency or nonprofit organization, through which the sponsor collects funds from an entity such as a port authority that is required to compensate for wetland loss it causes elsewhere.

Institution: Knowledge, values, and regulatory structures transmitted through culture and routine at multiple jurisdictional levels that provide stability and meaning to social behavior.

Instrument: See "tool."

Interest group: A collection of people or organizations with similar values who unite to advance their desired policy outcomes.

Invasive species: A nonindigenous or alien species whose introduction does or is likely to cause economic, environmental, or human-health harm.

Iron triangle: A particular style of subgovernment in which there are mutually reinforcing relationships among a regulated interest, the agency charged with regulation, and the congressional subcommittee responsible for policy making that affects the interest.

Isostasy: The regional mass balance of rocks in the earth's crust and uppermost mantle.

Ladder of citizen participation: A hierarchy of steps that characterizes public involvement and empowerment in policy by starting with nonparticipation, moving to degrees of tokenism, and ultimately according citizens direct power in making decisions.

Levee (artificial): An embankment built parallel to the streambed in an effort to prevent flooding.

Logrolling: The legislative practice of trading commitments to vote for members' preferred policies.

Mangrove: Salt-tolerant trees that grow in low-energy tropical and subtropical intertidal zones, commonly on the lee shore of islands and within lagoons. Types include red, black, and white mangroves.

Mariculture: Cultivation of marine species in tanks, in cages suspended in the water column, in rafts, or in ponds on land.

Marine protected area (MPA): Geographic region including benthos and overlying waters that is set aside to protect wildlife and habitat, advance recreation, or improve the stock of a commercially important fish or shellfish species.

Marine Protection Research and Sanctuaries Act (MPRSA): A federal law that controls ocean dumping and created the National Marine Sanctuaries Program to place limitations on uses of federal waters.

Market: Any structure that allows buyers and sellers to exchange any type of goods, services, or information.

Maximum sustainable yield (MSY): The density of fish that theoretically provides the maximum catch obtainable per unit time under an appropriate fishing rate.

Mobile offshore drilling unit (MODU): Self-contained floatable or floating drilling equipment such as a jackup (a barge with long legs that can be lowered to the seafloor), semisubmersable (a vessel with a deck high above the water that floats on submerged pontoon–like structures), or drillship (a vessel modified with special station-keeping equipment and a drilling rig).

Multiple use: Coordinated management of resources and uses focused on productivity, relative value of resources, and sustained yield without necessarily maximizing economic return as the best way of meeting the needs of people.

National Environmental Policy Act (NEPA): An act that requires agencies to address the environmental consequences of their proposed actions through an Environmental Impact Statement for all major federal projects that could significantly affect the quality of the human environment.

National marine sanctuary: An area of U.S. waters that is designated by the federal government for the purpose of enhancing ecological, recreational, cultural, scientific, educational, or aesthetic values.

Natural resource trustee: A government official who acts on behalf of the public when there is injury, destruction, or loss of natural resources as a result of a release of oil or another hazardous substance.

Networked program (in coastal zone management): A program that integrates an array of state laws and policies that have a bearing on coastal resources into an overarching policy and regulatory framework, rather than passing a new state law to do so.

No net loss (of wetlands): A policy created to prevent future wetland losses by requiring the creation of replacement wetlands if a given project destroys or reduces the ecological value of a wetland.

Nonpoint source pollution: Introduction of sediments, nutrients, toxins, and pathogens to surface waters from land use activities that are diffuse and may include agriculture, lawns, mining, and construction, as well as pollutants from the atmosphere.

Oil seep: A flow of oil from within the earth that emerges at the surface in a somewhat dispersed pattern.

Outer continental shelf: Submerged lands greater than three nautical miles (5.6 kilometers) from the shore (except for Texas and an area in Florida, where the boundary is three nautical leagues [16.7 kilometers]) out to the seaward extent of the continental margin or 200 miles (322 kilometers) from shore, whichever is greater.

Outcome: The result on the coastal environment from the implementation of a policy.

Outputs: The things in government that the policy process produces, such as laws, regulations, rules, organizations, and the like.

Overburden: Upper sedimentary strata that cover, compress, and consolidate sediments beneath.

Overfished: The condition that results when the biological viability of a fish population has been reduced by fishing activity.

Overfishing: Harvesting fish at a nonsustainable rate that causes a fish stock to rapidly decrease and, if continued, causes the fishery to become overfished.

Ozonation: When ozone gas contacts pathogens it destroys cell walls, forms by-products with great oxidizing capacity, and damages constituents of nucleic acids, which disinfects wastewater.

Paradigm shift: Occurs when the current ruling theory cannot explain anomalous information. If the anomalies persist, this will produce a crisis in understanding that results in a battle over a new paradigm and often a scientific revolution supported by a new universal theory.

Pathogen: Parasite, bacterium, or virus that causes disease.

Permeable: Having pores or openings through which fluids can flow.

Point source pollution: Pollution that can be traced back to a single origin or source, such as a pipe from a sewage treatment plant.

Policy process framework: A way of understanding the many factors that influence policy making and the activities that go into producing a policy.

Pore space: The total continuous and interconnected void space in a volume of sediments or rock.

Pork: Spending that is intended to benefit constituents of a politician in return for their political support, either in the form of campaign contributions or votes.

Precaution: Preventive measures for or suspension of activites that are potentially damaging to the environment until the resource user can demonstrate that severe or irreversible damage will not occur.

Presidential withdrawal: Potentially permanent removal of specific offshore areas from consideration for leasing at the discretion of the president.

Pretreatment: A process that either partially or totally treats effluent before it enters the sewage system (or receiving waters) by reducing or eliminating a portion of the pollutants.

Primary production: The production of living matter through the process of photosynthesis or chemosynthesis.

Primary treatment: Simplest form of sewage treatment in which only solids are removed from the waste stream, amounting to about thirty percent biological oxygen demand removal.

Privatization: Transfer of any government function to the private sector.

Problem definition: The process whereby conditions become defined as public problems through the activities of interested parties in and outside of government.

Production stage: Bringing oil and gas to the surface and separating the materials (sediment, oil, gas, water) for transportation and sale or discharge.

Rational policy process: Decision making in which it is assumed that decision makers have nearly all information about a problem, its causes, and its solutions at their disposal, whereupon a large number of alternatives can be systematically assessed and the best one selected.

Regime: A system of social control through specific rules that apply to a geographic area and are agreed upon by governments.

Relative sea level: The sea level at a specific location that is the result of local changes in the land elevation (subsidence, isostatic rebound, earthquakes, and others) as well as changes in global sea level.

Reservoir rock: A porous and permeable rock found in the earth in which oil and gas are found.

Resilience: The ability of a coupled social and ecological system to return to its original state, function, and identity if it is perturbed.

Responsible party: An individual, company, or government agency responsible for an oil spill or hazardous substance release.

Restoration: Practice of renewing a degraded ecosystem through human intervention. Assumes that damages are somewhat reversible.

Rivers and Harbors Act: Starting in 1899, this act made it illegal to (i) discharge refuse matter of any kind into the navigable waters or tributaries without a permit and (ii) excavate, fill, or alter the course, condition, or capacity of any port, harbor, channel, or other area without a permit.

Rotary drilling: The rotation of a drilling bit at the end of a drill string with downward force applied.

Royalty: Payment to resource owner, usually based on a percentage of the total value of the oil and gas produced.

Salt marsh: A vegetated intertidal mud or sand flat.

Sea level rise: A global rise in sea level caused primarily by thermal expansion of seawater and addition of water to the oceans from melting of ice on continents. Ultimately results in inundated wetlands, beach erosion, coastal flooding, and other changes.

Seaweed rebellion: Conflicting views between federal and state governments about the distribution of costs and benefits from development of outer continental shelf energy resources.

Secondary treatment: A sewage treatment process that removes up to eighty-five percent of biological oxygen demand of the waste through biological consumption of organic materials facilitated by the addition of oxygen either mechanically or chemically.

Sector-based management: Separate actions that implement the provisions of law that address single issues such as dredging, waste disposal, fishing, or energy development, rather than providing a comprehensive solution for multiple coastal issues through a holistic response.

Setback: The required distance that a building and other type of development must be located from streets, easements, other structures, or the coastline.

Sludge: The organic solids that remain after sewage treatment.

Spatial management: Proactively allocating marine and terrestrial space among multiple users and activities to achieve specified social objectives. Commonly implemented through a comprehensive map of a region with zones for approved uses and regulations concerning activities within the zones.

Special area management plan (SAMP): Plans under the Coastal Zone Management Act that provide for increased specificity in protecting significant natural resources, reasonable coast-dependent economic growth, improved protection of life and property in hazardous areas, and enhanced predictability in governmental decision making.

Species richness: The number of species present within a given ecosystem.

Sprawl (urban/suburban): Spreading of a city and suburbs over rural land. Lack of transportation options and pedestrian-friendly neighborhoods characterizes the style of development.

Stakeholder: Individual, community, or other group in society that is potentially affected by a management action.

Subsea completion: A system of high-pressure valves placed at the seafloor to control the flow of fluids. Fluids are transferred from here to the shore, a fixed platform, or more recently a floating processing facility.

Subsea production system: A complex of pipes, valves, and related equipment used to produce oil and gas from individual or connected subsea completions.

Subsidy (agricultural): Government funds paid primarily to farmers to affect the supply and cost of agricultural products, to influence farming practices, and/ or to supplement incomes.

Surface runoff: Water that does not infiltrate into the soil and therefore runs to a stream, lake, reservoir, or the ocean.

Suspended solids: Solid particles suspended in the water column.

Sustainability: The state of meeting current needs without compromising the ability of individuals to meet their needs in the future.

Takes: Harassing, harming, pursuing, hunting, shooting, wounding, killing, trapping, capturing, or collecting organisms listed for protection under the Endangered Species Act.

Targets (of policy): Persons whose actions are most likely to deliver goals.

Territorial sea: Part of the ocean adjacent to land where a coastal state has sovereignty subject to rights of passage. For the United States, the territorial sea extends out to twelve miles from shore.

Tertiary treatment: Sewage treatment that exceeds secondary levels by removing primarily nitrate and phosphate from the liquid waste stream.

Tool (in policy): Element in a policy design that causes agents or targets to do something they would not do otherwise so that the modified behavior solves public problems and results in attaining policy goals.

Total allowable catch: A catch limit set for a particular fishery for a year or fishing season. Usually expressed in tons of live-weight equivalent, but can be set as numbers of fish.

Total maximum daily load (TMDL): The pollutant load that a water body can accept without violating water quality standards. This load is allocated between point and nonpoint sources that constitute the total load.

Trends: Over time, the increase or decrease of environmental quality, social values, or other features in a coastal region.

Trophic efficiency: The rate at which energy or biomass is transferred from one trophic level to the next.

Turbidity plume: An elongated and mobile column or band of sediments in water.

Typhoid: A bacterial infection characterized by diarrhea, systemic disease, and a rash. Most commonly caused by the bacteria *Salmonella typhi*.

Ultraviolet disinfection: To reduce pathogens in sewage, electromagnetic energy from a lamp penetrates pathogens' cell wall, destroying the genetic material and retarding or eliminating reproduction.

Voluntary organization: A collection of individuals who choose to form a body, such as a nongovernmental organization, to accomplish a purpose.

Water Resources Development Act: An act that authorizes the U.S. Army Corps of Engineers, subject to appropriations by Congress, to engage in federal construction projects for flood control, navigation, or environmental purposes.

Watershed: Geographic area separated from other regions by drainage divides. All water, sediment, and dissolved constituents within a watershed flow to a common outlet, such as a stream, river, lake, or ocean.

Wetland mitigation bank: An area of wetland that has been created or restored to mitigate any unavoidable wetlands losses that occur through a project elsewhere.

Working waterfront: A parcel of land abutting the intertidal zone that is used primarily to provide access to or support the conduct of traditional maritime industries such as commercial fishing.

Zoning: Separate, mapped portions of an area to which different uniform sets of regulations apply.

Index

Figures/photos/illustrations are indicated by an "f" and tables by a "t".